The ArtScroll History Series®

Rabbi Nosson Scherman / Rabbi Meir Zlotowitz

General Editors

by Rabbi Shimon Finkelman
with Rabbi Nosson Scherman

Foreword by Rabbi Meir Zlotowitz

Published by

Mesorah Publications, ltd

in conjunction with
MESIVTHA TIFERETH JERUSALEM / YESHIVA OF STATEN ISLAND

Reb Moshe

The Life and Ideals of
HaGaon Rabbi Moshe Feinstein

FIRST EDITION
First Impression . . . December, 1986
Second Impression . . . November, 1990
Third Impression . . . January 1998

Published and Distributed by
MESORAH PUBLICATIONS, Ltd.
4401 Second Avenue
Brooklyn, New York 11232

Distributed in Europe by
J. LEHMANN HEBREW BOOKSELLERS
20 Cambridge Terrace
Gateshead, Tyne and Wear
England NE8 1RP

Distributed in Israel by
SIFRIATI / A. GITLER — BOOKS
10 Hashomer Street
Bnei Brak 51361

Distributed in Australia & New Zealand by
GOLDS BOOK & GIFT CO.
36 William Street
Balaclava 3183, Vic., Australia

Distributed in South Africa by
KOLLEL BOOKSHOP
Shop 8A Norwood Hypermarket
Norwood 2196, Johannesburg, South Africa

ARTSCROLL HISTORY SERIES ®
REB MOSHE
© Copyright 1986, by MESORAH PUBLICATIONS, Ltd.
4401 Second Avenue / Brooklyn, N.Y. 11232 / (718) 921-9000

Photo Credits
Many of the photographs in this volume are by courtesy of various members of the Feinstein family.
Grateful acknowledgment is made to them and to the following sources for use of their copyrighted
photographs: Rabbi Avrohom Biderman/Chinuch Atzmai/Elite Photographers/Ezras Torah/Moshe Maline/
Jerry Meyer Studio/Rabbi Eliyahu Steger/S.Z. Stern/Trainer Studio/Nachman Wolfson/Yacobi Studio,
Jerusalem/Zelman Studios

A special acknowledgment of gratitude is made to the Agudath Israel Archives and its director Rabbi
Moshe Kolodny, and to Moshe D. Yarmish, who have made their extensive collections available to the
publishers.

The portrait appearing on the cover is reproduced courtesy of Jerry Meyer Studio.

None of these photographs may be reproduced without permission of the individual copyright holders.

Typography by Compuscribe at ArtScroll Studios, Ltd.
4401 Second Avenue / Brooklyn, N.Y. 11232 / (718) 921-9000

Printed in the United States of America by Noble Book Press
Bound by Sefercraft, Quality Bookbinders, Ltd. Brooklyn, N.Y.

זֶה סֵפֶר תּוֹלְדֹת אָדָם
This is the book of the generations of man
(Genesis 5:1)

This volume is dedicated to the memory of

שלימה בת מרדכי ע"ה

Sylvia Zerring

August 20, 1986 / ט"ו אב תשמ"ו

Her life was a book of kindness and devotion, of nachas
and joy, of generations binding the future with the past.

— As the mother of Elliott, Jacqueline, and Marvin
— as wife of Sol
— as grandmother of Erin and Julie
— as sister of Goldie

she remains etched in our memories as a rare person
whose sensitivity and commitment were lavished
not only on her immediate loved ones, but on
her extended family — the entire Jewish people.

May we always be inspired by her kindness and concern,
and may we follow in her path of tzedakah and chessed.

קָמוּ בָנֶיהָ וַיְאַשְּׁרוּהָ בַּעְלָהּ וַיְהַלְלָהּ
Her children arise and praise her;
her husband, and he lauds her
(Proverbs 31:21)

Sol, Elliott, Marvin, Jacqueline, Erin,
Julie, Goldie and family

בתודה לבורא עולם שזיכני לראות את הקולות של תורה
בראותי את המנהגות של מורי ורבי רבן של כל ישראל זצ״ל
וחס ושלום שתשתכח תורה זו מישראל
לכן מלאני לבי לזכות בהדפסת הספר הזה
שהיא כטפה מן הים ממדותיו וגמילות חסדיו.

וזכות הברכה של כל אשר יקים את ספר התורה הזאת
תהי׳ לרפואה שלמה של אמי מורתי

עטיא בת רייזל שתחי׳

ולזכר נשמת אבי מורי

אלתר יוסף בן שלום ז״ל

נפ׳ ג׳ מרחשון בשמו״ת

יצחק דזשייקאבס

This volume is dedicated to the memory of our parents

Louis and Fanny Miller

ר׳ אליעזר בן ר׳ מרדכי ע״ה
מרת פייגא בת ר׳ אריה לייב ע״ה

who nurtured seeds of Jewish growth
during their exemplary lifetimes;

and to our brother and his wife and son

Emanuel, Lillian, and Philip Miller

ר׳ עמנואל בן אליעזר ע״ה
וזוגתו מרת לאה אסתר בת ר׳ פייוועל ע״ה
ובנם פייוועל ע״ה

whose lives ended in a tragic accident
with their futures still ahead of them

Mr. and Mrs. Milton Miller

We are privileged to dedicate
this biography of a giant of our century
in honor of our parents

Mr. and Mrs. Meyer Ratner

Mr. and Mrs. Joseph Saperstein

and their grandchildren

Richard and Tracy Ratner

*Reb Moshe added steel to the thread
that binds us to our glorious Torah heritage;
future generations will be linked to Sinai
because he was here to teach and inspire us.*

*What was his strength? The Torah!
It was his essence and he was its embodiment.*

*May his memory continue to inspire and guide us;
may we build upon the foundations he laid for us;
and may we be worthy of the sacrifices
he made for us.*

Joan and Sheldon Ratner

This volume is dedicated to the memory of
our beloved father

SAM KLAGSBRUN

ר' יהושע שלום בן ר' שמעון הכ"מ

ט' באב תשמ"ו

and our beloved mother

ESTHER KLAGSBRUN

מרת אסתר סעריל בת ר' אברהם ע"ה

ט"ו בשבט, תשמ"ג

Our paternal grandmother

Sima Klagsbrun

מרת סימא בת ר' משה יוסף הי"ד

who was martyred with nine of her children
and many grandchildren by the Nazis, in Melitz, Poland

Shimon Klagsbrun, Rose Srebro, Shirley Wininger

In honor of

David H. and Raizel Schwartz

❧ Table of Contents

◂§ Author's Acknowledgments

In eulogizing the *Chofetz Chaim*, Rabbi Elchonon Wasserman, זצ״ל, noted that, generally, the more one becomes acquainted with a person, the more he notices that person's character flaws and other deficiencies. In the case of the צדיק וגאון האמיתי, quintessential *gaon* and *tzaddik*, however, the opposite is true: the closer one becomes to such a person, the more one is awestruck by his sublime attributes and ways. In the course of my work on this book, Reb Elchonon's observation seemed more perceptive day by day. In conducting interviews with scores of people, I began to realize that the stature of מרן רשכבה״ג הגאון ר׳ משה זצ״ל was far beyond anything I had imagined. Those who revered him most were those who knew him best.

My personal contact with Reb Moshe was limited to a few cherished encounters, certainly not enough to gain even a minimal insight into his incomparable greatness. Perhaps this was my saving grace in writing this biography. Had I known Reb Moshe well, I might have portrayed him based on my own perceptions and experience; the absence of a personal relationship makes such an attempt impossible. This book, then, is an effort to convey, to the best of my ability, the recollections of his relatives, contemporaries, *talmidim*, and others who were privileged to have known him. I pray that I have succeeded at this in some small way, and that the book serve as an inspiration to all.

The material herein is based almost exclusively on interviews, first-person articles, and eulogies delivered by those who had a personal relationship with Reb Moshe.

Anecdotes which were popularized following Reb Moshe's passing (both in writing and through word of mouth) were included *only* after verifying them with people in a position to testify to the veracity of such material. Much effort was expended in this area, even after the manuscript was completed, resulting in numerous corrections and deletions. These inquiries were בעזהי״ת particularly rewarding, for they not only separated fact from legend, but also served to uncover many new points of information.

I am deeply indebted to the REBBETZIN, תחי׳, for her cooperation. It became increasingly apparent that her own strength and faith were indispensable components of her husband's greatness. I am equally indebted to Reb Moshe's illustrious sons, שליט״א, HAGAON HARAV DAVID FEINSTEIN, *Rosh Yeshivah* of Mesivtha Tifereth Jerusalem, and HAGAON HARAV REUVEN FEINSTEIN, *Rosh Yeshivah* of Yeshivah of Staten Island, for having consented to this project and having shared their recollections and insights. My thanks also to the other members of the family who graciously provided information.

I am deeply grateful to two of Reb Moshe's esteemed friends and colleagues יבל״ח, HAGAON HARAV TUVIA GOLDSTEIN, שליט״א, *Rosh Yeshivah* of Yeshivah Emek Halachah, and HAGAON HARAV MICHEL BAREN-BAUM, שליט״א, *Mashgiach* of Mesivtha Tifereth Jerusalem, for sharing their recollections and insights.

My deep appreciation to all those who contributed to this volume. The following distinguished *Rabbanim* (listed alphabetically), all of whom were privileged to have had a personal relationship with Reb Moshe, had a noteworthy share in this book: RABBIS ELIMELECH BLUTH, AHARON FELDER, NECHEMIA KATZ, NATHAN LOMNER, CHAIM MINTZ, MOSHE RIVLIN, BARUCH SICKER, YAAKOV YITZCHAK SPIEGEL, CHAIM TWERSKY, GERSHON WEISS, and MOSHE MEIR WEISS. My appreciation also to RABBI HILLEL DAVID for his continued guidance and encouragement, and to RABBI NISSON WOLPIN for his amiable advice and assistance.

Since his days as a *talmid* in Mesivtha Tifereth Jerusalem, RABBI EPHRAIM GREENBLATT of Memphis, Tennessee, remained close to Reb Moshe. Although my contact with him began close to the time of the passing of his father, ז״ל, Rabbi Greenblatt took the time to provide an hour-long tape of recollections and always made himself available for my inquiries.

My sincerest thanks to RABBIS YEHOSHUA BLOOM, YOSEF BRICK, AMOS BUNIM, YISRAEL H. EIDELMAN, SHLOMO EIDELMAN, DOVID GROSSMAN, HESHY JACOB, YERUCHAM LAX, EPHRAIM SPINNER, and YOSEF TANNENBAUM, most of whom were *talmidim* of Reb Moshe and all of whom enjoyed a personal relationship with him, for their contributions to this work. My thanks also to GERSHON SPIEGEL, a neighbor of Reb Moshe.

The untimely passing of RABBI NISSAN ALPERT, זצ״ל, who was among Reb Moshe's closest and most prominent *talmidim*, came shortly prior to the start of this project. However, his eulogies, and information provided by his mother תחי׳ and by his son, R' MORDECHAI ALPERT, were most helpful.

It has been an added privilege for me to have included in this volume a biographical sketch of Reb Moshe's late son-in-law, the *gaon* and *tzaddik* Rabbi Eliyahu Moshe Shisgal, זצ״ל. I am deeply grateful to HAGAON HARAV

AVRAHAM YAAKOV HAKOHEIN PAM, שליט״א, Rosh Yeshivah of Mesivta Torah Vodaath, and HAGAON HARAV ELIYAHU SIMCHA SCHUSTAL שליט״א, Rosh Yeshivah of Yeshivah Bais Binyamin, who shared their recollections of their dear friend, Rabbi Shisgal. My thanks also to RABBI PERETZ STEINBERG who provided a major portion of the material on Rabbi Shisgal; and to RABBI YITZCHAK MEIR SCHORR, who contributed as well.

My deepest thanks to REBBETZIN FAYA SHISGAL תחי׳ for her gracious help, and to REBBETZIN SHEILA FEINSTEIN תחי׳ who graciously provided information on both Reb Moshe and Rabbi Shisgal. My appreciation also to Rabbi Shisgal's brother-in-law and sister, MR. AND MRS. DAVID H. SCHWARTZ and his son-in-law and daughter, RABBI AND MRS. MENDY GREENFIELD.

Useful in the preparation of this work were writings of (listed alphabetically): RABBIS CHASKEL BESSER, AVRAHAM FISHELIS, JOSEPH FRIEDENSON, ASHER KATZMAN, MOSHE SHERER, and MORDECHAI TENDLER. Rabbi Tendler is a grandson of Reb Moshe and served him for many years as a talmid, companion, protector and more. Rabbi Tendler's piece in Dos Yiddishe Vort was invaluable and he was a major contributor to the lengthy article on Reb Moshe that appeared in the Jewish Observer, a major portion of which was assimilated into this work. That article was also reviewed and commented on prior to publication by Reb Moshe's son-in-law, יבל״ח RABBI MOSHE DAVID TENDLER.

I am deeply grateful to the many young men at Yeshivah of Staten Island's summer location who, during my visits there this past summer, assisted me in every way possible, especially RABBIS DOVID AUERBACH, PESACH BROYDE, DOVID FEINSTEIN (grandson of Reb Moshe), YISRAEL KLEINMAN, YISRAEL KOHN and YEHUDAH SOMMERS.

My sincerest apologies to the many others who knew Reb Moshe well and who would surely have shared their recollections had they been asked. Time did not permit me to seek out everyone who would have been helpful.

The driving force behind this work was, without question, RABBI MEIR ZLOTOWITZ, a talmid of Reb Moshe and a close friend of his sons who was determined that ArtScroll/Mesorah Publications offer its own contribution toward the perpetuation of Reb Moshe's ways and ideals. I am grateful to Rabbi Zlotowitz for his guidance and assistance, as well as for his comments and suggestions that greatly enhanced the finished work.

RABBI NOSSON SCHERMAN has served as mentor, advisor, gentle critic and source of encouragement through the course of this project. His total involvement in the book during the weeks prior to publication, his masterful editing, his contributions to the text, and inspiring biographical article in the Jewish Observer have raised the quality of the work immeasurably.

The aesthetic beauty of ArtScroll publications bears ample testimony to REB SHEAH BRANDER'S brilliant artistry, which he employs with unsurpassed zeal. During the course of our association, I have come to recognize that the source of this zeal is his desire to enhance k'vod shamayim and k'vod haTorah through the quality of the printed word. He has succeeded.

My thanks also to RABBI AVIE GOLD who read and commented, corrected and advised, always with good cheer; to REB ELI KROEN for his fine graphics work; and to the rest of Mesorah Publications' dedicated staff: SHIMON GOLDING, YOSEF TIMINSKY, MICHAEL ZIVITZ, YEHUDAH NEUGARTEN, LEA FREIER, MRS. SIMIE KORN, MRS. FAIGIE WEINBAUM, MRS. ESTHER FEIERSTEIN, MENUCHA MARCUS, and ESTHER ZLOTOWITZ.

MOSHE D. YARMISH, formerly a talmid at Yeshivah of Staten Island, is well-known for his beautiful photographs of gedolim, many of which appear in this volume. My thanks to him, as well as to RABBI AVROHOM BIDERMAN of Yeshivah of Staten Island and the many others who provided photographs for the book.

The reverence that my father and mother, שיחיו, have always shown for gedolei Yisrael and their ideals has served as an inspiration to their children. May they be granted many more years together in good health.

My wife Tova תחי׳ has been a pillar of support through the course of this project. To paraphrase the words of R' Akiva, what is mine is hers. יהי רצון שימלא ה׳ משאלות לבה לטובה.

I thank the Ribbono shel Olam for permitting me to carry out this project. May this book be a נחת רוח to the neshamah of Reb Moshe, זצ״ל, and serve to spread the glory of his Maker, Whom he served so faithfully all his life.

Shimon Finkelman

Kislev 5747

FOREWORD

"In the Rosh Yeshivah's Presence — as His Talmidim Saw Him"

by Rabbi Meir Zlotowitz

פגע בו רבי עקיבא מן קיסרי ללוד היה מכה בבשרו עד שדמו
שותת לארץ [והיה צועק ובוכה ואומר "אללי לי עליך רבי, אללי לי
עליך רבי ומורי, שהנחת כל הדור יתום!" (אבות דרבי נתן כה:ג)]
פתח עליו בשורה ואמר "אבי אבי רכב ישראל ופרשיו! הרבה
מעות יש לי, ואין לי שולחני להרצותן!" (סנהדרין סח)

Rabbi Akiva encountered [the bier of his rebbi, Rabbi Eliezer ben Hyrcanus] being brought from Caesaria to Lod. He began striking his flesh until his blood flowed to the earth. [He was crying out, weeping and saying "Woe is to me, my rebbi over you! Woe is me, over you, my rebbi, my master, for you have left the entire generation orphaned!" (Avos d'Rabbi Nassan 25:3)].

In the row of mourners, he introduced his eulogy with this verse, " 'My father, my father, chariot of Israel and its rider!' (II Kings 2:12). I have many coins, but I have no money-changer to evaluate them!" (Sanhedrin 68a; see Tos. there and Yevamos 13b; Yoreh Deah 180:6)

◄§ Orphaned

R ABBI AKIVA EXPRESSED his grief with the verse that the prophet Elisha exclaimed when his teacher and guide Eliyahu was taken from this world. *Maharsha (Sanhedrin 68a)* explains that Eliyahu was likened to the chariot and riders that lead the way in battle, overcoming defenses and conquering new lands and peoples for the service of their sovereign.

So, too, Eliyahu waged the battles of Torah, refining and reinforcing old concepts, resolving impregnable difficulties, and opening new vistas of knowledge.

Rabbi Akiva compared himself to the possessor of a horde of coins; some ordinary and some precious, some negotiable and some invalid. How can he know the value of each unless he can find a trustworthy, experienced, knowledgeable money changer who can teach and guide him? Rabbi Akiva was a repository of Torah but he needed his teacher, Rabbi Eliezer, to polish his brilliance, direct his knowledge, resolve his questions. Now Rabbi Eliezer was gone and the world was orphaned. Rabbi Akiva was overcome with grief, as his tears and blood flowed to the ground.

This was the reaction of Rabbi Akiva, who lived in a world still peopled by giants of Torah. The Sanhedrin was in Yavneh and the *Tannaim* of the *Mishnah* were the acknowledged leaders of the nation. If in such a generation a sage of Rabbi Akiva's stature could feel bereft and adrift, what words have we to describe our world without Maran HaGaon HaRav Moshe Feinstein, the *gadol hador* and father of his nation? Rabbi Akiva had coins, what have we? Rabbi Akiva at least had the words to shriek in grief, we are mute.

Our sense of orphanhood is compounded by the quantum loss within less than a year of three of our era's most revered and venerable sages: Maran HaGaon HaRav Yaakov Yisrael Kanievsky, the Steipler Gaon; Maran HaGaon HaRav Yaakov Kamenetzky; and finally, the *Rosh Yeshivah,* Reb Moshe, זכר צדיקים וקדושים לברכה. We have often heard that the passing of a great man signifies the end of an era, but for American Jewry, surely, the twin losses of Reb Moshe and Reb Yaakov — especially coming within two weeks of one another — marked a sunset. In his *hesped* on the *Chofetz Chaim,* Reb Elchonon Wasserman asked how one can know when an era is over. He explained that when a great leader dies and there is no one left to compare with him, no one who can be a bridge to *his* level of greatness, then an era has ended and the world moves down a rung. With the death of the *Chofetz Chaim,* he said, a period was closed. There was none to succeed him. In our time, we have faith that the sun will rise again — meanwhile Reb Moshe is gone and an era is over.

If a third of a million Jews in America and Israel came to bid the *Rosh Yeshivah* farewell, then it was because his people recognized him as their *gadol hador* and father.

Everyone perceived the *Rosh Yeshivah* in his own capacity, according to his own experience and needs, but one thing is indisputable: there is not an observant family in the world that has not been touched by the *Rosh Yeshivah* in some way, by his person or by his halachic decisions.

Many have noted that his funeral was the largest in *Eretz Yisrael* since the time of Rabban Yochanan ben Zakkai. Not coincidental. Rabban

Yochanan ben Zakkai and Reb Moshe led their people after unprecedented destructions; both elevated the stature of Torah and the authority of *Halachah* in generations when the faint-hearted feared for the future of *Klal Yisrael*. Heroically and farsightedly they prepared the way for others. Rabban Yochanan ben Zakkai laid the groundwork for Rabban Gamliel. Reb Moshe and his illustrious fellow *gedolei Yisrael* laid the groundwork for — we know not yet the history of the next generation, but one thing is clear: these *gedolim* had faith that Torah will never be forgotten from the Jewish People, and by their self-sacrifice and greatness, they assured that it would not be.

◄§ Totality of Greatness

THE *ROSH YESHIVAH* LEFT US many legacies, and an entire book could be written about each one. He was a giant in *Halachah* and *Aggadah,* a giant in fear of *Hashem,* a giant in prayer, a giant of inspiration to his countless *talmidim,* a giant in modesty, a giant in kindness, a giant in understanding people and situations with a perception born of the profundity of Torah. No one knew the *complete* Reb Moshe. Certainly the *moreh hora'ah* [halachic authority] who came to him with a complex question of *agunah* knew a different Reb Moshe than the woman who regularly asked him to translate a letter in Russian from her sister. The people who came to him for blessings and miracles knew a different Reb Moshe than those who marveled at his phenomenal intensity in prayer.

In the responsive reading of the Song at the Sea, *Chazal* tell us that Moshe called out אָשִׁירָה לַה' כִּי גָאֹה גָּאָה, *I will sing to Hashem for He is exceedingly great,* and the Jewish people responded, סוּס וְרֹכְבוֹ רָמָה בַיָּם, *He has hurled the horse and its rider into the sea.* Moshe saw the total greatness of *Hashem,* but the rest of the people could not perceive that — they could see only that *Hashem* had toyed with mighty Egypt and exerted His mastery over horse and rider. So it was with the *Rosh Yeshivah.* Great men saw him in all his grandeur; the rest of us saw him according to our own needs and experiences. That, too, was part of his greatness. He could relate to each of us according to his individual needs. And the miracle of the man was that in every one of his roles, he was great beyond measure. I write as a *talmid* who felt a personal closeness to him as to no one else. My picture of the *Rosh Yeshivah* is in many ways personal but it is also the reflection of the way countless others saw him.

One of the most distinguished of today's middle-aged *rabbanim* is an exceptional *talmid chacham* with the mind of a genius who has written a major halachic work. When he was working on his own *sefer,* he found it difficult to make time to respond to complex halachic inquiries and to attend *simchos* and institutional affairs. He was so totally engrossed in his own subject that he could not immerse himself into foreign subjects. "I am not Reb Moshe," he once told me. "I'm thankful that the *Ribbono shel Olam* lets me devote all my time to my *sefer;* I don't have the capacity to be available for so many things and to do each one as if that is the only thing on my mind." To him, the *Rosh Yeshivah's* greatness was demonstrated by his incredible ability to retain total command of every area of activity — to respond with equal facility to every manner of halachic question, to teach, to write, to comfort troubled Jews, to lead organizations, to attend weddings and *brisos* — and to do each without seeming distracted or preoccupied with something more important.

As HaGaon Reb David, the *Rosh Yeshivah's* older son and successor as *Rosh Yeshivah* of Mesivtha Tifereth Jerusalem and as *posek,* puts it, "My father had more than a photographic memory. He had a total grasp of the entire spectrum of Torah. Whatever subject one brought to him, he could instantly and without distraction focus upon it every source and nuance from his lifetime of immersion in Torah."

ৰ্ঙ Immersion in Torah

TOTAL IMMERSION IN TORAH — that was the *Rosh Yeshivah's* essence. The public is familiar with the legends that he finished *Shas* more than two hundred times and *Shulchan Aruch* more than six or eight hundred times. Those who knew him best insist that these are exaggerations; what truly matters is that learning was his life and that if it could be said of anyone that he was a living Torah, it was the *Rosh Yeshivah.* When he was saying the twice weekly *blatt shiur* for us, he lived in the *Gemara.* When there was a humorous passage, he smiled and laughed with obvious pleasure. When there was a tragic story or a discussion of Jewish sorrow, pain and grief would be etched on his face and tears would come to his eyes.

To him a *mitzvah* was a joyous privilege and never an effort. As part of his role as *Rosh Yeshivah,* he would invite groups of *talmidim* to be present at a *chalitzah* so that we could learn how such rare *mitzvos* are to be practiced. With a basin of water beside him, he would go down on his hands and knees and examine the bare foot of the man, to make sure it was free of any extraneous matter that might disqualify the performance of the *mitzvah,* and he would wash the foot himself, if necessary. A lack of dignity? Not at all! What could be more dignified than the performance of a *mitzvah?*

His extreme simplicity was misunderstood by some as naivete, but he had a full grasp of every facet of a situation. The most intractable disputes came to him and he had to sift the truth and apply the *Halachah* in disputes at which both sides were presented by forceful, learned, influential people. Once, during a recess of a heated *din Torah,* he remarked to one of his senior *talmidim,* "They think they are fooling me."

Disputes between institutions invariably came to him. Often they were cases where both sides were right, but one was a bit more right. He had to decide the *Halachah* in cases that were clear cut only to him. The *Rosh Yeshivah* had his ways of deciding who was sincere and identifying the underlying, truly crucial issues. For example, during the course of a celebrated, long-running dispute, he wanted to force one gentleman to forgo long-winded rhetoric and articulate the real issues as he saw them. The *Rosh Yeshivah* asked him, "If it were up to you, what would you want the result to be, realistically?"

⋖§ A Talmid's Eye View

HIS *TALMIDIM* CAN BEST DESCRIBE the *Rosh Yeshivah* from the vantage point in his *beis midrash.* The *Rosh Yeshivah* was utterly devoted to his institutions, on the Lower East Side and in Staten Island, and he was always available to anyone, especially his *talmidim.* He always seemed to be writing and learning. After *Shacharis,* he would review *Mishnayos* while removing his *tallis* and *tefillin.* In the earlier years, he would eat breakfast in the dining room, but when walking the steps became difficult for him, he began eating at his desk in the *beis midrash.* Breakfast was always the same: a roll, a soft-boiled egg, and a glass of coffee. As soon as he finished eating and *bentsching* he would begin writing in his hard-cover composition notebooks with usually only a *gemara* open before him. Then he would go into his office to prepare for his *shiur.*

We hesitated to disturb him because we knew that every second was so precious to him, and we knew how he avoided *bitul Torah.* But we knew that if we ever had to speak to him, he was warm and gracious. Our consciences told us to beware of interrupting, but nothing he ever did or said ratified that reluctance. When we went over to him, we would stand and wait until he noticed us. It never took more than a few seconds, and then he would put down his pen and give us his complete attention. He was very happy if we had a *kashya* on the *Gemara* or a probing comment on his *shiur.* Rarely did we ever have to complete a *kashya* before he knew what we meant. He was always way ahead of us, but he never interrupted. We wanted to finish making our point and he wanted to hear us develop it, even though he knew what we planned to say. He would answer, and if we didn't understand him, he would repeat his answer until we did. If we came to him with a personal problem or request, he gave us the same uninterrupted attention, and all the thought and sympathy our dilemma required.

When we were finished and ready to leave him, he always gave a b'rachah or encouragement. We never left him without a good word. And we knew he was concerned with our problem. He expected us to report back to him, and if we didn't, he would seek us out and ask. There was an exception. If the query was of a very personal nature, he would not inquire because we might have felt embarrassed. He would never pry, and he scrupulously returned private letters or papers, lest they fall into the wrong hands.

We approached him with reverence, and that feeling of awe was still upon us as we left him. We knew we were standing before the gadol hador and we felt that his throat was our conduit from Mount Sinai. Whether or not he used a pasuk or quote from the Sages to buttress what he was telling us, we knew that his every word and thought were growing from the lush soil of kol haTorah kulah. Even if his judgments had been coming merely from a man of experience, concern and enormous wisdom, he would have been a treasure to us, but he was much more. Whether one studied Scriptures, Talmud, Midrash, or Mussar, the descriptions of the ideal human being could have been written about him. To be near him was to be in the courtyard of a Beis HaMikdash and to hear his word was like hearing a holy voice emanating from between the Cherubim. Even his genius at humility could not obscure that.

As he walked through the beis midrash, and noticed a group of talmidim learning well, disputing one another vociferously over the p'shat of some commentary, he would pause and look on with obvious pleasure. Sometimes he would diffidently look over a shoulder to see what the to-do was about, but he would not come close to us because he knew that would make us self-conscious and interfere with our learning. Yet we knew he was there, and the thought that the Rosh Yeshivah was pleased with our efforts made us extend ourselves further in the fray of Torah.

He understood talmidim well and pushed them gently to come closer to realizing their potential. When we were studying for semichah [ordination], he would test us whenever we said we were ready. We could ask to be tested on one chapter or on an entire section. He let us know that the main thing in learning was to know something thoroughly; then we would be able to find sources and apply them to questions as they arose. "Cramming" was not the way, because things that are learned hastily and under pressure are soon forgotten. A rav has to know how to decide Halachah; if he remembers everything clearly, so much the better. But memorization is not a substitute for thorough knowledge.

New talmidim were always flabbergasted by the way he looked up a page in the gemara. He did not look at the page number at the top of the page. He would turn up the bottom of the page and look at the few words at the bottom corner. That was enough for him to know what page he was on. Total recall!

◄§ Part of the Klal

HE FELT A TREMENDOUS RESPONSIBILITY for *Klal Yisrael;* that is why he always managed to find time for so many causes and individuals. People usually manage to do what they *must* do, and to him attending the needs of Jewry was something that must be done. He was fully cognizant of his personal role in the Jewish destiny, and he sometimes groaned that he was personally liable for Jewish tragedy, because if he were more worthy, the nation would have merited Divine help. In a sense, he felt he was like the *Kohein Gadol,* who was held responsible for those who were exiled to a city of refuge [עִיר מִקְלָט] for manslaughter. Since the most complex halachic questions came to him, he was subject to a constant flow of tragic news. He once remarked sadly to this writer, "Situations that the *Rishonim* dealt with as abstract, hypothetical questions come to me as realities."

The *Rosh Yeshivah* complained about few things, but those he did complain about were most expressive of the kind of person he was. It bothered him that his *talmidim* and others did not inform him of happy occasions. "People come to me with their problems and woes, why don't they come to me with their joys?" Those who would call him hysterically for his blessings and prayers in cases of illness or business crisis usually did not tell him when the patient recovered or the business remained solvent. In fairness, many of us did not do so because we knew how he treasured every second of Torah and we didn't want to intrude on him. We failed to realize that it was not an intrusion. We were all his children — does a father resent the interruption when he is told that his child has weathered a crisis?

It bothered him that he was seldom asked halachic questions about the distribution of *tzedakah* or about the education of children. He once remarked that almost the only people who consult him about giving *tzedakah* are *Kollel* scholars who, in many cases, are not required to give. Don't people realize that the *Shulchan Aruch* speaks about *tzedakah* and *chinuch* just as it does about *Kashrus* and interest?

He could not understand why many more people did not attend the *Melaveh Malkahs* and dinners of his institutions. The Mesivtha Tifereth Jerusalem and later Yeshiva of Staten Island, where his son HaGaon Reb Reuven is *Rosh Yeshivah,* were very precious to him. He took personal financial responsibility for the institutions because his allegiance to *talmidim,* to the Jewish community of the Lower East Side, and to the transmission of Torah to future generations was so intense. His salary was modest beyond belief; he took only what he needed to maintain his very simple standard of living. It pained and mystified him, therefore, that many people ignored his appearances on behalf of the yeshivos.

�◈ Where are They?

OCCASIONALLY, IN HIS LATER YEARS, he would voice this complaint publicly when he spoke at a *Melaveh Malkah.* Where are the people, he wondered, who call early in the morning and late at night with *she'eilos* and requests? When we devote time to fund-raising, we are torn from learning and responding to the questions that come to us from everywhere. Why does the Jewish public force its *roshei yeshivah* to steal time from Torah and *talmidim* to raise money? Shouldn't people who value Torah go out of their way to give the *roshei hayeshivah* the financial support to which they and their institutions are entitled?

He had a remarkable ability to detach himself from his role. It was hardly possible for a human being to be more modest and personally self-effacing, but he was very much aware of what he was. The *Rosh Yeshivah* accepted the homage that was due to his Torah, his responsibilities, his position — but he never considered that the individual Jew named Reb Moshe Feinstein was entitled to any honors. That is why he did not shrink from deciding complicated and consequential questions of *Halachah* that no one else in the world would touch, or why he was ready to oppose the consensus of *poskim* if he was sure he was right. Despite his enormous respect for the *Chasam Sofer* or the *Mishnah Berurah,* he would rule differently from them if his research so dictated. In someone else, this could have seemed arrogant, but there was no one in the world who could associate haughtiness with the *Rosh Yeshivah.* He had no ego; he had only the Torah of which *Hashem* had made him a caretaker. It was his duty to interpret the Torah, convey it to *talmidim* and apply it to situations. That he did, and if his Torah conflicted with the opinion of others, so be it. As he constantly reiterated, any qualified *rabbanim* had a right to differ with him, provided they were positive in their own minds that they had mastered all the relevant Talmudic and halachic sources.

�◈ Breadth of Halachah

IT IS ALMOST IMPOSSIBLE to convey a full picture of the amazing breadth of his expertise. However, we can glean an inkling of his Torah greatness from a very brief sampling of the halachic inquiries that came to him:

— Are heart and other organ transplants permitted?

— What is the halachic definition of "time of death"?

— What is the halachic status of marriages and divorces performed and witnessed by people who do not accept the Divine origin of the Torah?

— When a woman is in labor, may her husband ride with her to a hospital on *Shabbos?*

— A response to Governor Carey of New York who asked the *Rosh Yeshivah* to explain the halachic status of the civil death penalty.

— The permissibility of plastic surgery for purely cosmetic purposes.

— Responses to several long series of medical inquiries regarding such matters as "pulling the plug," deciding priorities on who is more entitled to receive scarce medical treatment, prolongation of life which would involve great suffering but no hope of cure, abortion, and so on.

— The use of frozen meat that was not washed within seventy-two hours after slaughter.

— Severing Siamese twins if only one will survive.

— Bringing a seeing-eye dog into a synagogue.

— The halachic status of a deaf-mute from birth, who had been trained to function to a significant degree.

— If a business in Israel is owned by a Diaspora Jew, may it open for business on the second day of *Yom Tov?*

— Under what circumstances may an *eruv* be constructed in a metropolitan area?

— How can a child make restitution to parents after a long period of minor pilfering from them?

— What is the status of the laws of interest with regard to corporations?

When we consider that the seven volumes of *Igros Moshe* respond to thousands of such queries and that the *Rosh Yeshivah* decided countless *agunah* questions, we must stand in open-mouthed amazement at how a single human being could know so much, write so much, be available to so many people and institutions, grace so many *simchos* and *tzedakah* affairs, and accomplish so much in just one lifetime, even though it was nine decades long!

The *Rosh Yeshivah* was more than merely the sum of many parts; he was the embodiment *par excellence* of many perfect wholes.

⊷§ The Greatest Miracle

IT IS TOLD THAT REB LEIB, the *Chofetz Chaim's* eldest son, once visited a town where he was surrounded by people who asked to hear of his father's miracles. "My father's greatest miracle," Reb Leib said, "was that he fulfilled, to the letter, the word of *Hashem.*" Similarly, those who were very close to Reb Moshe insist that the greatest lessons we must learn from him are not tales of miracles, but the far greater miracle of his personal behavior.

Though this book cannot offer even a bare glimpse of the *Rosh Yeshivah's* Torah greatness, it can give us some idea of the man and his character traits. This is a very important, very worthwhile undertaking, because there is so much for us to learn from him. He was our *Rosh Yeshivah* and model in virtually every area of sublime human activity. There is much to emulate; even if we but make the attempt we will have benefited ourselves and our surroundings.

Because he is no longer among us, it is even more important that we preserve his legacy. It is not enough to mourn, we must preserve. And to paraphrase the Sages, we must ask ourselves, "When will my deeds approach the deeds of the *Rosh Yeshivah?*"

The Talmud relates that Rabbi Eliezer wept upon observing the incomparable beauty of his teacher Rabbi Yochanan. He explained, ובכו להאי שופרא דבלי בעפרא קא בכינא; אמר ליה, על דא ודאי קא בכית. ובכו תרוייהו "Because of this beauty that will shrivel in the earth do I weep." [Rabbi Yochanan] said to him, "For this it is surely proper that you weep" — and then they both wept *(Berachos* 5a).

The *Avnei Nezer* cited the above passage in his eulogy of the *Nefesh Chayah.* He commented that Rabbi Yochanan was a very old man, probably over a hundred years of age, when that meeting took place. How beautiful could he have been and why did Rabbi Eliezer cry? The *Avnei Nezer* explains that Rabbi Yochanan's beauty was spiritual. In his long lifetime he had unceasingly scaled the ladder of Torah, piety, kindness, and service to his people. This spiritual glow radiated from him — and this beauty was his alone. He was not born with it and no one presented it to him as a gift. It was the product ·of a lifetime of striving and self-perfection. Rabbi Yochanan and Rabbi Eliezer both knew that he would not live forever, and that children with the potential to succeed him would and had been born. But would they ever become great enough to duplicate his glory? Who would replace the spiritual radiance of Rabbi Yochanan when his time would come? At that thought, they both wept, as well they might.

The *Rosh Yeshivah* is gone. His beauty is gone. His wisdom is gone. Who will replace him? Well may we weep. At the same time, we are reassured by our faith and our history. *Klal Yisrael* survives and new *Gedolei Yisrael* have always arisen. The *Rosh Yeshivah's* heroic work for Torah will not be in vain.

In his *hesped* after the *shivah,* Reb David Feinstein noted, "Just as my father was accessible during his lifetime, his final resting place is accessible to everyone, even to *Kohanim.* He was laid to rest at the side of the road, where every Jew can come to pour out his heart and beseech him to pray for us now, just as he did in life."

He is still accessible. He still prays for us. May he implore our Maker to help his children. We mourn him and we miss him. May we learn from him and be worthy of his lifetime of dedication to *Klal Yisrael.*

תנצב״ה

CHAPTER ONE
Origins of Greatness

RABBI YISRAEL MEIR HAKOHEN, better known as the *Chofetz Chaim*, was wont to say that the Heavenly map of this world differs greatly from our own. In Heaven, major cities are not **Moshe** determined by population, level of industry or **Rabbeinu's** seat of government; rather, a place is deemed worthy of note if its inhabitants are especially **Namesake** G-d-fearing, steeped in the study of Torah and meticulous in their observance of its *mitzvos*.

The village of Uzda was one such place. Tiny in size, it would most likely go unnoticed by someone scanning a map of nineteenth-century White Russia, but this small suburb of Minsk dwarfed a host of famous landmarks as a wellspring of holiness and purity. It was there that Rabbi David Feinstein, an outstanding *talmid chacham*, *posek* and *tzaddik*, served as *Rav;* and it was there that on the seventh of Adar, 5655 (1895), a son was born to Reb David and his wife, *Rebbetzin* Faya Gittel. Having been born on the birthday of Moshe *Rabbeinu*, the child was named Moshe.

It would seem as if a flash of *ruach hakodesh* had inspired Reb David and his *Rebbetzin* to give their child this name. For, like his namesake Moshe *Rabbeinu*, their son would one day sit from early

Rebbetzin Faya Gittel Feinstein

morning until evening, studying and teaching Torah and answering *Klal Yisrael's* questions. And like Moshe *Rabbeinu*, their son would be so devoted to his people that he would always be ready to sacrifice himself for their benefit.

REB DAVID FEINSTEIN, who descended from a lineage studded with brilliant *talmidei chachamim*, was a direct descendant of the brother

Distinguished Lineage of the *Vilna Gaon*. He had been named after his paternal grandfather, who earned a livelihood as a common laborer, but was an exceedingly devout and G-d-fearing Jew, as can be seen from the following incident:

When Reb Moshe's great-grandfather was hired by a gentile employer, he stipulated that he be granted time off from work each day to recite the daily *tefillos*. While the gentile agreed to this condition, he seethed inwardly that precious time would be "wasted" because "the Jew had to say his prayers." His anger increased manifold when he saw that Reb David's *Shemoneh Esrei* was recited carefully and with intense concentration — and took far more time than was necessary, as far as the employer was concerned. This the gentile would not stand for. He decided to send a message to his worker, one which the gentile was sure the Jew would not forget for a long time.

One day, as Reb David stood with his eyes closed, praying the *Shemoneh Esrei*, his employer moved stealthily behind him, a shotgun poised in his hands. As Reb David bowed at one point, a shot rang out and a bullet whizzed above his head. The gentile watched gleefully, expecting to see the Jew collapse from fright or make a mad dash for the door.

He was greatly disappointed. Reb David continued to pray as if nothing at all had occurred. The employer told Reb David later that he had been angry enough to kill him if he had run or even turned around when the shot was fired. But when he saw how intensely Reb David was concentrating on his prayer, he realized that Reb David was truly a G-d-fearing man. Never again did the gentile complain about the length of "his" Jew's *Shemoneh Esrei*.

The greatness of Reb Moshe's father and mother is described in the introduction to *Dibros Moshe* to *Bava Kama*, the first of many *sefarim* which their son was to write during his incredible lifetime. Of his father, Reb Moshe writes:

"He was a great *gaon*, a *tzaddik*, *chassid* and *anav*; there is hardly a likeness to him, in *middos* and in the performance of every deed for Heaven's sake alone, as well as his love of Torah and those who study it, and in his love for every Jew." Elsewhere he wrote, "I lived near his town, and as long as he lived I consulted him in all complicated halachic questions; his responses were as if from Sinai itself."

The Ponevezher *Rosh Yeshivah*, Rabbi Eliezer Shach, remembered Reb David as "an angel of *Hashem*." Another person recalled that "*ahavas Yisrael* simply gushed forth from him."

❀ ❀ ❀

Reb Moshe's mother was of royal Torah lineage.

Her father, Rabbi Yitzchak Yechiel Davidowitz, was the scion of a rabbinic family that went back for many generations, and included Rabbi Yom Tov Lipmann Heller (author of *Tosafos Yom Tov*), and Rabbi Yechiel Halprin (author of *Seder HaDoros*), while her mother's family traced itself back to Rabbi Yeshayah HaLevi Horowitz, the famed *Shelah HaKadosh*.

Reb Moshe writes of his mother, "She has no peer in fear of *Hashem* and love of Torah. All she aspired for was that we become great in Torah; she expended every effort in seeing that we not waste any time at all from our learning." All his life, Reb Moshe was awestruck when speaking of his mother's sublime righteousness.

He humbly credited his accomplishments in Torah to the merits of his parents, and said that his mother taught him the value of time.

There is an elderly woman on New York's Lower East Side who remembers the Feinstein family from Russia. The men and boys were always learning, she says, all of them; Torah was their life.

Miracle of the Yeast
UZDA AND ITS ENVIRONS abounded with wondrous stories about Reb David. One such tale centered around his means of livelihood — the sale of yeast by his *Rebbetzin*. The income from this business could not have been much, but together with the small salary Reb David received as *Rav*, it was enough to provide his family of twelve children with their basic needs.

Then, a gentile opened a store in Uzda in which he sold baking supplies, including yeast. His sales were enough to damage the *Rav's* business, to the point that he, his *Rebbetzin* and their children were actually going hungry. Reb David, however, steadfastly refused to seek help in having the gentile cease his yeast sales; instead, he placed his full trust in *Hashem*.

One day, the gentile's wagon, laden with yeast, chanced down a path that brought it past Reb David's house. As it came directly in front of the house, the horse pulling the wagon came to an abrupt halt, for no explicable reason. The driver's repeated whippings and commands were to no avail; the horse simply would not budge.

Well aware of what effect his business had had on the *Rav's* livelihood, the gentile understood the horse's strange behavior as a heavenly warning that he had done wrong. He jumped off his wagon, knocked on Reb David's door and begged forgiveness for having caused anguish to him and his family — and he promised not to sell another speck of yeast.

The gentile then returned to his wagon — and the horse started down the road without a moment's delay.

MOSHE'S BIRTH BROUGHT HIS PARENTS special joy, for his mother had suffered a number of miscarriages before receiving a

In his Father's Footsteps blessing for a child from Reb Yisrael, the Karliner-Stoliner *Rebbe*. The joy of this noble couple surely increased manifold as it became apparent that their son possessed many rare qualities.

It was evident from his early youth that Moshe Feinstein was destined for greatness. He had been blessed with a brilliant mind, possessed sterling character traits and had an appreciation for the value of Torah study that belied his young age.

When about six years old, Moshe and a friend became involved in a "serious" discussion.

"When I grow up," the other boy said, "I would like to become a tailor, like my father."

"It is good for a child to go in the ways of his father," young Moshe replied. "When I grow up I hope to become a *Rav*."

He was a talented chess player in a country where chess was a popular pastime among Talmudic scholars. Yet, at age eight, he gave up playing the game. In later years he explained why. "I told myself that if one is already using his mind, it should better be used in the study of Torah."

An elderly contemporary remembers him as a child. He was popular and used to play with the other boys, but after five or ten minutes of play, he would excuse himself and go back to his *sefer*.

Reb David was his son's prime teacher in his youth. Before reaching his tenth birthday, Moshe already knew all the tractates *Bava Kama*, *Bava Metzia* and *Bava Basra*, a total of four hundred and ten *blatt* in three of the Talmud's most difficult tractates. On a Yom Kippur eve before his *bar mitzvah*, Moshe remained awake all night studying *Masechta Yoma* with his father. By the time morning services began, the two had completed the entire tractate.

Reb Moshe told how his father not only studied with him, but also carefully supervised his education. Reb David personally paid for a private *Gemara rebbi* for his son and three other boys, to foster their maximum growth. Indeed, the group completed the entire tractate *Gittin* with all of *Tosafos* that year. Here in the United States, Reb Moshe told that story to the president of a yeshivah who had argued that he could not afford the expense of a second *rebbi* for an oversized class.

Reb David knew that the youngster had unlimited potential and, as Reb Moshe wrote in the introduction to the first volume of his responsa *Igros Moshe*, " ... my father said to me that he hoped and was virtually positive that many would inquire of me regarding *Halachah*, which is the word of *Hashem*, both orally and in writing, and that I would answer correctly, with G-d's help."

That comment illustrated a unique characteristic of Reb Moshe, a trait that represented another of his similarities to Moshe *Rabbeinu*. On the one hand, his modesty was unbelievable. He was uncomfortable with honor, never felt that he had learned or accomplished enough, and gave respect and honor even to children and unlearned people. On the other hand, like Moshe, he knew that he had a responsibility to lead, to rule on the most complex questions of *Halachah*, and even to disagree with other great rabbis if he was sure he was right. He had the very unusual ability to differentiate between himself as an individual Jew and the Torah that he knew. As a person, no one could be more humble; but he felt he had no right to be humble where *Hashem's* Torah was concerned.

EVEN AT THAT EARLY AGE, Moshe was committing his original Torah thoughts to writing. It is told that when a thought would **Unlimited** come to mind and there was no paper on hand, he **Potential** would record the *chiddush* on any available substitute, even a stone.

When Moshe was about eleven years old, he once entered a room where his father was meeting with a number of prominent *rabbanim*, including Reb David's famous brother-in-law, Reb Elya Pruzhaner. As soon as they noticed Moshe's presence, the *rabbanim* all rose in respect for the young Torah genius. He turned red from embarrassment, and his father was terribly upset.

"What are you doing to me?" he demanded of the others. "You are destroying my child! You will turn him into a *ba'al ga'avah* ... "

When Moshe was twelve years old, his family left Uzda for Starobin, a city teeming with Torah scholars. It was said that there were one hundred Starobin working men knowledgeable enough to serve as *rabbanim*. This was a play on the Russian words *sta* (one hundred) and *rabbin* (rabbis), but it was an accurate description of the quality of Starobin's Jews. It was this golden community that chose Reb David Feinstein as its new *Rav*.

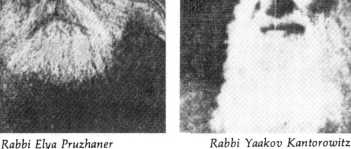

Rabbi Elya Pruzhaner   Rabbi Yaakov Kantorowitz

Uncles of Reb Moshe

SHORTLY BEFORE MOSHE BECAME a *bar mitzvah*, his father deemed him ready to leave home and study under one of the **Slutzk** foremost Torah giants of that time. Off to Slutzk he went, to the Yeshivah Eitz Chaim, headed by the famed Rabbi Isser Zalman Meltzer. It was through his closeness to the *Rosh Yeshivah* that, in later years, Moshe became friendly with Reb Isser Zalman's future son-in-law, Rabbi Aharon Kotler, with whom he worked hand in hand in guiding Torah Jewry in the United States and elsewhere after 1940.

In Slutzk, Moshe quickly earned a reputation for himself for his amazing brilliance and incredible diligence. The "Starobiner *Iluy*," as he was known, would remain in the *beis midrash* far into the night, sleeping barely five hours. By the time he turned thirteen, Moshe was fluent in two complete orders of *Shas*. Forty years later, Reb Isser Zalman would relate with admiration some questions and *chiddushim* of the thirteen-year-old Moshe Feinstein.

Aside from being headed by a *rosh yeshivah*, most yeshivos of higher learning are guided by a *mashgiach*, who is responsible for the spiritual growth of the *talmidim* in areas outside of actual Torah study. Yeshivah Eitz Chaim's *mashgiach* was Rabbi Pesach Pruskin, who himself had been a student of Reb Isser Zalman when he studied as a young man in Slutzk. Following his marriage, Reb

Rabbi Isser Zalman Meltzer   Rabbi Pesach Pruskin

Pesach became a night watchman in an orchard, which afforded him time to study alone and meditate while he sat among the trees. He became well versed in areas of Torah *hashkafah* (outlook), completing the *Rambam's* classic, *Moreh Nevuchim*. Meanwhile rumors abounded that Reb Pesach was one of the thirty-six hidden *tzaddikim* in whose merit the world exists.

During this period, he met Reb Isser Zalman, who invited him to return to Slutsk as *mashgiach*. After some delay, Reb Pesach accepted the offer, and proceeded to inspire the yeshivah's *talmidim* with his impassioned *mussar* talks and his own angelic ways.

WHILE REB PESACH was respected as a *tzaddik* and an expounder of *mussar*, he was deemed only average as a Talmudic scholar.

Reb Pesach's Transformation
Although he applied himself diligently, he was considered to have just an ordinary mind.

When a heated discussion on a topic in *Bava Kama* took place one day, Reb Pesach offered his opinion. Those taking part in the discussion were not impressed in the least by Reb Pesach's comment; they fell silent and a mocking smirk appeared on the lips of one or two of the participants. Reb Pesach noted the reaction and he retreated to his corner, deeply humiliated.

He began to weep until he fell asleep. He dreamt that he was commanded to continue his Torah study and was promised *siyata diShmaya* (Heavenly assistance) in achieving greater success in his learning.

Reb Pesach began to study with new confidence, and in a short time, a noticeable change had taken place. He spent a summer in the company of Rabbi Chaim Soloveitchik of Brisk, and, with his new-found depth and clarity, assimilated Reb Chaim's analytical approach to learning to an extent that amazed everyone. As time went on, he amassed a vast amount of knowledge and, combining this with diligence and his newly acquired sharpness of mind, Reb Pesach went on to become one of the foremost *gaonim* of his day.

Rabbi Nosson Tzvi Finkel (*"der Alter"* of Slabodka) advised Reb Pesach to leave Slutzk and start his own yeshivah in Shklov, which he would serve as *rosh yeshivah*. Seeking to assure the success of the new yeshivah, Reb Isser Zalman had lots drawn to select a group of outstanding *talmidim* who would accompany Reb Pesach and become the nucleus of his new *beis midrash*. Among those selected was the Starobiner *Iluy*, Moshe Feinstein, then all of fifteen years old.

Years later, when Reb Moshe was an acclaimed giant of his generation, a fifteen-year-old naively asked him, "Does the *Rosh Yeshivah* study only those tractates in *Talmud Yerushalmi* to which there is no *Bavli*, or does he study the others as well?"

Replied Reb Moshe with a warm and friendly smile, "By the time I was your age, I had already written *chiddushim* on the entire *Yerushalmi* tractates of *Bava Kama*, *Bava Metzia* and *Bava Basra*." It was his gentle way of encouraging young students to feel that they could accomplish much more in learning. He felt that people were usually held back not so much by lack of ability as by lack of confidence in themselves and ambition to attain major goals.

At the dedication ceremonies for the new yeshivah in Shklov, attended by many prominent *rabbanim*, Moshe offered a halachic discourse that amazed the entire gathering. Sixty years later, he included this *shiur* — with only minor changes — in a volume of his *Dibros Moshe*.

IN 1911, UPON THE ADVICE of Reb Chaim Soloveitchik, Reb Pesach accepted the invitation of the Jews of Amtsislav that he serve

A New Rabbi
as their *Rav*. The community accepted Reb Pesach's condition that his yeshivah be relocated in their city. Thus, when Reb Pesach departed Shklov he was joined

by his *talmidim*, including Moshe, who studied under Reb Pesach until he was nineteen, and always considered Reb Pesach his primary *rebbi*.

By age seventeen, Moshe had already mastered all of *Shas* with *Tosafos*, and in another two years he had completed all four sections of *Tur* and *Shulchan Aruch*. It was then that, at his father's urging, he began to write halachic responsa. One of these *teshuvos*, dealing with the complex laws of *shechitah*, was later printed in his classic *Igros Moshe*, a multi-volume collection of *teshuvos* [responsa], spanning a breathtaking array of halachic topics.

Around this time Reb Pesach remarked with pride about Moshe, "I have a student who has surpassed me in learning as well as in *Halachah*."

In 5729 (1969), many of Reb Pesach's lectures were published by his grandson under the title *Shiurei Rabbi Pesach MiKobrin*. (Kobrin, Reb Pesach's birthplace, was where he spent the last seventeen years of his life, serving as both *Rav* and *rosh yeshivah*.) The work contains a *haskamah* (approbation) from Reb Moshe, in which he writes, "I was extremely joyful to hear that the writings of my *rebbi*, the great *gaon* ... (are being published) ... Many great giants and geniuses in Torah became great by serving him and learning his holy ways in the method of Torah study. I recall the great pleasure I experienced when hearing his *shiurim* and *chiddushim* in the years I merited to serve him ... "

More than fifty years after Reb Moshe had taken leave of his *rebbi* (who passed away in 1939), he sent a wedding gift to one of Reb Pesach's grandchildren, with the following note: "This gift which I send you is nothing in light of the deep appreciation I feel towards my *rebbi* ... "

AT THE OUTBREAK of World War I in 1914, Moshe left Amtsislav and rejoined his father in Starobin, where they studied together and **Chofetz** where he soon began teaching local youths. His **Chaim's** *shiurim* gained broad acclaim and he was soon being hailed as a young giant of Torah and *p'sak*. **Blessing** During the second year of the war, with the Czar's army being mauled on the western front, a conscription order went out for all young men of Moshe's age. Aside from the dangers of fighting in a war, serving in the Russian Army meant forced transgression of certain *mitzvos* and, of course, little time for Torah

The Chofetz Chaim   Rabbi Elchonon Wasserman

study. To Moshe and his parents, these considerations were sufficient reason to seek a deferment from service through any means available. He traveled many miles to see an attorney who was said to have connections with government officials. However, the attorney proved to be of little help and Moshe began his journey home empty-handed.

On the way back to Starobin, Moshe stopped off in Smilovitz where the Chofetz Chaim and his yeshivah had been forced to relocate because of the war. Moshe headed for the yeshivah's beis midrash to seek the blessing of the Chofetz Chaim, whom he had never met.

When Moshe entered the beis midrash, he found the Chofetz Chaim with his most famous disciple, Rabbi Elchonon Wasserman. As Reb Moshe retold the story to his students half a century later, "I went to see the Chofetz Chaim and he was sitting with Reb Elchonon. We spoke in learning and when he saw that I knew (ven ehr hot gezehn az ich ken), he gave me his blessing." *

---

* It was typical of Reb Moshe's modesty that all his life he never said much about his visit to the Chofetz Chaim. Even to his family, he would say only that he had spoken to the Chofetz Chaim very briefly, and only to ask for his blessing. On Purim afternoons, his students used to visit his New York home to celebrate the festival with him. At those times he would be unusually jovial and outgoing, and on a few occasions, told about the conversation with the Chofetz Chaim.

The *Chofetz Chaim* had heard much about the "Starobiner Iluy" and was concerned when Moshe explained the gravity of his situation. The *Chofetz Chaim* and Reb Elchonon both rose and escorted their young visitor out of the *beis midrash*. The *Chofetz Chaim* then turned to Moshe and said, "Our Sages tell us, *Whoever accepts upon himself the yoke of Torah — the yoke of government and of worldly responsibilities are removed from him (Avos 3:6)*. It would seem that, rather than 'removed from him,' a more proper phrase would have been 'are not placed upon him.'

"There is, however, a fundamental message in this carefully worded statement of our Sages. One whose deeds are purely for the sake of *Hashem* will merit that even decrees that have already been proclaimed upon him will be removed." With these words, the *Chofetz Chaim* bade Moshe farewell.

Not long afterward, the government proclaimed that, in view of the successful mobilization of the Russian Army, all call-ups of rabbis were suspended until further notice. In that proclamation, Reb David saw a legal way to protect his son from the draft. Uzda, Moshe's birthplace, had no rabbi at the time, so — at Reb David's suggestion — they accepted Moshe as their *Rav*. His trials were not over, however, because he was ruled too young and able-bodied for a deferment. Nevertheless, he eventually succeeded in gaining an exemption. Despite the superficially natural means through which he gained his freedom, he attributed his success to the *Chofetz Chaim's* blessing.

WHEN REB MOSHE WAS INVITED to serve as *Rav* in Uzda, the inhabitants were filled with pride over the glowing reports concerning **The First** their former *Rav's* son. Twenty years old and as yet **Position** unmarried, Reb. Moshe assumed his first rabbinic position. Years before, his father had declared his confidence that his son would become a respected *posek*. In Uzda it became clear that Reb David's words were indeed prophetic.

In his very first year as *Rav*, a delicate halachic query came before him, involving a man and woman who had been wed in a marriage ceremony whose validity was questionable. After carefully reviewing the case, Reb Moshe issued a thirteen-page *teshuvah* in which he concluded that the ceremony was invalid, thus permitting the woman to remarry without obtaining a *get*. Forty-four years later, this *teshuvah* too was published in *Igros Moshe (Even HaEzer* 82).

Reb Moshe's halachic rulings were also sought by many people outside of Uzda, for already then his *p'sak* was known to be clear, concise and based on a knowledge of Torah that was breathtaking in range and dazzling in depth.

In his first years in Uzda, Reb Moshe wrote an intricate *teshuvah* (found in *Igros Moshe*) on the complicated laws of *ribis* (interest). Many years later, Rabbi Tuvia Goldstein, *Rosh Yeshivah* at Yeshivah Emek Halachah, expressed amazement to Reb Moshe that he could have had such a broad scope of knowledge at so young an age. In one of only two occasions when Reb Tuvia saw him display a touch of pride, Reb Moshe responded by commenting that he had sent the *teshuvah* for review to Reb Isser Zalman Meltzer, and his former *rosh yeshivah* had lavishly praised the piece as *emes la'amitta*, the quintessential truth.

IN UZDA, as wherever he went, Reb Moshe was loved and admired not only for his greatness in Torah, but for his angelic character

Appetite for Goodness
traits and his love for every Jew. The Jewish community in Uzda provided him with all his basic needs, some of which were slightly unusual for a *Rav*, since Reb Moshe remained unmarried during his years there. One of the local women was assigned the task of cooking his meals, a task she performed with relish.

One day, Reb Moshe's sister, Chana (who later became the *Rebbetzin* of Rabbi Isaac Small of Chicago), arrived in Uzda to visit her brother. "I see you are being treated very well," she commented upon seeing him. "You've put on a little bit of weight."

"I *am* being treated well," Reb Moshe replied. "The woman who cooks for me prepares a heaping plate of food for each meal. I always finish all that is served, not wanting her to think I find her food lacking. However, she sees my clean plate as a sign of hunger and she promptly serves me seconds — which I also partake of, for her sake. And so, yes — I have put on weight."

Later that day Chana joined him for a meal at the woman's house. She took one bite — and found it tasted so awful that she was tempted to spit it out. With a heaping plate of food staring at her and not wishing to insult her hostess, she saw no way out of her dilemma but to clear the food off the plate when the woman was not looking.

In later years, *Rebbetzin* Small would relate this story to her grandchildren, expressing her admiration for her brother, who day

Three renowned Lubanites: (left to right) Rabbi Chaim Kavalkin, Rabbi Yerucham Levovitz, Rabbi Nechemiah Yerushalemski.

after day, for three years, ate this woman's cooking, two portions at a time! Difficult as it may have been to eat the badly prepared food, Reb Moshe, who would one day be remembered as "a *gaon* in *middos,*" found it far more difficult to hurt the woman's feelings.

The Next Step

IN THE YEAR 1920, Reb Moshe accepted an invitation to serve as *Rav* in Luban, a town twenty miles from Slutzk. Torah and fear of Hashem were found in abundance in Luban. A group of working men formed a *Chevrah Shas,* in which the members divided the entire Talmud among themselves for study, with a *siyum* being held each Chanukah. Most parents sent their sons to study in the great yeshivos of Eastern Europe, where many of them developed into outstanding Torah personalities. Luban was the birthplace of Rabbi Yerucham Levovitz, legendary *mashgiach* of the Mirrer Yeshivah in Europe; and יבל"ח Rabbi David Povarsky, currently *rosh yeshivah* at the Ponevezher Yeshivah in Bnei Brak.

That Reb Moshe was chosen for such a distinguished position at so young an age says much for his stature in the Torah world at that time. Reb Moshe did not disappoint the people of Luban. There his brilliant light would shine forth ever stronger. There he would emerge as a courageous leader of his people.

CHAPTER TWO

A Rabbi under Communism

THE RAVAGES OF WORLD WAR I led to revolution in Russia immediately following the war's end. Relatively minor at its outset, the revolution quickly took on a different dimension when

Revolution and Violence government troops, ostensibly loyal to the Czar, banded with his enemies to force the government's collapse. A new government was formed, but this was not enough to satisfy the Bolsheviks (Communists) who sought full control of the state and total elimination of their opposition.

In October of 1917, the Bolsheviks took power, supported by their Red Army, and the country was then plunged into a four-year civil war as the counter-revolutionary White Army battled the Reds for control of the land.

As the scene of battle moved along the Russian terrain, soldiers on both sides of the conflict would often vent their fury on the Jewish communities that stood in their path. While the Red Army was, at least officially, opposed to such behavior, this was not so of its opposition. The fact that many Jews were in the forefront of the Revolution and most other Jews embraced it — because of its official stand against anti-Semitism — was enough to reinforce the age-old anti-Semitism of the Czar's supporters. Many battalions in the White Army were composed of Cossack forces, who popularized the battle cry, "Strike at the Jews and save Russia!" Countless Jews in the Ukraine, where the Cossacks were primarily to be found, lost their possessions, their homes and often their very lives at the hands of these beastly hordes. White Russia, the province in which Minsk, Starobin, and Luban were located, remained relatively quiet until mid-1920.

TOWARD THE END OF 1920, however, White Russia was invaded by bands of bloodthirsty Cossacks. Starobin became the scene of a **Reb David's** terrible pogrom. The Cossacks pillaged Jewish **Courage** homes, mercilessly slaughtering many of their inhabitants. Afterwards, they seized Reb David Feinstein and led him away to the outskirts of the town, while demanding an exorbitant ransom from the remaining Jews in exchange for the safe return of their beloved *Rav*.

Well aware of the poverty prevalent in his town, the untrustworthiness of the Cossacks and probably afraid that payment of the ransom would encourage the Cossacks to repeat this practice in other Jewish towns, Reb David was ready to die rather than have the townspeople submit to his captors' demands. He somehow sent word to the townspeople that as *Rav* he strictly forbade them to pay the ransom.

Reb David's grandson, Rabbi Yechiel Michel Feinstein, *Rosh Yeshivah* of Yeshivah Beis Yehudah in Bnei Brak, recalls that horrifying time vividly. Fearful for his grandfather's fate, he sat in a room together with his uncle, Reb Moshe, who began reciting *Tehillim* from memory. Reb Moshe said each word slowly and distinctly so that his young nephew could repeat after him.

Soon after, for no explicable reason, the Cossacks decided to release Reb David. However, before letting him go, they insisted that he repeat a certain declaration that they recited to him in Polish, a language with which he was unfamiliar.

To this, Reb David responded, "I will not say something that I do not understand." The Cossacks again threatened him with death, but he remained unshaken. Finally, Reb David was released unharmed and returned to his grateful community and family.

IN LUBAN, ON LAG B'OMER of 1921, Reb Moshe seemed to have sensed an ominous atmosphere. He packed his most precious

The Pogrom belongings — his Torah manuscripts — and fled the town. Minutes later, Luban was struck by a pogrom, and a bomb was detonated in the *Rav's* house. The assumption was that Reb Moshe had perished in the explosion.

Reb Moshe continued in his flight from the area until several days later when he simply collapsed. A Russian peasant found the package of writings and brought them to Reb Isser Zalman Meltzer who recognized them as belonging to Reb Moshe. He saw it as grounds to fear the worst, for Reb Moshe would never be separated willingly from his writings. Yet, when an inquiry came to him from Reb David Feinstein, asking if he had heard anything about Reb Moshe, Reb Isser Zalman replied, "I am confident that he is alive."

Sure enough, in a matter of days, a fatigued Reb Moshe Feinstein found his way to Slutzk, where he stayed with Reb Isser Zalman for an extended period of time.

When the Cossack threat had passed, Reb Moshe and the others who had survived the pogrom returned back to the ruins that had once been their homes. Infused with the *Rav's* spirit, faith and love, the survivors fought to overcome their personal tragedies and rebuild life anew. With the help of the surrounding communities, life in Luban slowly returned to normal.

To commemorate the *Lag B'Omer* pogrom, Reb Moshe never took advantage of the break in the *Sefirah* mourning period that *Lag B'Omer* offers. His *Sefirah* bridged the entire period without interruption.

After that short separation from his precious writings, Reb Moshe bought a handsome leather carrying-case for the sole purpose of taking his manuscripts with him whenever he traveled. A year later on the Tenth of Teves, on his way to visit his father and show him a manuscript of his *chiddushim* on *Yerushalmi*, the briefcase was stolen at a train station, probably because it was of such high quality. As a result, the fast of the Tenth of Teves always had an extra dimension of gravity in the Feinstein household.

IN THE FOLLOWING YEAR, Reb Moshe married Sima, the daughter of Rabbi Yaakov Moshe Kastonowitz, Luban's *shochet* and *mohel* **Marriage** and head of the Luban Jewish community. *Rebbetzin* Feinstein, who would be Reb Moshe's faithful partner in life for the next sixty-four years, bore him five children: two daughters, Faya and Sifra; and three sons, Pesach Chaim (who

*Reb Yaakov Moshe
Kastonowitz*

died of whooping cough as an infant) *, David and Reuven. All were born in Luban except Reuven who was born in the United States.

Reb Yaakov Moshe appreciated the great merit of having Reb Moshe as his son-in-law. Recognizing Reb Moshe's legendary diligence in Torah study, he did his utmost to insure that nothing would disturb it. Reb Yaakov Moshe was once present when his daughter was faced with the common dilemma of trying to wash the floor while the children required supervision. Seeing the possibility that Reb Moshe would be forced to close his *gemara* and tend to the children, Reb Yaakov Moshe quickly said to his daughter, "His job is to learn; I will wash your floor and *you* tend to the children." Years later, *Rebbetzin* Feinstein would recall this incident as having impressed upon her the value of her husband's diligence.

Reb Moshe's total concentration on Torah was legendary in Luban already in those years. One of his admirers was an elderly *talmid chacham* who could well appreciate the Torah greatness of the young *Rav*. In those days, the only time Reb Moshe took a nap during the day was on Shabbos. The elderly scholar would jokingly tell *Rebbetzin* Feinstein, "Don't let the *Rav* sleep! You are not allowed to let him sleep! Too much Torah is lost when he is not awake."

In general, the *Rebbetzin* took upon herself the burden of all material matters in the home, making certain that all was in order without interrupting Reb Moshe's holy work. She bore this responsibility with happiness and dignity, realizing full well that her husband's mission in life was greatly dependent on her. It can certainly be said that

---

* The heading to a *chiddush* in *Dibros Moshe* reads, " ... said at the *seudas bris milah* of my first son, Pesach Chaim, who was taken from us, due to our many sins, on the fifth of Elul, 5686 (1926), and who will be returned to us at the time of *techias hameisim*."

without the *Rebbetzin's* dedication, Reb Moshe may not have become the Torah giant that he was.

Rabbi David Povarsky, who lived in Luban as a young boy, recalls that the Feinstein household shone with exemplary *middos*. The respect this earned them among the town's inhabitants, including non-religious Jews and gentiles, would figure prominently in their surviving the many years of Communist oppression that lay ahead.

BY THE END OF 1921, the Communists had conquered all opposition and were in full control of what became known as the Union of

Communist Domination

Soviet Socialist Republics (U.S.S.R.). While the Communists were opposed to all forms of religion and especially Judaism, they were too preoccupied in the formative years of their regime to make a concerted effort at subverting religious practices.

There was, however, one section of the Communist Party that, from its inception, expended great effort to destroy Jewish religious life. This was the *Yevsektsia*, the notorious "Jewish Section." It was composed of Jews who had shorn all traces of their Jewishness in the hope that this would gain them acceptance among the Communists. The *Yevsektsia* advocated the death of the Jewish religion. They opened a network of kindergartens, schools and youth clubs where there was no mention of Jewish history or faith and where "G-d" was treated as a superstition of backward people, ר״ל. Instead, Communist ideology and culture was taught with enthusiasm and fervor.

The *Yevsektsia's* open war against the religion of its ancestors began with ridicule of Jewish laws and customs. On the eve of Pesach they would send the local *Rav* a loaf of bread; they would choose the night of Yom Kippur to hold their mass meetings at which non-kosher food was served; and they would demonstrate in front of *chadarim* (religious elementary schools) bearing placards with slogans such as: "Down with the *chadarim* and yeshivos!" "Down with the black rabbis!" and "Let freedom live!" As time went on, *chadarim* in Russia were forced to close and teaching Torah to the young became a crime against the State.

In his addresses delivered in the main *shul* of Luban, Reb Moshe would allude to the new regime's edicts against his people. In an address delivered on the Shabbos before

Pesach, 5682 (1922), he said:

"We are redeemed, in a sense, even while we are in exile, for our own spirit can never be exiled. No one can claim mastery over our spirit; the decrees against us can only affect our bodies ...

" ... This is cause for great rejoicing. We must, therefore, celebrate the *Yom Tov* with much beauty and splendor ... for we are not slaves ... We have no master but *Hashem.*"

In Luban, the Jewish community was spared the wrath of the Party and the *Yevsektsia* until 1930, when the ruthless anti-Semite Joseph Stalin crushed the last remnants of opposition to his power, thus allowing him to turn his full attention to the Jews.

IN FACT, REB MOSHE CONSIDERED the five years from 1925 to 1930 as the most productive of his life. It was during this period that

Most Productive Years he wrote a famous *teshuvah* that challenged a ruling by Rabbi Yechezkel Abramsky. The two responsa were brought to the attention of Rabbi Chaim Ozer Grodzenski, in Vilna, who sided with

Reb Moshe. He commented: "I have heard of the two brothers (Reb Moshe and his brother Reb Mordechai) deep in the Russian heartland, who learn Torah as it was studied a century ago!"

When, in 1936, Reb Moshe passed through Vilna on his way to America, he visited Reb Chaim Ozer, who was then the recognized leader of world Jewry and its foremost *posek*. During the course of their conversation, Reb Chaim Ozer mentioned that he had read Reb Moshe's above-mentioned *teshuvah*. "I have also written on this subject," he told his much younger visitor, "and my conclusion concurs with yours. However, your line of reasoning is superior to mine."

☙ ☙ ☙

Throughout the 1920's, Reb Moshe responded in writing to halachic questions, sending *teshuvos* to people in Slutzk, Starobin, Amstislav and elsewhere. Many of these *teshuvos* were subsequently published in *Igros Moshe*, where we find among his correspondents his father, Reb David; Rabbi Yechezkel Abramsky, then *Rav* in Slutzk; and יבל״ח, Reb Moshe's friend from his days in Slutzk, Rabbi Eliezer Shach.

IN THE EARLY 1930's, the Jews of Luban were subjected to the religious oppression that was already a way of life for communities **The War** in other parts of Russia. The *chadarim* and main **Against** synagogue were closed down. A heavy tax was levied **Rabbis** on the importation of religious articles. With many Jews suffering economically as punishment for their adherence to Torah, it became necessary for Luban and four neighboring towns to share in the purchase of a single *lulav*. Everyone fulfilled the *mitzvah* of *arba'ah minim* by the minimal requirement of lifting the species, save for the five *rabbanim* who performed the *na'anuim* ritual. After Succos, the *lulav* was carefully preserved and made to last for *another two years.*

The Communists levied special taxes against rabbis to force their resignations. Most rabbis gave in to the Soviets and left their positions. Those who did not, paid the consequences, and they were severe. The Lubavitcher Rebbe, Rav Yosef Yitzchok Schneersohn, had already been imprisoned and expelled from the country in 1927. Rabbi Yechezkel Abramsky was sentenced to hard labor in Siberia in 1930, and served for two years before foreign intervention gained his freedom. Many other rabbis were arrested and mistreated; many were never heard from again.

While Reb Moshe fell victim to Soviet oppression in the 1930's, he remained at his post as *Rav* in Luban until his departure for America in 1936. Whenever a rabbi resigned his position, the Communist press would feature the news with blaring headlines about how another rabbi had seen the true light. Reb Moshe considered this to be a public *chillul Hashem* and felt that it was forbidden for him to resign his position, even at the risk of death. In later years, Reb Moshe remarked that, ironically, the *rabbanim* who remained at their posts, though suffering for their recalcitrance, generally escaped deportation or prolonged imprisonment, while virtually all of those who acceded to the government's demands were exiled to Siberia.

Without a doubt, Reb Moshe's quiet, respectful manner and his avoidance of public encounters with the Communists kept him in relatively good standing with the regime and its supporters. Though there was no doubt where the *Rav* stood on religious issues, the government could tolerate a man who did not, at least publicly, attempt to show the fallacy of their brutal policies.

In private, though, Reb Moshe defied the Communists as much as anyone, if not more. When his father-in-law was forced by the

government to cease practicing *she-chitah*, Reb Moshe mastered the skill and became the town *shochet*. He continued to study *Gemara* with the men of the town, while inspiring and encouraging his people to remain strong in their faith and observance of every *mitzvah*, despite the persecutions.

Many years later, while discussing a particular page in *Masechta Kreisus*, Reb Moshe remarked wistfully, "This was the last *daf* I studied with the men of Luban."

Reb Moshe shortly before leaving Russia in 1936

The Mikveh

PERHAPS THE SINGLE most important factor in Reb Moshe's being allowed to remain *Rav* was the reverence he inspired from both Jew and gentile alike. While the religious Jews of Luban were in awe of his overall greatness, all were impressed by his wisdom and earnestness. Many *Yevsektsia* members were children of religious families and they could not bring themselves to make life difficult for the man whose mere mention evoked awe in their parents' home; in fact, some Jewish Communists tried secretly to protect him.

One particular incident illustrates both Reb Moshe's courage and effectiveness during those years. There was no possibility of maintaining a *mikveh* openly, but Reb Moshe found a way, nevertheless. With a combination of ingenuity, personality, daring and — most important — faith, he succeeded in having a *mikveh* built — with the aid of the Communists themselves.

A municipal bathhouse and swimming pool were being built in Luban. Reb Moshe prevailed upon the non-Jewish contractor to build the pool in such a way that it would be a kosher *mikveh*.

With the construction taken care of, a problem of a different sort had to be solved. Men and women were expected to use the pool at the same time, something no religious Jew in Luban would dream of doing. Unless this situation could be changed, the pool would be useless as a *mikveh*.

Reb Moshe approached a high-ranking official, whose respect he had earned, and put the dilemma to him this way: The religious community wanted very much to enjoy the new sanitary facilities generously provided by the government, but would not bathe in mixed company. It was important, then, in the interest of public hygiene, that the bathhouse have a few separate men's and women's nights. The official agreed and the Jews had themselves a *mikveh*, the only one for miles around.

A responsum in *Igros Moshe (Orach Chaim* I §126) begins: "In our city Luban, after it became possible, through *Hashem's* kindness, to construct a *mikveh* (during the years of evil decrees) in a bathhouse run by the government, which was unaware that it was, in fact, a kosher *mikveh* ... "

❀ ❀ ❀

The persecutions increased as time went on. The Feinstein family was forced out of its house by an exorbitant clergy tax, and Reb Moshe was harassed with the intention of forcing him to resign as rabbi. He answered that he was ready to turn over his meager earnings to the state — an offer the Communists graciously accepted — but he could not relinquish his position.

Reb Moshe's family moved into a room adjoining the *Schneider's Shul* [Tailor's Synagogue], the only synagogue in Luban still in Jewish hands. There, Reb Moshe, his *Rebbetzin* and their young children were forced to live — along with Reb Moshe's in-laws and two other relatives.

Even then, Reb Moshe's diligence in study did not slacken. He continued to write voluminously and the Jews of Luban continued to revere him. *Hashem* was their G-d, Reb Moshe was their king, and they clung to him tenaciously.

REB MOSHE WOULD LATER SAY that it was during this period, with so many others sharing the same room, that he learned to study **Tenacity** amid all sorts of distractions. When notebooks were often unavailable, he wrote his *chiddushim* on **under** anything he could find. The Feinstein family still has **Fire** old used ledger-sheets, on which he wrote between the columns of numbers.

What is incredible is how, throughout such frightening times, with the sword of interrogation and imprisonment constantly over him, Reb Moshe was able to put every fear and distraction out of his mind and grow uninterruptedly in Torah.

In his preface to *Dibros Moshe*, he writes, "I thank and bless

Shul in Luban where Reb Moshe learned

Hashem Yisbarach, for all the kindness He has done me, until this day. He took me and my family from the place of *shmad* ... and even there, in the days of my suffering and oppression, He helped me so that I should lose little time from my study and analysis of the Torah." One can only conclude that *Hashem* was rewarding his utter devotion to the Torah with divine assistance, for such greatness under such circumstances seems nothing less than supernatural.

Once, Reb Moshe was taken from his room in the middle of the night for interrogation by the secret police. A prime purpose of such interrogation was to trap the person into making a statement that could be used as a proof that he was an 'enemy of the State.' Responding with wisdom and forethought, Reb Moshe did not fall into such a trap. He acquitted himself so well that the inquisitor apologized, saying that he had only wanted to gain insight into Judaism. In addition, thirty Jewish political prisoners were released in Luban.

Rebbetzin Feinstein vividly recalls those fearful times. "When the government evicted us from our home it seemed as if the next step was Siberia; but *Hashem* provided us with great miracles ..."

As wife of the *Rav*, she suffered her share of abuse at the hands of the Communists. The Feinstein girls, Faya and Sifra, were among the honor students of the local government school, which they were required to attend, but they were hardly welcomed with open arms. When one of them attempted on her own initiative to join a kindergarten at the age of four, she was told, "We will be in trouble if we register you, because you are the Rabbi's daughter."

She went home in tears, feeling like an outcast. "Why did you have to marry a rabbi?" she wailed, as her mother cried with her.

When a gathering was to be held at the government school for a group of outstanding students — Faya among them — and their parents, the *Rebbetzin* was very reluctant to go. She had already experienced an unpleasant exchange with a school official in her own home and, as she put it, "If they treated me this way in my own home, what sort of treatment could I hope for in their school?" In the end, however, she decided to attend the gathering, for Faya's sake.

As soon as the gathering commenced, an official announced that those who did not follow Communist Party ideology — such as the *Rav's* wife — were not welcome. The *Rebbetzin* was roundly booed and forced to leave the auditorium, as her humiliated daughter looked on.

Such anecdotes vividly illustrate both the torment and the courage of those who refused to relinquish their rabbinical positions. It is easier to endure poverty and harassment than to see one's wife and children tormented and humiliated. The Communists understood this quite well; it was part of their psychological warfare against the rabbis who would not surrender.

※ ※ ※

In 1936, Reb Moshe and his family were evicted from their cramped dwelling which, along with the adjoining *Shneiders' Shul*, was being taken over by the government. Ignoring the risk involved in taking the *Rav's* family into his home, the old Jewish shoemaker of Luban invited Reb Moshe to come live with him. Of this brave Jew, the *Rebbetzin* says, "He, like the local wagon-driver, was fluent in all of *Shas*. During the time that we lived in the *shul*, I would see the two of them studying throughout the night."

The accommodations which the poor shoemaker could offer

Reb Moshe's family were not very much. He took planks from a barn, and used them to erect makeshift walls near the kitchen stove. It was in this 'room' that Reb Moshe's family lived, along with the mice who came to warm themselves near the fire.

SEVERAL YEARS AGO, A DISTINGUISHED *RAV* asked Reb Moshe why he remained at his post for so long and why he had let so many years pass before finally attempting to leave Russia. Reb Moshe answered simply that he was the only practicing *Rav* remaining in his area and he felt it an obligation to stay and guide the Jews of Luban and its neighboring towns. He sought to emigrate only after it became clear to him that there was no alternative.

Time to Leave

In 1939 in New York, Rabbi Moshe Bick was present at a conversation between Reb Moshe and Rabbi Elchonon Wasserman, who was visiting America to raise funds for his yeshivah. Reb Moshe remarked that there were people who were upset with him for "deserting" his brethren in Russia.

Reb Elchonon responded that the *Chofetz Chaim* said that a country where it is forbidden to speak *Hashem's* Name is tantamount to a bathroom. "No one," he concluded, "can be expected to spend his whole life in such a place."

Reb Moshe sent word to friends and relatives in *Eretz Yisrael* and America, requesting their help in gaining admittance to their respective countries.

Time after time, Reb Moshe's applications for an exit visa were rejected — with one exception. A cousin of Reb Moshe, reputed to be a millionaire, had fled across the Russian border to freedom. The authorities guaranteed Reb Moshe's family a visa if he would help them locate this man. Of course, Reb Moshe refused.

Once, Reb Moshe donned peasant's clothing and slipped into Moscow, in the hope of somehow procuring a visa there. A kind gentile family provided him with a place to sleep while he subsisted on a diet of potatoes and water. Whatever time was not needed for his mission he spent studying in a local *beis midrash*, where he blended in with the other Jews and would not be noticed by government agents.

One night while studying in the *beis midrash*, Reb Moshe became so engrossed that he failed to note the passage of time. When he finally looked up at the clock, the hour was well past midnight. Realizing that he would very likely wake someone in the household were he to return to his lodgings, Reb Moshe decided to spend the night in the *beis midrash*.

The next morning, he was greeted with incredible news. The previous night the secret police had raided homes in the district, in search of those who had gained illegal entry into the city. By not returning to his lodgings, Reb Moshe had escaped discovery and certain arrest.

A BROTHER AND SISTER of *Rebbetzin* Feinstein and a sister of Reb Moshe were able to get out of Russia and came to the United States.

American Intervention They were to become *Hashem's* agents in saving Reb Moshe and his family from the Communist purgatory and the Nazi Holocaust. Rabbi Nechemiah Kastonowitz, who shortened his name to Katz, became a rabbi in Toledo, Ohio, where he served for forty-eight years before his retirement. His sister *Rebbetzin* Zlata Levovitz lived in New York. Reb Moshe's sister *Rebbetzin* Chana Small lived in Chicago. Upon learning that Reb Moshe was trying in vain to leave Russia, they attempted to secure congressional assistance in gaining his family's freedom.

Senator William Edgar Borah (a Republican from Idaho) was one of the powers of the United States Senate. Until Roosevelt's Democratic landslide, Borah had been chairman of the Senate Foreign Relations Committee, and was still the ranking Republican of that committee. Although Borah was an arch-conservative and isolationist, he had been one of the first to champion the cause of United States recognition of the Communist regime. As a result, he enjoyed a personal friendship with Soviet Ambassador Yanovsky.

Rabbi Katz and *Rebbetzin* Levovitz were convinced, therefore, that if Senator Borah would be willing to use his influence with Yanovsky, an exit visa could be pried out of the Soviets. But how could they reach Borah? Their initial attempts failed. They went to visit two congressmen from New York to ask them to intercede with Borah, but New York's liberal New Dealers wanted nothing to do with Borah. Instead, they provided personal letters to Yanovsky on Reb Moshe's behalf. Undaunted, Rabbi Katz then took his case to his own congressman, who arranged an appointment with Senator Buckley of Rabbi Katz's state of Ohio, in addition to providing his own letter to Yanovsky. Buckley, too, gave Rabbi Katz a personal letter for the Russian ambassador and, having a good relationship

СОЮЗ
СОВЕТСКИХ СОЦИАЛИСТИЧЕСКИХ РЕСПУБЛИК.

ЗАГРАНИЧНЫЙ ПАСПОРТ.

Пред'явитель сего, гражданин

и Союза Советских Социалистических Республик

отправляется за пределы С.С.С.Р.

в удостоверение чего и для свободного проезда дан сей паспорт с приложением печати.

Настоящий паспорт действителен для прожива-ния вне пределов С.С.С.Р. в течение

со дня переезда границы.

Выдан 193 г.

в городе

СВЕДЕНИЯ О ПРЕД'ЯВИТЕЛЕ:

Время и место рождения

Семейное положение

ПРИМЕТЫ:

Рост Глаза

Нос Волосы

Особые приметы

Настоящий паспорт действителен:

для выезда из С.С.С.Р. 193 г.

через Контр.-Погран.-Пропускной Пункт.

для возвращения обратно в С.С.С.Р. в течение срока дей-ствия паспорта через любой Контр.-Погран.-Пропускной Пункт.

Взыскано 200 руб.

Квит. №

UNION
DES RÉPUBLIQUES SOVIÉTISTES SOCIALISTES.

PASSEPORT POUR L'ÉTRANGER.

Le porteur du présent, citoyen

et de l'Union des Républiques Soviétistes Socialistes

se rend au delà de la frontière de l'U. R. S. S. en

en foi de quoi et pour le libre passage le présent passeport est délivré avec apposition du sceau.

Le présent passeport est valable pour le séjour hors des frontières de l'U.R.S.S. pour la durée de

à partir du jour quand la frontière est franchie.

Délivré le trente premier mars 1936

ville Moscou

SIGNALEMENT DU PORTEUR:

Lieu et date de naissance 1891 Lubau

État de famille marié

SIGNES:

Taille Yeux brunes

Nez Cheveux

Signes particuliers

№ ПАС. 03851
РВ. 182123

Reb Moshe's passport and exit visa, 1936.

with Borah, he contacted the Senator, who agreed to provide his own letter as well.

When Rabbi Katz came to Borah's office, the senator was away, and one of his assistants, an elderly, sympathetic gentleman, received him very graciously. The man had instructions to give Rabbi Katz a letter on Borah's personal stationery — but his typewriter was broken. Seeing Rabbi Katz's disappointment, he placed a call to the Russian Embassy and requested, in the name of Sen. Borah, that the rabbi be given an audience with the ambassador. After some persuasion, the request was granted. As an elated Rabbi Katz was about to leave the office, the gentleman tried again to repair the typewriter and succeeded. He typed the letter and Rabbi Katz, accompanied by *Rebbetzin* Levovitz, who spoke an eloquent Russian, were soon heading toward the Russian embassy, carrying with them letters from two senators and three congressmen.

Meanwhile, Reb Moshe's brother-in-law, Rabbi Isaac Small, worked through his own congressman, Adolph Sabath of Chicago, one of the most senior members of the House, who also exerted efforts on Reb Moshe's behalf.

Yanovsky was not in the least sympathetic to the plight of a rabbi in Luban. Rabbi Katz and his sister pleaded that they were not anti-Soviet; they merely wanted to be united with their family. Finally, in deference to Borah's "personal request," the ambassador said that he would forward all five letters to Moscow. In Moscow, too, the strong congressional sentiment, given added weight by the venerated name of William Edgar Borah, turned the tide. The Feinsteins were granted an exit visa.

BUT THERE WAS STILL A FORMIDABLE HURDLE to overcome. Those were the years when it was impossibly difficult for Jews to come to the United States. Again Rabbi Katz thought of a plan. He appealed to the secretary of the Ohio Democratic Party, a gentile who was known as a warm, sympathetic person. The secretary enlisted the aid of the state's lieutenant governor, who beamed as he listened to Rabbi Katz's story. The American consul in Riga, Latvia was an old friend of his! He got word to the consul, who agreed to process the papers for the family. So it was that — as Rabbi Katz puts it — they had the indescribable privilege of saving the future *gadol hador!*

On Rosh Chodesh Elul, 5695 (1936), the Feinstein family — Reb Moshe and his *Rebbetzin,* and their three young children — and the Jews of Luban bid one another their sad farewells. Many of his

Free at Last

(left) Reb Moshe and his Rebbetzin with their son David and (behind them)
daughters Faya and Sifra; (center) Reb Moshe's brother-in-law Rabbi Yisrael Shaul
Yoffen with his son David, (behind him) his wife Shainda, nee Feinstein, and
daughter; (right) Reb Moshe's brother Rabbi Yaakov Feinstein and his family; in
Riga, 1937

dear ones remained behind in and around Luban: his in-laws, who
were later murdered by the Nazis; his brother, Rabbi Mordechai
Feinstein, the Rabbi of Shklov, who was taken from his holiday
table on Shavuos and deported to Siberia where he died; and many
others.

Even though the Feinsteins had all the documents they needed
to leave Russia legally and safely, they still had to fear that the
Communist authorities in Luban might prevent them from going.
To help avoid this possibility, they left town under cover of
darkness, in a horse and wagon that would take them to the nearest
railroad station. The townspeople, too, did not want to endanger
their beloved *Rav* and his family by a public farewell. They slipped
out of the town at night and parted from Reb Moshe on the road.

Reb Moshe had expected to encounter difficulties in taking
along his hundreds of pages of manuscripts, so he devised a method
for transporting many of them safely out of Russia. Every day he
would mail several pages of his writings to each of some thirty

relatives in America in the guise of correspondence, mailing them from different villages to ward off suspicion. He did not put a return address on the envelopes or enclose a signed personal note, lest the authorities concoct some accusation against him. He had hoped that the relatives would understand that the writings were his and why he mailed them. His hopes were vindicated, for almost all of the "mail" eventually was returned to him in the States.

The family went to Moscow to pick up its exit visa, and then to Riga. At the border between the USSR and Latvia, the Russian border authorities confiscated a package of his writings, claiming it was anti-Soviet propaganda. Other manuscripts were left behind in Luban. They were destroyed by the Nazis.

In Riga, Reb Moshe was invited to become *Rav* of Dvinsk, as successor to the famed Rogatchover *Gaon*, who had recently passed away. But he decided to go on to the United States, where he arrived in Shevat 5697 (1937).

When the boat carrying the Feinstein family docked at New York Harbor, it was met by a number of prominent *rabbanim* who had come to welcome the forty-one-year-old *gaon* from Luban. While the vast majority of America's Orthodox Jews had never even heard of Rabbi Moshe Feinstein, many *talmidei chachamim* had. The Iron Curtain had not blocked news of Reb Moshe's greatness in Torah.

An issue of the Torah periodical *HaPardes*, published soon after the Feinsteins' coming to these shores, heralded Reb Moshe's arrival:

"... This *gaon*, renowned in Europe as a great personage, is a giant in Torah, amazingly fluent in all of *Talmud Bavli, Yerushalmi, Rishonim* and *Acharonim* and (is known for) the many original Torah thoughts with which he responds to questions.

"... It is hoped that he will find a rabbinic position in this country, through which the glory of his Torah will be heard."

Little did anyone dream to what degree the "glory of his Torah" would shine forth for the next fifty years.

CHAPTER THREE

Rebbi of Talmidim

SOON AFTER REB MOSHE ARRIVED in America, he was invited to deliver a number of *shiurim* in the New York area. Following one such *shiur*, the Torah periodical *HaPardes* wrote,

Bleak Prospects "All the city's *roshei yeshivah* and *rabbanim* were delighted by his extraordinary *shiur*, wondrous *chiddushim*, reasoning and depth."

While all were impressed by Reb Moshe's genius, in no way did this assure him of a position connected with Torah. America in those days had few yeshivos and none of those that existed had anywhere near the large enrollment that so many yeshivos enjoy today. As such, the chances of Reb Moshe being offered a post as a *Rosh Yeshivah* were slim indeed. One yeshivah did offer him a respectable position soon after his arrival, but Reb Moshe rejected it, fearing that a certain member of the yeshivah's administration would resent the appointment as an infringement on his own position. Opportunities to serve as a *Rav* were also difficult to find.

Reb Moshe experienced more than one discouraging encounter as he tried to find a position. "What will you *do* in America?" people wondered. Such questions did not unsettle Reb Moshe. "I will do what Reb Shalom the *melamed* did back home," came his even reply.

Reb Shalom the *melamed* was a teacher of Torah to the Jewish children of Luban — until the Bolsheviks took control. After that, he was forced to spend his days cleaning the town's streets. (Reb Shalom merited having a son who became a *rosh yeshivah* in the Ponevezher Yeshivah, Rabbi Dovid Povarsky.) Reb Moshe, too, would not let his spirit be broken by the bleak forecasts of others. He was eternally thankful to have escaped the oppressive Communist rule. Certainly he would try his utmost to obtain a position that would afford him the opportunity to spread the word of *Hashem*, but he was prepared to accept whatever lay ahead — even something along the lines of poor Shalom the *melamed's* forced occupation.

A relative offered to establish Reb Moshe as a *mashgiach* (*kashrus* supervisor) in a large slaughterhouse, a post that would have allowed him to support his family in reasonable comfort. Reb Moshe, however, refused the offer, for he was not yet ready to give up on becoming a *rosh yeshivah* or *Rav*. Annoyed and surprised, the relative argued, "America does not *need roshei yeshivah;* you will never make a living your way!" However, Reb Moshe was adamant. He had lived in peril in Luban for the Torah's sake, and he was not yet ready to surrender the chance to instill America's Jews with its message, unless he had no choice.

RABBI YEHUDAH LEVENBERG, one of the pioneer Torah builders in America, who had established a yeshivah in New Haven,

Rosh Yeshivah Connecticut, had relocated his institution to Cleveland, Ohio. Reb Moshe accepted Rabbi Levenberg's invitation that he become a *rosh yeshivah* in his institution. Only a few months later, Rabbi Levenberg died and the yeshivah disbanded. Almost immediately came the call to serve as *rosh yeshivah* of Mesivtha Tifereth Jerusalem on New York's Lower East Side. It was this position that Reb Moshe held with such distinction for the rest of his life, nearly forty-nine years.

One of his original *talmidim* in Tifereth Jerusalem recalls how Reb Moshe was introduced to them. The yeshivah's principal was Rabbi Yosef Adler, a distinguished and popular local *Rav*. Rabbi Adler told the students, "Whenever we needed a *rosh yeshivah*, I brought a great *talmid chacham* from Europe. Sometimes, I went to Europe myself to recruit people. *Baruch Hashem*, you boys learn well and, before long, I have to bring you a new *rebbi* who knows even more Torah. I am not a young man anymore, so I decided to bring you someone who knows so much that no matter how much you learn, he will always know more than enough for you."

When Reb Moshe assumed the leadership of Tifereth Jerusalem, the Lower East Side was still a vibrant, teeming center of Jewish life, with synagogues on virtually every block. Down East Broadway from the yeshivah were *Ezras Torah*, where the great *tzaddik*, *gaon* and *posek* Rabbi Yosef Eliyahu Henkin, directed a world-wide *chesed* apparatus; and the *Agudas HaRabbanim*, the organization of European-trained rabbis who had the Talmud and *Shulchan Aruch* on their fingertips. Sadly, there was still an appalling shortage of yeshivos. The Jewish establishment looked down on Orthodoxy and had little respect for its rabbis or institutions, and younger generations of Jews were slipping away from Torah and *mitzvah* observance. There were a few strong Zeirei Agudath Israel branches here and there, but the Agudath Israel of America had not yet been founded in its present form. So Jewish life on the East Side was strong, but its future was not promising.

REB MOSHE AND HIS YESHIVAH quickly became a center of Torah life on the East Side. At its peak, Tifereth Jerusalem enrolled over five hundred *talmidim*, but it was more than a **Tifereth Jerusalem** yeshivah, just as Reb Moshe was more than a *rosh yeshivah*. Tifereth Jerusalem included a *shul* where Reb Moshe not only delivered *shiurim* to his *talmidim*, but the traditional *Shabbos HaGadol* and *Shabbos Shuvah drashos* to large audiences of *lomdim* (scholars) — usually on Talmudic themes related to *Kadoshim* (sacrificial order).

His primary role, however, was as decider of halachic questions, and before long, the word spread that a *posek* of the first rank was there — and available. Distinguished rabbis converged on him with knotty problems and so did local housewives with their strange-looking chicken parts — because he belonged equally to them all. Two middle-aged *talmidei chachamim*, whose fathers were butchers on the East Side, remember being sent frequently to Reb Moshe with *she'eilos*. As children they knew him as the nice, friendly man who never made them feel unimportant — as some others understandably did. As they grew older, they realized with a shock that their "friend" was one of Jewry's greatest people. It is not

Mesivtha Tifereth Jerusalem, 145 East Broadway, on Manhattan's Lower East Side

surprising that one woman used to call him every Friday afternoon to inquire about the time to light candles; he would answer and pleasantly wish her *a Gutten Shabbos* — as he would have done in Uzda or Luban. Did it make any difference whether he was a twenty-year-old beginner in a tiny *shtetl* or the teacher of *Klal Yisrael?* His responsibility was to answer the queries of all Jews who needed him.

REB MOSHE DELIVERED THREE KINDS of *shiurim:* a *blatt,* or a *shiur* on the text of the *Gemara* and the basic commentaries of *Rashi*
The Shiurim and *Tosafos;* a *pilpul,* in which he would discuss a breathtakingly broad and deep range of material and concepts, and relate them to the text being studied; and a *Halachah shiur,* in which he taught the text and basic commentaries of the *Shulchan Aruch.*

The *blatt shiur* was generally delivered on Mondays and Wednesdays, for an hour and a half to two hours. As Reb Moshe once told Rabbi Abraham Kalmanowitz, the legendary *hatzalah* figure and founder and *Rosh Yeshivah* of the Mirrer Yeshivah in

Reb Moshe with his first talmidim in Tifereth Jerusalem

Brooklyn, "When my *talmidim* come to the *blatt*, they already know the *Gemara*, *Rashi* and *Tosafos*. I have to show them *how* to learn it properly." In other words, the *blatt shiur* was intended to train his students to analyze and understand the basic textual material. What is the significance of a seemingly superfluous word or phrase? What has the *Gemara* added by citing a particular question and answer?

Reb Moshe and Rabbi Shmuel Greineman, menahel,
with the first semichah group of Mesivtha Tifereth Jerusalem

Delivering a shiur in Mesivtha Tifereth Jerusalem

What is the key to a Talmudic dispute? Why do *Rashi* and *Tosafos* differ? What forced *Rashi* to interpret the text a certain way despite the objection raised by *Tosafos*? The goal of this *shiur* was to deal with the text as it is stated, not with abstract theories. If the text was properly understood, the underlying principles and concepts would follow of their own accord and the major commentaries would have a framework on which to be understood properly.

As is true of all master teachers, the greater the scholar the more he puts into even his most elementary elucidation of a Scriptural verse or Talmudic passage. Reb Moshe's basic translation of a simple *Rashi* was colored and flavored by his thorough knowledge of the entire Torah.

The *pilpul shiur*, delivered every Friday, was entirely different. It was exceedingly complex. First would come a long list of as many as twenty *kashyos* [difficult questions] regarding the *Gemara* and then a series of intricately woven frameworks upon which an approach to the entire subject would be fashioned. Only the most accomplished of his *talmidim* could follow his reasoning. For the rest, the *shiur* provided flashes of insight and a demonstration of the vastness of Torah knowledge.

His preparation of the *pilpul* was exceptionally rigorous. He would arise at 2 a.m. Friday morning and go through all the major sources. Sometimes he would surround himself with chairs upon

Delivering a shiur in Mesivtha Tifereth Jerusalem

which he would put the many *sefarim* to which he referred, while he sat on the floor referring to several of them at once. After *Shacharis* in the yeshivah, he would lock himself in his office and rehearse the *shiur* aloud, perfecting it as he went along. These *shiurim*, which he wrote as he prepared them, later formed the bulk of his *Dibros Moshe* on the Talmud.

Until his later years, he would be in the *beis midrash* from *Shacharis* until after *Minchah*, to be available to the *talmidim* who had questions about their learning. After *Minchah*, he would leave and devote the rest of the day to study, responsa, individual petitioners and communal needs. The only exception was the one afternoon a week when he would return to Tifereth Jerusalem to deliver a *Halachah shiur*. This would be along the general lines of the *blatt;* but it would lay down the general principles upon which practical halachic decisions are based.

The general practice was that if a *talmid* wished to pose a *kashya*, he would first discuss it with the *Mashgiach*, Rabbi Barenbaum. Only if the *Mashgiach* said that the *kashya* was a genuine difficulty would *talmidim* feel free to pose it to the *Rosh Yeshivah*. There was a natural reluctance on the part of nearly all students to present a question to him unless they were sure it was worthy of his attention — and would reflect well on them.

NEVER DID REB MOSHE PERMIT his responsibilities to *Klal Yisrael* as a whole to interfere with his guidance of the yeshivah and its

For a Talmid's Sake students. His many *talmidim* who became *rabbanim* and *roshei yeshivah* would never forget the love, warmth and respect shown them by their revered *rebbi*.

Rabbi Ephraim Greenblatt, a prominent *Rav* in Memphis, Tennessee, and a renowned *posek*, is among Reb Moshe's closest disciples. He vividly recalls his first day in Tifereth Jerusalem on an *Erev Shabbos*, as a nineteen-year-old who had arrived by boat from Jerusalem only a day earlier. Rabbi Greenblatt entered the *beis midrash* while Reb Moshe was in his office, preparing his *shiur*. When Reb Moshe entered the *beis midrash* and noticed the newcomer, he hurried over and greeted him, asked his name and said that they would talk after the *shiur* had ended. When they spoke again, Reb Moshe told the newcomer to return on Sunday when they would "talk in learning" and he would arrange a study partner for him.

As soon as Reb Moshe recognized his new *talmid's* potential in deciding matters of *Halachah*, he began taking Rabbi Greenblatt aside when questions came before him, to demonstrate his method of analyzing a problem and arriving at a *p'sak*. Rabbi Greenblatt was often asked to be present when Reb Moshe was called to preside over the preparation of a *get* and at times he would accompany his *rebbi* to comfort a mourner. "Come with me," Reb Moshe would say. "You will meet a great person."

During the summer that followed, Rabbi Greenblatt spent a few days with Reb Moshe in his summer cottage in upstate New York. Reb Moshe would come in at night to check if his *talmid's* blanket had fallen off while he slept.

Rabbi Greenblatt recalls his feelings during those first months. "At first, I felt that he was going out of his way for me. As time went on, I realized that this was how he treated everyone. He brought every *talmid* close to him and made us each feel as if we were his *only talmid*."

Another of Reb Moshe's *talmidim* in those years recalls the time when a student with a very poor reputation was accepted in the yeshivah. The student was touched by Reb Moshe's sincerity and gentleness and became a changed person; today he is a respected member of a thriving Torah community.

REB MOSHE WOULD SAY that there are two primary deterrents to a Torah student's success: a lack of appreciation for the immeasurable

Sensitivity to Others value of Torah, and depression over not doing as well as he had hoped. One who diligently applies himself to his studies should never become depressed. He should have confidence in the teaching of our Sages that, if one claims, "I have toiled and not found [success in my studies]," do not believe him. As long as a student does his very best and keeps trying, *Hashem* will help him attain the Torah wisdom that he seeks.

Reb Moshe once entered his *beis midrash* and found a *talmid* sitting alone, a sullen expression on his face. Reb Moshe wasted no time in approaching his *talmid*. "עִבְדוּ אֶת ה' בְּשִׂמְחָה" ("Serve *Hashem* with joy!" — a verse in *Psalms*), he told the student. He then brought the *talmid* into his office and the two spoke together for some time. A student who observed the incident recalled, "I do not know what the *Rosh Yeshivah* told the boy, but I do know one thing — the *bachur* came out of the office a changed person."

It did not take Reb Moshe long to size up an individual. An aged *talmid chacham* recently passed away in Jerusalem after living

With Rabbi Michel Barenbaum;
rending his garment while viewing the Temple site in Jerusalem (1964)

in the same neighborhood for decades, but many of his closest acquaintances did not realize his true worth. When Reb Moshe was in Israel in 1964 to attend the *K'nessiah Gedolah* (World Conference of Agudath Israel) he met the man briefly, and remarked, "This man is a *nistar* (hidden *tzaddik);* he studies Torah for its sake alone."

He made use of this ability to guide his *talmidim* along the particular path best suited for each of them. To one of his students he suggested taking a position in a community that was then a spiritual desert, but the *talmid* could not foresee himself living in such an environment. Reb Moshe said, "If you settle there it will become a place of Torah." The young man heeded his *rebbi's* advice. He still lives in that same area, which today is a true center of Torah. Reb Moshe once accepted the *talmid's* invitation to visit him and his community. Afterwards, Reb Moshe told him, "I see that what I said has come true."

ANOTHER SOURCE of the special relationship that existed between Reb Moshe and his *talmidim* was the great respect he accorded

Respect for Talmidim

them. Rabbi Nathan Lomner, former Hebrew principal of Tifereth Jerusalem and a *talmid* of Reb Moshe, recalled, "When I was admitted into the *beis midrash,* I usually made a point of coming on time. One morning I came somewhat late. The *Rosh Yeshivah,* when passing near me, stopped for a moment and said, '*Nu,* you came a little late this morning; you probably couldn't come any earlier.' Then he turned and went his way." Reb Moshe had made his awareness of the occurrence known without making the *talmid* feel uncomfortable in any way.

❀　　❀　　❀

When testing a class or an individual, Reb Moshe was careful never to say anything that might possibly cause anyone humiliation. Rather than ask pointed questions, he would say, "Let us 'speak in learning,' " and then forge into a discussion of the topic. "*We* asked a question" or "*We* had answered" (rather than "*I*"), was Reb Moshe's general way of speaking during an examination. As he discussed, he attempted to draw the students into the discussion. In no way could he be fooled. When a class performed poorly they were told to review and prepare to be tested again. To a *semichah* candidate whose knowledge of a pertinent subject was not up to par, Reb Moshe said, "You *will* be getting *semichah.* But I want you to review the material and in two weeks we'll 'discuss' it again.''

A student from another yeshivah came to Reb Moshe for a *semichah* examination. After a few minutes it became apparent that the young man's knowledge was so sorely deficient that a few weeks of review would not do him much good. What the young man needed was to study the laws with someone knowledgeable. Reb Moshe volunteered to study privately with him. They studied together for some time until the young man was fit to receive *semichah*.

NEVER WOULD REB MOSHE DISMISS a *talmid's* question as irrelevant or lacking forethought. To one who thought he had disproven a statement of the *Maharam* — because he had totally misunderstood the statement — Reb Moshe said, "What the *Maharam* seems to be saying is *a little* different from your interpretation." If a boy would ask something totally irrelevant, Reb Moshe would say, "You probably mean to ask as follows," and proceed to raise a sound difficulty which the *talmid* had not intended to ask — but which was sure to prevent the student from feeling ashamed.

Self-Esteem

A *rebbi* once asked Reb Moshe if it was proper to use precious class time to give proper answers to foolish questions that students may sometimes ask. Reb Moshe replied, "The person asking the question never thinks of it as foolish."

Reb Moshe's own self-respect played no role when he and his *talmidim* were involved in Torah discussion. Once, during the course of a *shiur*, he made an original point. A *talmid* interjected to say that he thought he had come across the identical point in a section of *Mishneh L'Melech*. Reb Moshe immediately asked that someone bring him the necessary volume so that he could examine the *Mishneh L'Melech's* comment before continuing his *shiur*.

  ❦ ❦ ❦

Aside from attending his *shiurim* and observing his behavior, Reb Moshe's *talmidim* gained much from his private comments and observations. At times, he would give a *talmid* practical advice on how to get the most out of his studying. He discouraged a *talmid* who had difficulty understanding Reb Moshe's quickly spoken Lithuanian Yiddish from listening to a recording of the *shiur* (which he could play again and again) rather than hearing it live. One must *see* the *rebbi*, Reb Moshe would say, for his words to have their maximum impact.

TO ANOTHER *TALMID*, he said that the commentaries of *Maharsha, Maharam, P'nei Yehoshua* and Rabbi Akiva Eiger were most basic to a proper understanding of *Gemara* with **Priorities** *Rashi* and *Tosafos*. Reb Moshe would also stress the importance of review. At a *siyum* celebration he expressed the wish that "we merit to study, review and remember."

He encouraged all his students to adopt an 'early to bed and early to rise' schedule, for he placed great value in studying done during the early morning hours. Once, Reb Moshe became aware that a few diligent students were studying regularly until 4:00 a.m. in their desire to complete a *masechta* before the term's end. After a few hours' sleep, they would rise, *daven* without a *minyan* and then resume studying. Reb Moshe called the students aside. "Completing a *masechta* is a wonderful thing," he told them, "but it must not be done at the expense of *davening*."

As a senior student, Rabbi Shlomo Eidelman felt that the time had come for him to change yeshivos. Since he had become personally close to the *Rosh Yeshivah*, he felt embarrassed at telling him of his intention, but it would have been wrong not to do so. Trembling, he told Reb Moshe what he wanted to do. Reb Moshe answered, "The *Gemara* says that one should learn where he feels he will be most successful, so you *should* leave. But I think it is better for you to stay here, so after a few months in your new yeshivah, you should think it over. If you decide to come back, you will be welcome."

Indeed, Rabbi Eidelman *did* return to enjoy the privilege of learning from and serving Reb Moshe for many years.

❊ ❊ ❊

Reb Moshe stressed to his *talmidim* the importance of sharing their time to study Torah with those who lack background or ability. In *Dibros Moshe (Kiddushin 50:9)* he points out that Rabbi Preida (see *Eruvin 54*) would review the same lesson with a student *400 times*, though he certainly could have used his time to pursue his own studies. Reb Moshe writes, "From this we can prove ... [that just as] one must contribute to others in the areas of *tzedakah* and *gemilas chesed* and he may not be exacting even when he needs the money for himself — so it is with regard to the study of Torah. It is forbidden for a *talmid chacham* to be exacting with his time and to say that he needs it for his own studies, from which he will derive more benefit ... but he must give of his time and teach others, even when it is only the student who stands to gain.''

After suggesting that students of Torah devote one-tenth of their time for the benefit of others, Reb Moshe writes, '' ... In this merit, not only will they not lose from their own [success in] Torah, but, they will ascend to a more lofty level [than before] ... '' *

SINCE REB MOSHE VIEWED TORAH as "our life and the length of our days" *(Deuteronomy 20:30)*, he did his utmost to insure that **To Remain** each of his *talmidim* grow in Torah to the best of **in the** his abilities. Whenever a *talmid* considered leaving Tifereth Jerusalem in pursuit of a livelihood, Reb **Yeshivah** Moshe would carefully evaluate the *talmid's* personal situation. If he felt that the move should be delayed, he would do his best to keep the *talmid* in yeshivah for a while longer.

One student found himself in a dilemma. He respected the *Rosh Yeshivah's* feeling that it was too early for him to leave yeshivah, but could not convince his father of this. The father came to Tifereth Jerusalem to discuss the matter with Reb Moshe personally. Reb Moshe was not swayed by the man's arguments. "It is important for your son to remain in our *beis midrash* for at least a few years more," he said.

The man was frustrated by Reb Moshe's adamance. He shot back, "Fine, my son will stay in yeshivah — but don't expect to see a penny of tuition from me!"

Reb Moshe replied calmly, "I already carry the tuition load of many *talmidim.* I will manage to bear the load of one more."

His words, spoken with utmost sincerity, struck a responsive chord in the man. The *talmid* remained in yeshivah for a number of years while his father paid tuition and became a staunch supporter of Tifereth Jerusalem.

---

* A yeshivah student once asked the *Steipler Gaon* if he should cease learning with a student who had a poor grasp of the material, in favor of a far brighter partner. The *Steipler* replied, "If you will perform a *chesed* with one student then *Hashem* will repay you in your studies with a second partner, so that your own grasp of the subject material will be quicker than expected. It is not worth it for you to drop your present partner" (from הליכות והלכות ממרן קהלות יעקב).

Leaving Tifereth Jerusalem after Shacharis, accompanied by the Yeshivah's gabbai, Rabbi Mordechai Schiff (wearing tallis), Rabbi Mordechai Tendler and a talmid

IN ANOTHER ENCOUNTER, a parent's reaction to Reb Moshe's position was shocking. Rather than appreciate the concern shown for his child, the father took the opposite approach. "Mark my words!" he declared. "I have a younger son and I will not send him to a yeshivah at all!"

The Threat

This threat upset Reb Moshe tremendously. How could a father threaten to deprive his own child of the Torah's beauty? A very agitated Reb Moshe said to the man, "I will tell you something ... no, I had better not say it; once words are uttered they cannot be reclaimed."

Some *talmidim* who witnessed the episode had never seen Reb Moshe so upset and actually became fearful for his health. They escorted him to a room in the building and then placed before their *rebbi* the one thing that was sure to calm him — a *gemara*. Reb Moshe opened the *gemara*, immediately became immersed in the subject before him and remained there studying for two hours.

Meanwhile, the father had remained in the *beis midrash*, mistakenly thinking that Reb Moshe had been led out to attend to something and would be returning shortly to continue their discussion. When some time had elapsed, he asked a student why the *Rosh Yeshivah* had not returned.

"Didn't you notice how upset he was?" the student asked incredulously. "Your words hurt the *Rosh Yeshivah* so, that we feared, G-d forbid, he might suffer a heart attack. We escorted him out to allow him to calm down."

The man had not realized just how deeply his threat had affected Reb Moshe. He asked the student to direct him to the *Rosh Yeshivah* so that he could apologize. The student explained that Reb Moshe was now deeply immersed in his studies and it would be wise to leave him alone after the ordeal he had been through.

When Reb Moshe re-entered the *beis midrash*, the man rushed over to him. "Please forgive me," the father pleaded. "I will certainly send my younger son to the yeshivah. I apologize for having caused the *Rosh Yeshivah* such anguish. My sincerest ... "

"Apologize?" asked a smiling Reb Moshe. "Whatever for? Nothing happened, nothing happened."

RABBI NATHAN LOMNER served for a time as *rebbi* of the yeshivah's sixth grade. He once invited Reb Moshe to test the class **How to Teach** on the second chapter of *Masechta Bava Metzia*, which deals primarily with laws concerning the returning of lost objects. Reb Moshe began by asking the class, "What if someone sees two lost objects, one belonging to his father and the other to his *rebbi* — which does he return first? Why?" The children answered correctly that the *rebbi's* object takes priority, for he is the one who, through his teaching of Torah, places his *talmidim* on the path leading to the World to Come. Reb Moshe then asked a few more questions, all of which were intended to impress upon the *talmidim* the esteem in which they should hold their *rebbi*. His line of questioning then took a very unexpected turn.

"How do *Hashem's* commands affect the way we live?" Reb Moshe asked the boys. One of the students answered that were it not for the command that we study Torah, he could be outdoors playing ball. To this Reb Moshe responded, "Children may play ball. But how do *Hashem's* commands affect how one plays ball?" Now the entire class was stumped. After a short pause, Reb Moshe answered the question himself. Jewish boys, he said, should avoid fighting when they play and they should certainly never lie or use foul language. Even a Jew's recreation must be guided not by what is accepted in the world at that time, but rather, by the timeless teachings of the Torah.

In a similar vein he once explained at a meeting of *rebbeim* in Tifereth Jerusalem why it is common practice for students to be introduced to the study of *Gemara* with the second chapter of *Bava Metzia*, as opposed to a more practical topic such as the laws of *Shema* or *Shemoneh Esrei*. He said that one reason was to impress upon children that the Torah dictates how a Jew is to behave in the street as much as it teaches him how to conduct himself in *shul.*

ONE DAY, one of Rabbi Lomner's students found a dollar in the classroom. Putting into practice a law that the class had learned in

By Example

the *Gemara*, Rabbi Lomner had the finder announce that he had found money, so that the loser could prove his ownership by stating the amount and where the money was lost. However, before anyone had a chance to claim the find, one of the boys raised his hand and unwittingly announced that he had seen the finder pick up a dollar in front of the lockers. Almost as soon as this revelation was made, another boy raised his hand and claimed that he had lost a dollar and that it had probably fallen out of his pocket when he had taken out a key to open his locker. To this, the finder retorted that the claimant had probably contrived the whole story after hearing the other boy's announcement.

The case was then brought before Reb Moshe for his ruling. After listening to the finder and claimant state their respective positions, Reb Moshe turned to the finder and said, "It is wrong to accuse your friend of lying. A *yeshivah bachur* would not claim something that was not rightfully his.

"However, you are not obligated to give away the dollar, since the amount of money and the location of the find were made public and, as such, cannot be used as proof."

Reb Moshe then took a dollar out of his pocket and in his gentle and sincere manner said that he did not need this dollar and was therefore giving it to the boy who said he had lost the money. When the finder saw this, he immediately exclaimed, "If the *Rosh Yeshivah* believes him, then I also believe him and I'll give him back the dollar."

"No," Reb Moshe insisted, "You keep your dollar and you take this dollar; both of you should have a dollar."

The younger students of Tifereth Jerusalem savored their personal encounters with their revered *Rosh Yeshivah.* Rabbi

Lomner recounts his first personal encounter with the *Rosh Yeshivah*, as a youngster of eleven. He had come to the United States with his parents from Germany and was behind his class because he did not know Yiddish and had not learned *Gemara* as yet. Accompanied by Rabbi Shmuel Greineman, Reb Moshe tested the class, but young Nathan Lomner performed poorly. Recognizing that the young refugee would be hurt by his failure, Reb Moshe patiently and sympathetically taught him the *Gemara* — and then gave his *rebbi* a good report about his performance!

For many years, it was a much-sought-after privilege for a student to hold open a *Chumash* for Reb Moshe when he moved close to the *bimah* better to hear the Torah reading. Aside from the privilege itself, the boy went away with another reward — a gentle pat on the back from Reb Moshe.

ONE *TALMID* WAS SENT by his family to live with relatives in Israel when he was thirteen years old. When Reb Moshe attended

Simplicity and Concern the *K'nessiah Gedolah* in 1964, the boy stood outside the site of the gathering in Jerusalem waiting to greet him. When they met, Reb Moshe warmly greeted the boy and then stuffed a ten-dollar bill into his hand. "Here," he said, "you'll need this."

❧ ❧ ❧

In earlier years, many of Tifereth Jerusalem's students were out-of-towners whose hometown had no yeshivah. The parents of these boys, having been convinced of the importance of providing their son with a Torah education, sent them to attend Tifereth Jerusalem and live in the adjoining dormitory. Naturally, parents were often anxious about such arrangements and whenever Reb Moshe became aware of this, he did his best to calm these fears. He could sometimes be found speaking to a mother who sat nervously in the hallway of the yeshivah while her son sat in his new class for the first time. Once, he was seen assuring the mother of a nine-year-old newcomer to the yeshivah that her son would surely overcome his homesick feeling in due time.

❧ ❧ ❧

One Friday night, as the congregation filed out of the *beis midrash* after *Ma'ariv*, Reb Moshe noticed a bewildered-looking out-of-town student. The boy was only too happy to explain his dilemma to the *Rosh Yeshivah*. It had been arranged for him to eat the Shabbos meal at the home of a neighborhood couple and he was to have met his host in yeshivah after *Ma'ariv*. However, the man was nowhere to be seen and the boy did not know where he lived. Reb Moshe told the student to wait while he looked for the man. (In those days, a few Friday night *minyanim* were conducted simultaneously in the yeshivah.) Reb Moshe found the man *davening* with a different *minyan* and then went to get the boy.

This student later related that it was as a result of this incident, where he saw such extraordinary concern and simplicity from a man so great, that he decided to emulate Reb Moshe in dedicating his life to the spreading of Torah.

RABBI NISSAN ALPERT, whose untimely passing came only a few months after Reb Moshe's, was a prime and beloved disciple of his.

For the Sake of a Talmid In his eulogy, delivered at the funeral for Reb Moshe in New York, Reb Nissan told of how their close relationship developed. At the conclusion of Reb Moshe's *shiur* on Friday afternoons, students would usually rush out. Reb Moshe would remain behind to return the *sefarim* to their shelves and climb on benches to shut the lights. As Reb Nissan related, "The *Ribbono shel Olam* put an idea into my mind that I should remain with the *Rosh Yeshivah* and help him shut the lights and return the *sefarim*. When we went home, I would take his briefcase and carry it for him. Through this, I merited a tremendous closeness; I was like a member of the family to the *Rosh Yeshivah* and יבל״ח the *Rebbetzin* ... "

While Reb Nissan spoke of how he achieved a special closeness with Reb Moshe, their relationship actually began well before that time, when Reb Nissan was twelve years old and the first refugee child to become enrolled at Tifereth Jerusalem during World War II. One day, young Nissan was given an envelope containing a tuition statement which he was to take home to his parents. Unknown to the yeshivah administration, Nissan's father was not well at the time and was unable to work. In no way could he and his wife afford to pay tuition. Nissan noticed that his parents were upset by the bill. Realizing that his parents could not honor the request, he felt ashamed to be seen in yeshivah. The next day he remained at home, rarely venturing out of his room.

A few days went by with no change in the situation. Then, one afternoon, there was a knock on the Alperts' door. It was *Rebbetzin*

Rabbi Nissan Alpert

Feinstein, accompanied by two other neighborhood women. Nissan was a bright, charming child and had quickly become a popular face in the yeshivah. His absence had been noticed. Was he perhaps not well? the *Rebbetzin* wondered. The Alperts told her the truth.

The next day there again was a knock on the Alperts' door. This time it was Reb Moshe. He asked to see Nissan. When the boy appeared, Reb Moshe asked him, "Do you want to study Torah?"

"Yes," came the shy reply.

"Then there is nothing to be concerned about. Come with me." Reb Moshe took Nissan's hand in his own and in this way the *Rosh Yeshivah* and the young immigrant walked together to yeshivah. Needless to say, Nissan no longer felt ashamed to attend yeshivah and rose to become one of Tifereth Jerusalem's most outstanding products.

REB MOSHE OFTEN SPOKE OF the importance of performing *mitzvos* with true spirit and joy, even at a time when they require

Pride in Yiddishkeit

much personal sacrifice. He remarked that in the early part of this century, Shabbos observance in America was far from easy. Often a religious Jew would have to search for a new job every Sunday, since his employer had fired him on Friday for his refusal to work on Shabbos. How people reacted to such difficulties had a great effect on the way their children grew up. A well-known Orthodox leader recalls that he was a young teenager the first time he saw Reb Moshe. The *Rosh Yeshivah* was the guest speaker at a *siyum* in a small out-of-town *shul*. His *hadran* was beyond the listener's comprehension, but one part of the address made an indelible impression. "People destroyed their children by always repeating *es iz shver tzu zein a Yid* (it is hard to be a Jew). No — it is *not* hard to be a Jew. It is beautiful and joyous to be a Jew."

His face glowed with pride and happiness when he said those simple words, and the young listener recalls that he too became suffused with pride in his Jewishness.

Reb Moshe did his best to instill in his *talmidim* a true love for *mitzvos*, especially Torah study. Once, when addressing the high school of Tifereth Jerusalem, he said, *"Moshe commanded the Torah unto us, an inheritance for the congregation of Yaakov (Deuteronomy 33:4).* What is the significance of the Torah being our inheritance?

"Imagine a bride purchasing a new set of candlesticks before her wedding. Certainly she will be happy, but this will not compare to the joy of a bride who inherited her beloved grandmother's candlesticks. Those are priceless to her; she would not trade them for any pair in the world.

"The Torah that we study is the very same one that Moshe transmitted to our people at Sinai. It is our inheritance!"

When his younger son, Reb Reuven, was a young boy, Reb Moshe would spread out his child's clothing on the radiators in the early hours of cold winter mornings. Then he would dress his son under the covers, before sending him off to yeshivah. Reb Reuven sees more than a father's concern in this act. "My father did not want me to dread getting out of a warm bed to study Torah. He wanted me to feel that Torah study was something to look forward to, not something that was a burden."

A thirteen-year-old boy remarked that he could see Reb Moshe's deep love for Torah from the way he embraced and kissed a *sefer Torah* whenever it was carried in *shul.*

A former *talmid* recalled, "When I first attended the *Rosh*

Celebrating the completion of a new Sefer Torah;
standing behind Reb Moshe is Herman Wouk;
Jack Gartenhaus is holding the chuppah *pole*

Yeshivah's shiur I was too young to grasp it, but it was worth coming just to see the look on his face — his *ahavas haTorah*, his love for relating a Torah thought. When someone would interrupt with a question, the *Rosh Yeshivah* would explain himself again and again (if necessary). When the *bachur* would finally understand, the *Rosh Yeshivah* would smile — and sometimes even laugh — from joy!"

IN 1966, A BRANCH OF MESIVTHA TIFERETH JERUSALEM was founded in Staten Island, New York, with Rabbi Reuven Feinstein
The Yeshivah Expands as its *rosh yeshivah*. Today, the Yeshivah of Staten Island is a major Torah institution, where students can escape the tumult of city life and immerse themselves in Torah learning. Until his very last years when illness confined him to his home, Reb Moshe would deliver a weekly *shiur* in the yeshivah in addition to his visits there for Shavuos and other occasions. Even when not there in person, Reb Moshe guided the yeshivah from afar, as his son consulted with

him in formulating yeshivah policy.

Almost since its inception, the *talmidim* of Staten Island have enjoyed the summer months, which they spend in upstate New York, combining a somewhat lighter learning schedule with recreation. Until the last summer of his life, Reb Moshe would join the yeshivah for at least one month each summer. In earlier years, on summer Shabbos afternoons, *Rebbetzin* Feinstein would prepare refreshments for a group of high school boys whom Reb Moshe would join for an *oneg Shabbos* gathering. He would always say a *d'var Torah* and answer any questions the boys might have.

In his last years, Reb Moshe's physical condition did not permit the members of Camp Staten Island much more than an opportunity to observe him learning outside his bungalow, going for a short walk or *davening* in the camp's *beis midrash*. A few years ago the *beis midrash* was relocated from its original site to a structure only a short distance from Reb Moshe's bungalow, and a path was paved from the bungalow's back door to the *beis midrash*, so that Reb Moshe could walk to *davening* on level ground. When, in his very last years, even this short walk became too difficult for Reb Moshe,

Present and proposed buildings of the Yeshivah of Staten Island Campus

a golf cart would take him to the *beis midrash*. Reb Moshe would wave to the small children who would sometimes stand along the path as he rode by.

IN THE SUMMER OF 1982, a group of thirteen-year-old yeshivah boys from Camp Torah Vodaath (in Highland, New York), accompanied by their counselor, set out on a twenty-five-mile hike to Camp Staten Island, where they hoped to visit Reb Moshe. It was common knowledge that Reb Moshe was not well and was allowed few visitors. The group did not call the camp in advance of their journey, but instead

**The
Visitors**

With Rebbetzin Feinstein at their bungalow in Camp Staten Island

hoped that when they would arrive there and tell of the sacrifice they had made in coming, they would be permitted to see him.

It was a hot, sunny day, and by mid-afternoon the group — which had set out very early in the morning — had covered only thirteen miles. The counselor feared that some of the boys could not continue for much longer. Not about to see their efforts wasted, he hired taxis to take the group the rest of the way.

When they arrived at Camp Staten Island, the story of their journey was told over to the grandson who was attending Reb Moshe. Though Reb Moshe was officially not seeing anyone that day, his grandson did not have the heart to disappoint the weary campers. He asked them to wait in front of the bungalow's screened porch, to which he would bring Reb Moshe. In this way the boys would at least get a chance to see him. When Reb Moshe heard what they had gone through to come, he exclaimed, "Such *mesiras nefesh!*" Before he could say more, his *Rebbetzin* entered and, upon hearing of the boys' self-sacrifice, suggested that her grandson bring them to the back door of the bungalow where Reb Moshe would greet them individually. He shook each boy's hand, asked him his name, and gave his blessing. He then instructed his grandson to get

At Camp Staten Island with his elder son, Reb David, and a grandson

food for them from the camp's dining room and make sure that they go for a swim before returning home — by car! Reb Moshe then wished the boys well, and told them not to undertake such an arduous trip ever again.

THE ABOVE ANECDOTE ILLUSTRATES the feeling that *all* students of Torah, young and old alike, had for Reb Moshe. However great

Everyone's Father the physical distance may have been between them, Reb Moshe was still *their* guide, *their rosh yeshivah, their rebbi.* This was indicative of Reb Moshe's status as *gadol hador* and the "father of all yeshivos." Torah students understood that when they had the privilege of being with him, they were in the presence of a spiritual grandeur that gave light to Jews everywhere. It was this understanding that influenced scores of yeshivah students in the New York area to rise early every so often and take the subway to East Broadway for a chance to observe Reb Moshe as he *davened,* and perhaps even shake his hand and receive his blessing. It influenced elementary school *rebbeim* to schedule buses to take their classes to Tifereth Jerusalem. It influenced hundreds of yeshivah students to press

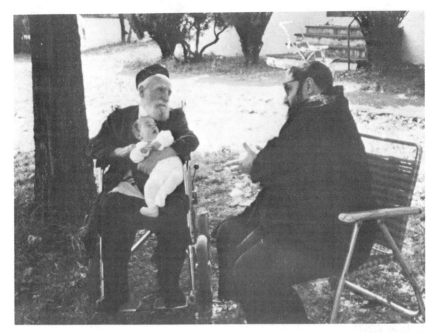

With his younger son, Reb Reuven, and a great-grandchild

against police lines a few months before Reb Moshe's passing, in an attempt to catch a glimpse of him as he attended the wedding of a grandson.

For his part, Reb Moshe was exuberant whenever he heard of a new undertaking for the spreading of Torah and he rejoiced whenever being introduced to a Torah student. Once, when he was forced to reprimand a yeshivah student for a gross misdeed, Reb Moshe exclaimed, "I have a headache from chastising a student of Torah! It had to be done, but it does my health no good."

How Torah students the world over prayed, in the last two years of Reb Moshe's life, that his failing health be preserved. How they hoped that he would lead them in greeting *Mashiach*.

The *Ribbono shel Olam* willed it otherwise.

⚜ ⚜ ⚜

Following Reb Moshe's passing, a student of a prominent American yeshivah told his father, "Since I was old enough to go to funerals of *gedolim*, I would hear speakers say that now we are like orphans. But I never felt like an orphan because I knew that Reb Moshe was still here. Now I am an orphan." They both cried.

CHAPTER FOUR

Keys to Torah Greatness

I N 1947, REB MOSHE PUBLISHED the first of his many works — *Dibros Moshe* to *Masechta Bava Kama*. * Rabbi Chaim Shmulevitz, legendary *Rosh Yeshivah* of Mirrer Yeshivah in Jerusalem, examined its contents carefully and then told his *talmidim*, "A fabulous *gaon* has written this *sefer*. I was able to go through his questions. But his answers and expositions? They are so lengthy, it is incredible to what depths he has gone. He is truly among the greats of this generation." Reb Chaim suggested to his *talmidim* that in studying a given topic in *Gemara*, they examine all of Reb Moshe's questions and observations on the subject, and then seek to find answers on their own.

Genius Recognized

Rabbi Nachum Pertzovitz, a son-in-law of Reb Chaim and a *gaon* in his own right, added the following: "I met Reb Moshe when

---

* Reb Moshe viewed the publishing of one's Torah thoughts as a sacred obligation. In the preface to the first volume of *Dibros Moshe*, he writes, "The benefit of publishing that which *Hashem Yisbarach* has helped me to understand [in the words of our Sages] through much toil and effort, ... is obvious ... It seems to me that one who has the ability to publish his *chiddushim* and does not, has not fulfilled the *mitzvah* of teaching Torah to others, in its fullest sense ..."

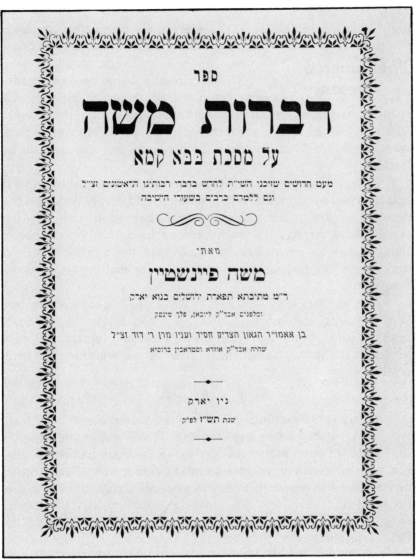

Title page of the first published volume of Dibros Moshe

I was in America. He is much more than a *gaon* in learning. He is a *gaon* in *Bavli, Yerushalmi, Halachah, Aggadah, drush, chesed, tzidkus* ... He is of a type that we simply do not find today, an אִישׁ מוּשְׁלָם (a complete and consistent person).''

Rabbi Aharon Kotler is said to have commented after studying *Dibros Moshe* to *Bava Kama* that every meaningful opinion and concept on the tractate is contained in the *sefer*.

REB MOSHE'S LEVEL OF TORAH greatness cannot be accurately described, for we cannot begin to fathom it. He knew all of *Shas* and

Phenomenal Memory

Shulchan Aruch along with many of their commentaries virtually *verbatim*, and had a flawless command of scores of other works, spanning the many centuries of *Rishonim* and *Acharonim*. That he had been blessed with a phenomenal memory was obvious to those who knew him, from incidents both related and unrelated to his learning.

Once, he learned that a fifteen-year-old student of his yeshivah had criticized someone else and in doing so had deeply wounded that person's feelings. Reb Moshe knew that while the boy had committed a wrong, his intention had been to correct what *he* thought was an error. Reb Moshe judged the boy too young to understand his mistake and therefore let the matter rest — for the time being.

Twelve years later, Reb Moshe was alone in a car with the boy, then a young man of twenty-seven. "You know," Reb Moshe began, "some years ago you made a certain remark ......" He reminded the young man of the incident before beginning his gentle reproof.

❀   ❀   ❀

Whenever he was introduced to a yeshivah student, Reb Moshe would ask where the boy was studying. To one student he remarked that some ten years earlier the boy's *rosh yeshivah* had enlightened him with an excellent interpretation of a comment by *Rashi*. Surely he intended also to elevate that *rosh yeshivah's* stature in the eyes of his student.

❀   ❀   ❀

To appreciate how amazing such incidents are, one must bear in mind that, in the words of one of Reb Moshe's closest associates, "The *Rosh Yeshivah* was the busiest man in the world." Countless numbers of people came before him each year in search of his halachic expertise, blessings, counsel and comfort. Yet Reb Moshe did not forget anything or anyone.

The thoroughness of his knowledge was phenomenal. A leading *rosh yeshivah* once called him with a list of difficulties in *Eizehu Neshech*, one of the most complicated chapters in *Shas*. After they had discussed all the questions and Reb Moshe had resolved all the problems, the caller remarked that he was fortunate to have called at a time when Reb Moshe had obviously studied the chapter fairly recently. In the course of the conversation it emerged that it had been more than eight years since Reb Moshe had studied the chapter thoroughly.

❁   ❁   ❁

A group of senior yeshivah students were delving into a certain halachic subject. Slowly and deliberately, they studied the *halachah* as it is developed in the original sources, *Shulchan Aruch* and its commentaries. Finally, they opened the *Igros Moshe* and examined a *teshuvah* relevant to the topic. It seemed that Reb Moshe's opinion contradicted that of the *Pri Megadim* (a classic commentary to *Shulchan Aruch*). The students brought the question to their *rosh yeshivah* — and he was as surprised as they were. There was only one thing to do, he told the students. Soon, one of the yeshivah's scholars was on his way to East Broadway.

Reb Moshe welcomed the student and asked what had prompted him to come. The young man, pointing to the particular *teshuvah* in *Igros Moshe,* said that he had found an apparent difficulty in it. Reb Moshe did not need to familiarize himself with the *teshuvah,* one of the thousands he had written on subjects that cover the entire range of Jewish law. Nor did he wait to hear the student's question. "Yes," came the instant reply, "it seems to contradict the *Pri Megadim.* However, there is really no contradiction at all, for ... "

❁   ❁   ❁

Some years ago, two *talmidei chachamim* found a number of difficulties with a *teshuvah* written by Reb Moshe some thirty years earlier on a complex Talmudic subject. The two were anxious to confront Reb Moshe with their questions, but first they spent days researching and studying all related material. When they finally felt very well prepared, they went to the *beis midrash* of Tifereth Jerusalem following *Shacharis,* as Reb Moshe was folding his *tallis.* He listened patiently to their arguments and then quickly refuted every one of them. Stunned, the two thanked Reb Moshe and turned to leave. As they walked toward the exit of the *beis midrash,* one was overheard remarking to the other, "A *gaon* of *gaonim;* the entire Torah is at his fingertips ... "

Those who were privileged to observe Reb Moshe as he put a *teshuvah* in writing were amazed to see him cite source upon source while rarely referring to a *sefer*. On the other hand, he took no question lightly. As the Sages teach, it makes no difference whether a question involves a penny or a huge fortune; the Torah must be interpreted accurately because it is the word of *Hashem*.

Reb Moshe's amazing power of reasoning and analysis is plainly apparent in his many volumes of *Dibros Moshe* on *Gemara* and *Igros Moshe* on *Halachah*. His longtime friend and neighbor, Rabbi Tuvia Goldstein, an eminent *posek* in his own right, commented that we find various authors of the *Mishnah* and Talmud praised for the characteristic in which they were most outstanding. Rabbi Elazar ben Hyrkanos retained all that he learned, while Rabbi Elazar ben Arach was known for his sharpness of mind and power of understanding (*Avos* 2:11); Rav Yosef was called *Sinai* because of his wide-ranging knowledge, while his contemporary Rabbah was called *Oker Harim* (the Uprooter of Mountains) because of his penetrating analysis (*Berachos* 64a). "What can we say," asks Reb Tuvia, "of someone who is most outstanding in both his breadth *and* depth of Torah knowledge? Such a person comes along but once in a generation. This was Reb Moshe."

As Rabbi David Feinstein put it, "My father's greatness was not simply that he remembered all of the Torah, but that he could apply any relevant thing he ever learned all his life to any question that ever came to him."

RATHER THAN DWELL ON Reb Moshe's inborn genius and extraordinary memory, it is important for us to analyze his attainment

Always Learning

of his greatness and see how it applies to ordinary people. Reb Moshe used to say that one can retain what he has learned even without the benefit of a very good memory. When a person views an unusual event, he can often recall it years later with perfect clarity. It does not take a good memory for one to remember something that made a deep impression on him. Similarly, one who appreciates the inestimable value of Torah and savors its every new thought and teaching as priceless, will find it possible to recall what he has learned. As the *Chasam Sofer*, a great Moshe of a previous era, used to say, "It is not that I have such a good memory. I invested so much time and hard work in mastering a Torah topic that it is a shame to forget it."

We may venture to say that Reb Moshe's deep love for Torah and his recognition that life had no meaning without it were important factors in his ability to recall what he had learned with the freshness of one who had studied it that very day.

A yeshivah student who was very close to Reb Moshe once asked him directly how he had become so great in Torah. Realizing that the questioner was sincere, Reb Moshe suppressed his deep humility and gave the boy an honest answer. "Of course, one is fortunate to be blessed with a good head, but hard work and *hasmadah* (diligence) are crucial to success in Torah."

A father once brought his young son before Reb Moshe for a blessing. The father said proudly, "My son learns very well. In fact, his *rebbi* says that if he continues along this path he will grow up to become another Rabbi Moshe Feinstein!" Reb Moshe responded sincerely, "I hope he will be even greater than I, but I must tell you that success in Torah does not come easily. The main thing is to love learning, work very hard and not waste a minute."

REBBETZIN FEINSTEIN WOULD HALF-JOKINGLY tell her husband, "The *gemara* to you is like a bottle of whiskey to an alcoholic … You

A Toraholic

can't live without it."

She was right. Torah was his life and he could no more be without it than he could be without oxygen. His love for Torah began very early in life and continued to the end of his days.

Rabbi Yitzchak Chaim Krasnitsky, dean of Yeshivah LiMetzuyanim in Israel, knew Reb Moshe from his boyhood days in Russia. When asked to relate interesting episodes from those days involving young Moshe Feinstein, he replied, "There is nothing to relate. All his time was spent learning."

An elderly Jew in the Bronx told a *talmid* of Reb Moshe, "I remember him as a little boy in Uzda. He was always learning. We all knew he would be a great *talmid chacham*, but we never dreamed that our friend would become the *gadol hador!*"

The Telshe *Rosh Yeshivah*, Rabbi Mordechai Gifter, observed that Reb Moshe was always "in the middle of learning." Even when he was engaged in some other activity, it was only a temporary

interruption of his studies; Torah was his love, his comfort, his ambition. Whenever there was a half-minute to spare he would be glancing at his *sefer*. While he put away his *tefillin*, as he walked in the street or sat at a wedding waiting for the *chupah* to begin, whenever he was involved in light activity, he was reciting *mishnayos* by heart. He was always adding to his thousands upon thousands of pages of writings.

Rabbi Gifter recalled arriving early for a meeting at Reb Moshe's home. While he and Reb Moshe waited for the other participants, they both sat and studied. The *Rebbetzin* asked Reb Moshe to come and eat lunch before the meeting began. He got up from the table without closing his *gemara*, although one should do so when he stops learning. He explained to Rabbi Gifter that he was not required to close his *gemara* because he would be returning to it the instant his meal was over, so he still had the status of being engaged in his studies.

Once, a granddaughter and her husband came to visit him and found him learning in his study, his back to the door. Not wanting to disturb him, the couple stood silently in the doorway, waiting for Reb Moshe to pause in his studies. Some time passed and Reb Moshe remained immersed in his learning. When the *Rebbetzin* came by and observed the scene she exclaimed, "If you are waiting for him to stop learning, you will be standing here all day!" Hearing this, Reb Moshe turned around to his grandchildren and said laughingly, "How I wish that you should never find me sitting idle."

Once, when Reb Moshe was called to the Torah reading, a *talmid* brought his volume of *Mishnah* to the *bimah*, so that he could study it between *aliyos.* * Someone told the *talmid* that he was

---

* Until he reached his late eighties, Reb Moshe's procedure during the Torah reading was to study *Mishnah* until the first *oleh* would begin to recite the opening blessing, then rush to stand near the *bimah* and listen to the reading while a child held a *Chumash* for him, then rush back to his seat at the conclusion of the *aliyah* to resume his *Mishnah* study until the next blessing.

*In the beis midrash of Mesivtha Tifereth Jerusalem,
listening to the Torah reading*

taking things too far and in the future should allow Reb Moshe to stand at the *bimah* without a *sefer*, like everyone else who was called to the Torah reading. When the *talmid* asked Reb Moshe about this, he was told to continue bringing the *sefer* to the *bimah*. No matter where one found himself, time was too precious to waste.

※　　※　　※

For most of his life, Reb Moshe slept between five and six hours a night, and took a short nap in the afternoon. As a student in Yeshivah of Staten Island, Rabbi Moshe Meir Weiss was privileged to attend to Reb Moshe for some time and once observed him arising from a nap. As Reb Moshe opened his eyes, he instinctively reached for a small *Tanach* that he took with him almost everywhere he went. He arose and, carrying the *Tanach*, made his way to the sink and rested the *Tanach* on the sink's edge while opening the faucet. As he filled a cup with one hand his other hand turned the pages of the *sefer* until he found the proper place. After washing his hands and face, he began — or rather resumed — learning without a moment's delay.

He once remarked, "In America I have heard people say, 'I have plenty of time!' I wish they could give me some of that time — I never have enough of it!"

THOUGH HIS MEMORY WAS INFALLIBLE, Reb Moshe did not cease to review all that he had mastered. He once remarked that

Constant Effort many geniuses had fallen far short of their potential in Torah study, for they were satisfied with having amassed more knowledge than most others and therefore made no effort to gain the maximum benefit from their G-d-given abilities. Reb Moshe was anything but this type of genius, for he used every bit of his mental and physical ability to its utmost.

The time Reb Moshe devoted to study was outstanding as much for its quality as for its quantity. At the wedding of a son of Rabbi Gifter, Reb Moshe got up to leave at 11:00 p.m., before the end of the meal. He apologized to Rabbi Gifter, explaining that he had to sleep a few hours because it was his practice to get up at 4:00 a.m. to learn for three hours before *Shacharis*. Only then, he said, was he able to study without interruption and achieve the maximum benefit from the time.

He would frequently cite the *Vilna Gaon's* teaching that Torah study without proper toil is equivalent to wasted time. "Praiseworthy is he whose *toil* is in Torah" (*Berachos* 17a) — only when one studies Torah with proper effort and concentration, using his G-d-given abilities to the fullest, has he performed this greatest of *mitzvos* properly.

Rabbi Yaakov Kamenetzky, himself a *gaon* of towering stature, once remarked that Reb Moshe's posture was indicative of the reason that he had surpassed his peers in Torah scholarship. He never leaned back in his chair to relax. He always leaned forward, his brow furrowed, straining to uncover the true meaning of the Torah's holy words.

In the *battei midrash* of Mesivtha Tifereth Jerusalem and Yeshivah of Staten Island, *talmidim* study at desks or tables as opposed to the high *shtenders* (lecterns) found in many other yeshivos. It was Reb Moshe's feeling that *shtenders*, which a student can easily pull toward his chair as he leans back, can breed lethargy and hinder the proper toil in Torah study.

Reb Moshe would encourage *chavrusos* (study partners) not to have one student listening silently while the other reads the *Gemara* aloud. Both should toil equally, reading together, explaining the *Gemara* to one another, sharing in each other's insights. Difficulties should be written down for future reference; most will in all probability be resolved as the *Gemara* becomes clearer and its meaning begins to take form. With proper toil, success is inevitable.

While Reb Moshe stressed toil as a vital ingredient in learning, he also felt it important that Torah be studied in comfort, not to be confused with leisure. His approach is best demonstrated by his custom of studying outdoors in the summertime in his shirtsleeves, hunched forward in intense concentration — toil and comfort, one complementing the other.

REB MOSHE'S SELF-DISCIPLINE was another factor in his greatness. He was an exceptionally well-organized person. His day was **Internal** governed by a carefully arranged schedule that usually began at 4:00 a.m. and ended at around 11:00 **Clock** p.m.. He did not wear a watch and did not use an alarm clock, but somehow never overslept and was always on time for *tefillah.*

Someone close to Reb Moshe recalled that when they would travel together, he would sometimes say, "I'm going to nap now for half an hour." He would then lie down, without asking to be awakened. Sure enough, he was always up half an hour later.*

Reb Moshe once confided that no matter how exhausting his schedule was on any given day, he never fell asleep while learning. Yet, whenever he retired for the night or lay down for a nap during the day, he always fell asleep moments after his head touched the pillow.

He would arise on Friday morning at 2:00 a.m. to prepare for his weekly *pilpul shiur*. Somehow his body knew that once a week it had to manage on less sleep.

Though Reb Moshe had hundreds of *shiurim* in writing, he would still construct new *chiddushim* in the early hours of Friday morning to be used in that day's *shiur*. Rabbi Tuvia Goldstein once asked him why he strained himself so to prepare new material when he could have certainly managed well with his existing *shiurim*. Reb Moshe replied, "As long as the *Ribbono shel Olam* gives strength,

---

* Rabbi Shneur Kotler once told a *talmid* that as a *yeshiva bachur* in Europe, he had learned to awaken himself at a specific hour without any assistance. He remarked that every person has the ability to discipline himself in this manner.

one must seek to originate anew." Reb Tuvia then remarked that one evening might not always be sufficient to construct the kind of involved *shiurim* for which Reb Moshe was famous. What did Reb Moshe do when time was running out and the *shiur* was not near completion? Reb Moshe allowed himself a slight smile and said simply, *"Baruch Hashem, Baruch Hashem."*

Reb Moshe once felt dizzy minutes before he was to deliver a *shiur* and asked someone to get him a glass of water. After doing so, the person said, "I will take the *Rosh Yeshivah* home so that he can rest." Reb Moshe replied, "What do you mean? I must say the *shiur!"*

REB MOSHE POSSESSED an incredible power of concentration. Neither a loud noise, a bang on the table or anything else could

Concentration startle him. Often, he would look up to see if someone needed him — he could even hear a footstep on a carpeted floor — but always calmly. While he took to

---

* In relating this story, the person involved said, "Reb Moshe did everything according to the *Shulchan Aruch*. No doubt, he was sure that saying the *shiur* would not endanger his health, otherwise he would have gone home. Once he decided that his health was not endangered, he felt obligated to go on with the *shiur*."

heart the suffering of others to the point that their pain was his pain, this in no way disturbed his total immersion in his studies after they had gone. Through the course of a day, Reb Moshe could be confronted with news of travail after travail. Those who were with him could see the anguish on his face as he heard a piece of bitter news, and they could often hear him groan in anguish. But Torah, for which heaven and earth exist, still had to be learned. And by Reb Moshe's definition, learning meant that one apply himself to the fullest under all conditions.

Many of the notebooks containing Reb Moshe's *chiddushei Torah* start and end in the middle of sentences.* In a sense this sums up his entire life: a never-ending flow of Torah from a most unusual wellspring of thought.

> Incredibly, he had the ability to resume his writing after an interruption, without pausing to collect his thoughts. Once he put down his pen to hear the case of an *agunah* (a woman whose husband is missing and may be dead). Reb Moshe listened to the story, probed and considered the available evidence, and finally issued his *p'sak* as to whether or not the woman was permitted to remarry. The instant that the parties had left, Reb Moshe picked up his pen and without a moment's hesitation continued from where he had left off. A man who had observed the entire scene could not believe his eyes. Unable to contain himself, he asked, "How could the *Rosh Yeshivah* deal with so delicate a question and not lose track of what he had been thinking of before?" Reb Moshe replied simply, "I have worked on this."

This was a skill that was very important to him. He told his brother-in-law Rabbi Isaac Small that a paramount factor in his success was the ability to stop in the middle of a subject and return to it many hours later exactly where he had left off, without needing to refresh his memory by review.

He also had the ability to do two things at once. He could, for example, answer a question on the phone and at the same time correct galleys of a forthcoming *sefer*, a task that requires a great

---

* His notebooks were outstanding for their orderliness. Each had a table of contents in the front that listed the many chapters contained within by title. Often, Reb Moshe would revise a chapter and insert new material. He would always note which parts had been written earlier and which had come later.

degree of concentration. Rabbi Alpert recalled many conversations during which Reb Moshe listened and responded regarding weighty matters, but, under his breath, would review *Mishnah* while others were speaking.

It is interesting that while he was best known for his *Igros Moshe* on *Halachah*, in his own mind, Reb Moshe placed greater emphasis on his *Dibros Moshe* to *Gemara*. Following her husband's passing, *Rebbetzin* Feinstein recalled the tremendous self-sacrifice Reb Moshe had endured in composing his *Dibros Moshe*, of which fifteen volumes have been published and many are still in manuscript form. The *Rebbetzin* remembers well her husband's boundless joy when he would receive a letter pertaining to something he had written in *Dibros Moshe*.

Many of his *chiddushim* had to be reconstructed after being destroyed in Russia. Yet this did not deter Reb Moshe, who viewed the writing of his *chiddushei Torah* as an important part of his mission on earth.

> His writing was not only an end, but a means as well. Rabbi Elimelech Bluth, a prime disciple of Reb Moshe who stood faithfully at his side for many years, was once present when Reb Moshe did not have an immediate answer to a difficult question. He said, "I will commit my thoughts on the matter to writing. Perhaps things will become clear as they are written."

IN *PIRKEI AVOS* (6:1), Rabbi Meir teaches, "Whoever engages in Torah study for its own sake merits many things." Among those

Heavenly Assistance rewards is an unusual level of success in one's learning. "The Torah gives him ... analytical judgment; the secrets of the Torah are revealed to him; he becomes like a steadily strengthening fountain and like an unceasing river." As Reb Moshe's dedication to Torah was of the highest degree, he was granted great *siyata diShmaya* (Heavenly assistance) in his learning. This is obvious simply from the depth and breadth of his enormous store of *chiddushei Torah* and *teshuvos*.

When Reb Moshe once visited Rabbi Ephraim Greenblatt, the two became involved in a halachic discussion, and Rabbi Greenblatt expressed surprise over the *p'sak* he had seen in a certain *sefer*. Reb Moshe said, "I too am surprised. In fact, I hold that what this author has forbidden is actually permissible."

Later when the two were in Rabbi Greenblatt's study, Reb Moshe noticed the sefer *Sh'eilos U'Teshuvos Shoel U'Meishiv*, by the classic *posek* of the last century, Rabbi Yosef Shaul Nathanson. He reached for it while saying, "Just yesterday, someone told me that a *p'sak* of mine differs with that of the *Shoel U'Meishiv*. I would like to see if this is so." Reb Moshe then opened the *sefer* randomly and there, staring back at him, was the *first* question which Rabbi Greenblatt had put to him. The *Shoel U'Meishiv's* ruling concurred with Reb Moshe's. Rabbi Greenblatt was amazed. "This is *siyata diShmaya*," he said. Reb Moshe tried to make light of the matter. "It can happen sometimes ... ," he replied. Rabbi Greenblatt recalls that during his days in Tifereth Jerusalem, Reb Moshe would very often open a *sefer* to the exact page he was seeking.

In 1981, when Reb Moshe suffered from attacks of sciatica, a neighborhood boy who often attended him once initiated a discussion in learning, only to realize that Reb Moshe was in agony. "Please forgive me!" the boy said. "I will ask the *Rosh Yeshivah* another time ... "

"No!" Reb Moshe insisted. "We can continue talking now. *'For they* (i.e., the words of Torah) *are our life and the length of our days'* — this is what I live for ... "

CHAPTER FIVE

Posek of the Nation

ITHOUT A DOUBT, Reb Moshe achieved his greatest renown in the area of *Halachah*. His *Igros Moshe*, in which thousands of his responsa spanning the full range of Torah law are collected, was acclaimed as a classic decades before his passing. In recent times, the *Steipler Gaon* said that Reb Moshe was the leading authority of the era. Rabbi Shlomo Zalman Auerbach of Jerusalem, one of the greatest *poskim* of our time, declined to eulogize Reb Moshe, saying, "Who am I to eulogize him? I studied his *sefarim*; I was his *talmid*."

Universal Acceptance

Several years ago, Rabbi Yaakov Kamenetzky sent one of his closest disciples to Reb Moshe, saying, "Only Reb Moshe has shoulders broad enough to rule in this matter. But if he tells you that you are permitted to follow a lenient course, your conscience should not bother you at all. If he says so, it is permitted by the Torah."

A difficult halachic question was sent from London to Jerusalem. Two of the leading authorities of the Holy City, Rabbi Shlomo Zalman Auerbach and Rabbi Shalom Yosef Eliyashiv, both insisted that only Reb Moshe was competent to render a decision.

A prominent Chassidic *rav* ruled a certain act permissible, unaware that Reb Moshe had ruled to the contrary. One day, the two met and debated the matter. The *rav* was not convinced of Reb

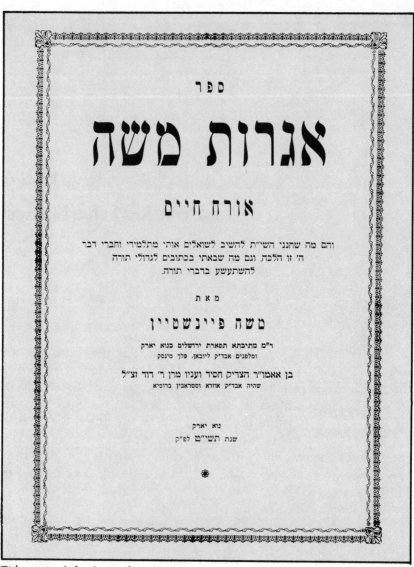

ספר

אגרות משה

אורח חיים

והם מה שחנני השי״ת להשיב לשואלים אותי מתלמידי וחברי דבר
ה׳ זו הלכה, וגם מה שבאתי בכתובים לגדולי תורה
להשתעשע בדברי תורה.

מ א ת

משה פיינשטיין

ר״מ מתיבתא תפארת ירושלים בנוא יארק
ומלפנים אבד״ק ליובאן, פלך מינסק

בן אאמו״ר הצדיק חסיד ועניו מרן ר׳ דוד זצ״ל
שהיה אבד״ק אוזדא וסטראבין ברוסיא

נוא יארק
שנת תשי״ט לפ״ק

❋

Title page of the first volume of Igros Moshe

Moshe's reasoning; nevertheless, from then on, when asked
regarding this *halachah*, the rav would respond, ''Reb Moshe
forbids it.'' He also instructed his own household to abide by Reb
Moshe's *p'sak*.

Similar reverence for Reb Moshe was shown by the Torah
giants of a generation ago. When he was well into his nineties, Rabbi
Eliyahu Lopian, legendary *mashgiach* of Yeshivah K'far Chassidim,

Reb Moshe's personal inscription in a volume of Igros Moshe which he would present to his close talmidim as a wedding gift. The inscription reads:

בעה"י
לאות ברכה וידידות נאמנה
להחתן המופלג הרב מאיר יעקב בן
הרה"ג ר' אהרן זלאטאוויץ שליט"א
ליום חתונתו ושמחת לבו עם
ב"ג הכלה הכבודה פיגא רחל תחי'
בת ר' חיים חייקל שוהלמאן שליט"א
יתברכו בכל הטוב והשלום והצלחה
בתורה וביראה ובגדולה עשר
וכבוד ויזכו לבנות בית נכון
ונאמן בישראל לתפארת
משה פיינשטיין ורעיתו

insisted on attending the *K'nessiah Gedolah* held in Jerusalem in 1964, so that he could fulfill the *mitzvah* of standing up for Reb Moshe.

❈   ❈   ❈

Rabbi Yonasan Steif, formerly *Rav* of Budapest, Hungary, was among the leading halachic authorities of the past generation. After Rabbi Steif's passing, Reb Moshe once attended a wedding at which *Rebbetzin* Steif was also present. She asked to be introduced to Reb Moshe and when he was told who she was, he stood up, because he had known and had greatly respected her late husband. Flustered, she said, "Please, *you* should not stand up for *me*. Once, when my husband was already suffering from a heart condition, I watched him put on his hat and stand up while speaking on the phone. When I demanded that he sit down for his health's sake, he protested, 'How can I sit down? I am speaking with Rabbi Moshe Feinstein!'"

Rabbi Aharon Kotler, who until his passing in 1962 was the recognized leader of the American yeshivah world, declared Reb Moshe to be the leading halachic authority of his generation. Reb Aharon once could not contain his surprise upon hearing a *p'sak* that had been recently issued by Reb Moshe. Nevertheless, he said, "The *halachah* is like him at all times. If the *posek hador* says that the *halachah* is so, then we must listen to him."

Yet another *gadol* of yesteryear, Rabbi Yaakov Yechiel Weinberg, author of *S'ridei Eish*, once compared Reb Moshe to Rabbi Yitzchak Elchonon Spector, the *posek hador* of a century ago, in explaining why he had the authority to dispute a ruling of the *Chasam Sofer* while other *poskim* did not.

IN HIS PREFACE TO *IGROS MOSHE*, Reb Moshe humbly explains how one has the right to propound new halachic rulings in this

Genesis of a Posek

generation, even though we are so far below the level of wisdom of earlier generations that one should fear that his opinions are not in accordance with Torah truth. It was such a fear, writes Reb Moshe, that caused many Torah luminaries of the past to abstain from *p'sak*, "and certainly [this should apply] to those of little worth like me, who has neither Torah nor wisdom in proper measure ... " Still, Reb Moshe continues, one who is fit to rule in matters of *Halachah* is permitted and even obligated to do so, "... after he has toiled and strained to clarify the *halachah* through (studying) *Shas* and *poskim* as much as his strength allows, with a serious sense of responsibility and with fear of *Hashem* ... and, as *Rabbeinu Yonah* writes (*Avos* 4:12), that one review until he does not forget a thing and until he has plumbed to the depths of the matter ..."

Toiled and strained ... as much as his strength allows ... with a sense of responsibility and with fear of Hashem ... *that one review until he does not forget a thing* ... These guidelines say much for how Reb Moshe came to be the greatest *posek* of his day.

Someone once expressed his amazement at how Reb Moshe ruled on every sort of question that came to him, without doubt or concern that perhaps he had not analyzed the problem correctly. Reb Moshe told the person that he had accepted upon himself the yoke of *p'sak halachah* only in response to the needs of his generation. He then said, "From the time that I accepted this yoke upon myself, *Hashem* granted me a special degree of *siyata diShmaya*. At times when I have been asked to rule on extremely difficult and complex questions, it has been obvious to me that *Hashem* has illuminated my eyes."

With his son Reb David

With his son Reb Reuven

That Reb Moshe merited such *siyata diShmaya* is certainly no cause for wonder. *Sh'iltei HaGibborim* (to *Mordechai, Shabbos* 2:265) writes: "When a man toils in Torah for its sake, then *HaKadosh Baruch Hu* illuminates his darkness so that he will not come to sin and will not rule against the *halachah* ... "

❀   ❀   ❀

Reb Moshe's son, Reb David, who has succeeded his father as *Rosh HaYeshivah* of Mesivtha Tifereth Jerusalem, says that while Reb Moshe did everything in a very natural and simple way, his sense of responsibility and fear of *Hashem* were obvious from his method of formulating a *p'sak.* In determining the *halachah* he would leave no stone unturned, straining and struggling to adduce proofs to either side of the question. Reb Moshe's *teshuvos* are replete with proofs to back up their conclusions. This firm basis for his rulings was a source of pride to Reb Moshe, his son recalls.

Reb David once sought to determine the basis for a certain *halachah.* After spending some time researching the matter, he then studied his father's *teshuvah* on the topic and saw that not a single source related to the question was missing from it. Reb David notes that his father was granted great *siyata diShmaya* in locating the necessary sources to any given question with amazing speed and he had such total command of his fund of knowledge that he could unerringly relate to everything that had a bearing on the topic at hand.

In exhorting his *talmidim* to strive for greatness in Torah, which, he said, was within everyone's reach, Reb Moshe would name diligence and *siyata diShmaya* as the two prime ingredients for success. Diligence is in the hands of the individual, while *siyata diShmaya* is granted by the *Ribbono shel Olam*, according to what the individual deserves.

REB MOSHE'S CONFIDENCE that Heaven guided his decisions along the path of truth was visibly apparent. Once, he ruled that an

Halachah as Reality *agunah* was permitted to remarry. After she did so, a story began to circulate that her husband was still alive — which would have meant that she was now living in sin. The woman's family was horrified and those who were closest to Reb Moshe were dismayed that he would be humiliated by an error with such tragic consequences. The only one not daunted by the news was Reb Moshe. As his grandson Rabbi Mordechai Tendler recalls, Reb Moshe remained confident that he had ruled according to the *halachah* and that *Hashem* would not permit such a calamity to occur as a result of his *p'sak*. The rumor *had* to be false. In due time, Reb Moshe was proven right. The first husband was not alive.

❁　　❁　　❁

Rabbi Meir Zlotowitz was present when a related incident was brought to Reb Moshe. A Holocaust survivor was permitted to remarry on the basis of evidence that her husband had perished in the concentration camps. Then, after more than twenty years, when she had grown children of marriageable age, she met her first husband! The distraught woman had come with her rabbi from South America to seek Reb Moshe's guidance.

Reb Moshe asked the woman to tell her story. She told of how she had brought her case before a well-known *rav* in one of the

Displaced Persons Camps after the War. Based on available testimony and evidence, this *rav* had ruled it correct to assume her husband dead, and had given her a document containing this decision. It was on the basis of this ruling that she had remarried. The *rav* had passed away not long after the War, and, due to the chaotic post-War conditions, she had lost the document. Now she and her family were suffering indescribably from a mistake that was not theirs!

Reb Moshe asked her to repeat her story, and she did so. He asked her to tell it a third time. The atmosphere in the room was tense. Why was Reb Moshe tormenting the poor woman so? What could be added by another repetition of her sorrowful tale?

> Reb Moshe's brow was furrowed in intense concentration, while everyone in the room was silent. Then, abruptly, he rose, leaned across the table and said agitatedly to the woman, "It cannot be! I knew the *rav* of whom you speak. He was a *gaon* and a *tzaddik*, and I do not even approach his ankles in Torah. I have permitted over two thousand *agunos* to remarry and never did the first husband reappear. Now you are telling me that such a thing could have happened to that *tzaddik*? It is impossible! It cannot be!"

The people in the room were shocked that Reb Moshe, who was famous for his mild manner and compassion, could have spoken in such a way to a woman in distress. But their shock gave way to incredulity when the woman broke down in tears and admitted that her story was indeed false. She had been sure that her husband was dead — how could he have survived, she had asked herself. When she heard that a highly respected rabbi had passed away, she made up the story concerning the document, using that rabbi's name.

To Reb Moshe's mind, a person's complete obedience to the Torah even when it involved personal suffering was a source of very great merit. A young man, whose marriage had been childless for some time, once came to ask whether it is permissible to undergo a certain medical test. Reb Moshe would not permit the procedure. The questioner became very upset and begged the *Rosh Yeshivah* to find some way to permit it. With love and concern, Reb Moshe took the young man's hand and said, "Often a childless couple will seek the blessing of a *tzaddik*. You should know that obeying the *halachah* is greater than any blessing." The man followed Reb Moshe's decision and did not undergo the test. Nevertheless, the young man's wife eventually bore him a number of children.

REB MOSHE'S MEMORY was of utmost importance to him, because he could not undertake to decide complex and serious questions of

Passion for Accuracy

Halachah unless he could be sure that he had not overlooked any sources. Once he and several rabbis were sitting in the large communal *succah* of the apartment complex in which he lived when a Talmudic passage came under discussion. Reb Moshe said that it was explained in a commentary of *Tosafos* in *Sanhedrin*, while the others all agreed that the source was not in *Masechta Sanhedrin* but in *Makkos*. He rose and rushed from the table. The others were surprised. True, he had completed his meal, but it was out of character for him to leave the table without saying *Gut Yom Tov*. Several minutes later he returned. He had crossed the courtyard and climbed the steps to his apartment to look up the *Gemara*. As he had thought, it was in *Sanhedrin*, but he simply could not wait until later to verify his recollection, because truth was his most important value, his most pressing concern. If his memory was challenged, then the source must be checked — now, not later.

Once a *talmid* inquired where he could find references to a particular *halachah*. Reb Moshe told him the chapter and paragraph numbers where the *Magen Avraham* discussed it. A while later the student reported that he had found what he needed, but the paragraph number of the *Magen Avraham* was different. Reb Moshe asked him to check the number again and to report back. As it turned out, Reb Moshe had been right, but the *talmid* was curious as to why the *Rosh Yeshivah* had been so concerned about the proper paragraph number. He explained, "I decide halachic questions from memory, and if my memory is becoming faulty, then I would not be allowed to continue doing so."

Once Reb Moshe urged a *talmid* to enter the rabbinate and undertake to decide questions of *Halachah*, but the young man felt he was not qualified. "I have spent most of my time in yeshivah studying *Gemara*, not *Halachah*." Reb Moshe replied, "You have strained to understand Torah? You are truly fortunate! But you can still acquire the halachic knowledge you will need. Study each section of *Shulchan Aruch* with its primary commentary, and then review it again and again. Then you will know where all the major topics are discussed and you will be able to research individual questions as they arise."

With Rabbi Lipa Eidelman, a rosh yeshivah in Mesivtha Tifereth Jerusalem

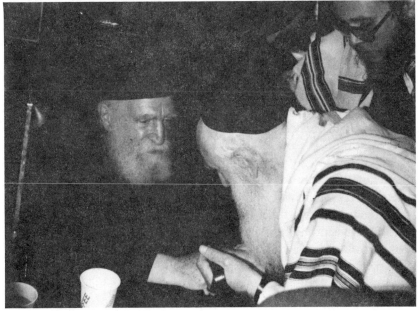

With the mashgiach, *Reb Michel Barenbaum*

Of course, there is a vast difference between knowing where to find existing answers to questions and offering one's own original rulings, as Reb Moshe did in thousands of cases, many of which required applying the Torah's unchanging statutes to areas of modern medicine and technology. Only by meeting the most exacting standards he had established for himself would he rule so often, on so many complex and delicate issues, with such certainty.

REB MOSHE WOULD CITE *Yam Shel Shlomo (Bava Kamma* 4:7) that a judge must not back down from a Torah ruling even when

Fearless Posek

threatened with death. To alter a *halachah* is to alter the Torah, G-d forbid, and this must be avoided regardless of the consequences. Reb Moshe's longtime friend and colleague Rabbi Michel Barenbaum, *mashgiach* of Tifereth Jerusalem who served for forty years under Reb Moshe, recalls Reb Moshe's tenacity in standing by his decisions. Even on the rare occasions when a ruling was opposed rather forcefully in certain circles, both verbally and in writing, Reb Moshe remained unshaken. He was ready to back down if proven wrong, but until that time there could be no wavering from what he held to be truth.

His passion for truth was apparent in one of the very first

With members of Agudath HaRabbanim: (left to right) Rabbi Noach Chadash; Rabbi Ephraim Yolles; Rabbi Meir Zvi Ginsberg; Reb Moshe; Rabbi Simcha Elberg; Rabbi Baruch Leizerowski; and Rabbi Yaakov Neiman

dinnei Torah that he judged in America. The case involved the *Agudath HaRabbanim*, the Union of Orthodox Rabbis, an organization that was doing much to spread Reb Moshe's fame among the American Torah community and to help him become established. Reb Moshe ruled *against* the organization. Would this leave its directors with bitter feelings and damage Reb Moshe's relationship with them? There were those who said that his future in the American rabbinate was doomed. Perhaps, but this did not figure an iota in his decision. All that mattered was that truth be determined and justice be carried out. In fact, Reb Moshe did not suffer because of his decision; rather, he gained esteem for his noble character and courage.

During most of his career, he was constantly asked to rule in disputes between individuals, businesses, and institutions. People knew that a *din Torah* at which Reb Moshe presided would be decided fairly and correctly. At such sessions, he would listen to the arguments intently and respectfully, without revealing by word or expression that he could tell which side was being more truthful. Some people misunderstood his evenhandedness; they thought he was being fooled. But, as he told a *talmid* after a *din Torah* session, with an amused look on his face, "They think they are deceiving me." In private discussions he held with the parties to work out compromises, he had a way of defining which issues were most important to each of the sides. He would say to a party in the dispute, "Tell me how you would want the result to be."

No question was too big or too small for Reb Moshe. He could closet himself in a room for days researching and studying before deciding a life-and-death matter, a decision which the current Surgeon General of the United States and a team of doctors awaited before going ahead with a delicate and dangerous operation. And he could listen just as carefully to the question of an educator regarding which text to use for an *al hamichyah* poster for children.

> In a *teshuvah* he writes (*Orach Chaim* 1:109), "It is unnecessary for his honor to excuse himself for disagreeing with me. This is the way of the Torah, to clarify the truth, and G-d forbid for one who disagrees to remain silent ... Therefore even if you view me as a man of stature, it is permissible to disagree and you are therefore obligated to state your opinion ... but, in any case, with regard to the actual question, what I have written is correct ... "

Someone close to Reb Moshe was once sent to ask him a halachic question — and to make an unusual request. "The *Rosh Yeshivah* should please forgive me," the emissary began, "but if I do not present the following request then I will not have properly fulfilled my mission. I was asked to tell the *Rosh Yeshivah* that the person wants a decision that is strict *Halachah* without any leniencies."

"I do not rule with leniencies," replied Reb Moshe. "I rule according to the law."

That is certainly true, but it is also true that often Reb Moshe arrived at a lenient *p'sak* when no other recognized *posek* felt able to. How could *he* do so?

A STORY IS TOLD of an *agunah* who came before the Kovno Rav, Rabbi Yitzchak Elchonon Spector, seeking his authorization to

The Role of Compassion remarry. Reb Yitzchak Elchonon reviewed the case again and again but could not find the necessary proof for such a ruling. He was about to consider the case closed when, out of pity for the distraught woman, he decided to go over the case one last time. It was then that Reb Yitzchak Elchonon, the leading *posek* of his era, discovered that there *was* a basis in *Halachah* for the woman to remarry. Reb Yitzchak Elchonon's compassion had driven him to strain his mind even more than was required of him until, somewhere in his vast storehouse of knowledge, he discovered what was needed for a lenient ruling. Had he not been so compassionate, he would not have taken the extra effort to rule as he did. True, his lenient ruling was made possible by his compassion, but it was not *based* on his compassion, for Torah truth can *never* be compromised, no matter what the consequences. The woman could remarry because Reb Yitzchak Elchonon understood that the *Halachah* indeed permitted her to.

So it was with Reb Moshe. As Rabbi Michel Barenbaum expressed it, "Reb Moshe was the man of *Halachah,* but from studying his *teshuvos,* one can see his *chesed* and the concern he felt for others." His knowledge of Torah was incomparable, and his *siyata diShmaya* in *p'sak* was unusual. These two factors permitted him the 'broad shoulders' needed to be lenient when others may have hesitated to do so. And his concern for others often drove him to search tirelessly for a leniency *within the confines of Halachah* as established by the sages of past generations.

Once, he involved himself in a very sensitive case and as a result was the target of verbal attack by one party. Someone asked Reb Moshe, "Why does the *Rosh Yeshivah* allow himself to get involved in such cases? He has nothing but aggravation from these matters!" Replied Reb Moshe, "Had you seen the tears of the person that brought the problem before me you would not have asked such a question."

❀ ❀ ❀

A young woman who was going through difficult times was scheduled to see Reb Moshe regarding a halachic matter related to her problem. The day after the appointment was made Reb Moshe told someone, "The thought of a *bas Yisrael* suffering so disturbed my sleep last night."

❀ ❀ ❀

An important Jewish leader once asked to bring a visitor to

him. Reb Moshe answered that he was ill, but would be glad to see them in a few days. The caller said that the man he wanted to bring along had begun a hunger strike to publicize the plight of Jews in the Soviet Union. When Reb Moshe heard this he said, "Come immediately. Don't waste a moment!"

The two arrived at his apartment and Reb Moshe was waiting for them. He told his fasting visitor that it was forbidden for him to endanger his health that way despite the nobility of his cause. Then he asked the *Rebbetzin* to bring food to the table and insisted that the man break his fast and pursue other ways of helping his brethren. Reb Moshe succeeded.

IT UPSET HIM GREATLY to hear that someone had distorted or misquoted one of his rulings, thereby deducing proof for a leniency that

Dedication to Truth

was false! Someone once told Reb Moshe a story of how a famous nineteenth-century *tzaddik* would swallow steaming hot food without chewing it so as not to enjoy earthly pleasures. Reb Moshe replied that he could not believe that so great a *tzaddik* would do something that could be so damaging to his health. "But they say it's a true story!" the man insisted. "Yes," Reb Moshe responded, "and people also say things about me which are not true, although I am alive to deny it. So why is it hard to believe that a story about someone who passed away over one hundred years ago is, in fact, a fabrication!"

Reb Moshe's commitment to truth in his everyday life was unswerving; nothing in the world could ever cause him to stray from it. Undoubtedly this attribute was another important reason why *Hashem*, Whose seal is truth (*Shabbos* 55a), granted him the help needed to arrive at the truth in *Halachah*.

His passion for truth went to unusual lengths. He always insisted on paying for the breakfast he ate in Tifereth Jerusalem. While the yeshivah administration felt that he was entitled to the breakfast — and a great deal more — Reb Moshe would not hear of it. He received a salary from the yeshivah for his services and he would not accept a penny more than had been agreed upon. Of course, when it came to making appeals, attending functions or doing anything else to raise funds for the yeshivah, Reb Moshe was always ready to be of service, without the slightest notion of accepting payment for such voluntary services.

Through an error, the government began sending him Social Security checks before he was legally entitled to them. He returned the money, along with a note of explanation.

❈ ❈ ❈

People often donated money to Tifereth Jerusalem so that *Mishnayos* would be learned in memory of the deceased. As time went on, the membership of the *Chevrah Mishnayos*, which had always fulfilled such requests, dwindled. This prompted Reb Moshe to set aside more time each day for the study of *Mishnayos*, which he dedicated to the memory of those for whom money had been donated.

FORTY YEARS AGO, a man whose son was studying for *semichah* (rabbinic ordination) at Tifereth Jerusalem loaned the yeshivah

Personal Integrity

twenty thousand dollars, thereby rescuing it from financial disaster. As the time of his son's ordination approached, the man sent out printed invitations to a gala affair celebrating the event. Meanwhile Reb Moshe was told by someone that the man's son was not conducting himself as a student of Torah should. Reb Moshe investigated and found the allegations to be true. Fully aware of the consequences, Reb Moshe told the young man that he could not be awarded his *semichah*. The enraged father then demanded that his loan be repaid without delay. It was.

Reb Moshe expected students of Torah to live up to the Torah's high standards of truth and honesty. He once received an unusual phone call from a yeshivah student. The young man had become engaged in a friendly argument with a friend. The two had bet that whoever would be proven wrong would not shave on the coming *Erev Shabbos*. The caller had lost the argument, and now he wanted Reb Moshe's help in finding a way to be released from his vow.

Instead of helping the caller, Reb Moshe chastised him. "Whatever happened to the commandment of *Guard that which escapes your lips?*" he demanded. "Is it proper for a student of Torah to utter a vow without a serious intention to honor it?" While Reb Moshe could have found the student a way out, he refused to do so. The young man would have to learn to weigh his words more carefully.

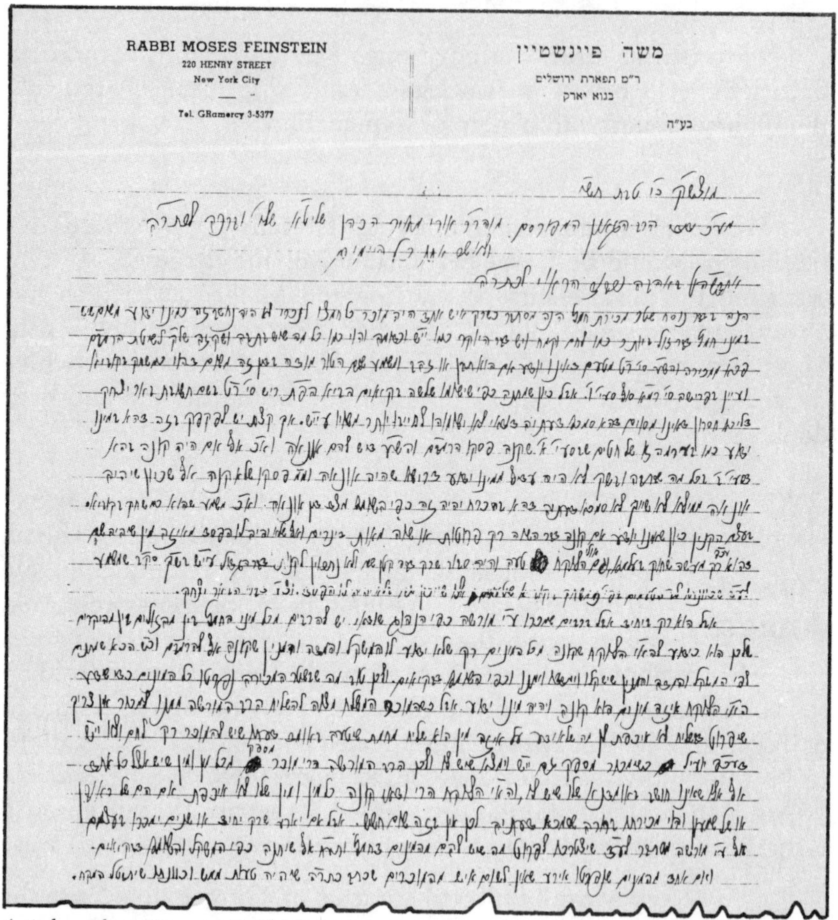

RABBI MOSES FEINSTEIN
220 HENRY STREET
New York City

Tel. GRamercy 5-5377

משה פיינשטיין
ר"ם תפארת ירושלים
בנוא יארק

בע"ה

[Handwritten Hebrew responsum]

A teshuvah *written to Rabbi Uri Meir Kahanow, a* rosh yeshivah *at Mesivta Torah Vodaath in its early years (this responsum appears in the first volume of* Igros Moshe §150)

A YOUNG MAN purchased a home that had belonged to a ninety-five-year-old Jewish woman who had passed away. The seller of the

The Hidden Treasure house was the woman's seventy-year-old daughter, who had neither the desire nor the strength to clear out her mother's possessions from the house. She therefore stated that the house was being sold along with all its contents (furniture, clothing, etc.), and had this written into the contract of sale.

The young man planned to renovate the house before moving into it. One day, before the renovations began, his children were looking for something to do. The young man gave them the key of their new home, only a few blocks from where they were then living, telling them to go there and play. The happy children excitedly ran off.

They made their way through the house until they reached the master bedroom. The old woman's family had left the house virtually untouched since her death and her bed was still perfectly made, just as she had left it. This did not prevent the young man's little boy from climbing onto the bed and jumping on the mattress. Up and down he went until, suddenly, something popped out from underneath the mattress. It was a securely locked metal box.

Before telling his father of his find, the boy decided to find out what he had discovered, so he got a screwdriver and pried the lid open. He and the other children could not believe their eyes. The box was filled with cash, bonds, and assorted jewelry, some of it studded with diamonds. They raced home with the box.

It was obvious to the young man that the contents in the box were worth tens of thousands of dollars. It was also obvious to him that the old woman had not told her children about the small fortune she was leaving behind. Were he to remain silent, they would never know, and even if they *were* to learn of his discovery, it was quite

possible that they had no legal claim to the box, for did not the sales contract stipulate that the house was being sold *with all its contents?*

However, all this meant nothing to the young man; there was no question in his mind as to what he should do. He would not even consider holding on to the box unless the *halachah* declared it rightfully his. The old woman had not been observant, nor was her daughter, but that did not matter. He *did* live by the Torah and that meant that everything he did had to be governed by its teachings.

The young man called Reb Moshe and told him the story. Reb Moshe said that he needed some time to think the matter through and asked that the young man call back the next day. When the two spoke again, Reb Moshe was prepared with his *p'sak.* "You must return everything," he said with finality. "The clause stating that the contents were being sold along with the house did not include cash contents. People sell furniture, clothing or other commodities along with a house; they don't sell money with it. In this case, jewelry has the status of cash. There was never any intent to sell such things."

The young man complied with the *p'sak* and returned everything to the seller, with the suggestion that she donate some of her new-found fortune to charity.

TO REB MOSHE, anything stated in the Torah or decided by *Halachah* was reality. Once, at an Agudath Israel convention, he

Convenience Comes Second

was making his way to a meeting of Torah leaders, when he suddenly stopped. There in front of him was a man praying the *Shemoneh Esrei.* There was no way for Reb Moshe to reach the doorway without passing in front of the man, something which the *Halachah* does not permit.

A while passed and the man was still *davening.* Someone who had accompanied Reb Moshe to the convention and was now standing next to him whispered that the hour was late. "What shall I do?" Reb Moshe responded. "There is a wall in front of me!" To Reb Moshe, passing before a man who was reciting *Shemoneh Esrei* was as impossible as walking through a wall, because the *Halachah* declared it forbidden.

❀ ❀ ❀

In 1968 Reb Moshe traveled with Rabbi Yisrael Eidelman, his *talmid* and Executive Vice-President of Tifereth Jerusalem, to the

With Rabbi Yisrael H. Eidelman

town of New Square in upstate New York to attend the funeral of
Rabbi Yaakov Yosef Twersky, the saintly *Rebbe* of Skver.
Unavoidable circumstances caused the start of the funeral to be held
up for some time, while thousands of mourners stood in the streets
waiting. Had the organizers known that Reb Moshe was present and
standing, they surely would have provided him with a place to rest.
However, Reb Moshe, in his usual humble way, did not make his
presence known and remained standing along with everyone else. A
young Skverer *chassid* went into the *Rebbe's* home and brought Reb
Moshe a chair, but he refused it. More time passed. Realizing how
strenuous the standing must have been for Reb Moshe, then
seventy-three years old, the *chassid* again offered him the chair. Reb
Moshe said, "One does not stand when others are sitting; one does
not sit when others are standing." Once the person heard this he did

not make the suggestion again. He had thought that Reb Moshe had simply not wanted to trouble him, but now he understood that there was more to it than that. Reb Moshe's refusal was rooted in a teaching of *Chazal,* and if such was the case he would not change his mind.

❀　　❀　　❀

Reb Moshe once arranged for a *get* (bill of divorce) to be written for a certain man and then had a *talmid* act as the man's emissary (*shaliach*) in delivering the *get* to his wife in the presence of the required two witnesses. The woman, however, was not Torah observant and refused to accept the *get.* The emissary and witnesses returned to Reb Moshe, their mission not accomplished.

Soon Reb Moshe, accompanied by the emissary and witnesses, was making his way up the four flights of steps leading to the woman's apartment, in a run-down Manhattan tenement. He was met at the door not by the woman, but by her father, who yelled at Reb Moshe to leave his daughter alone. Reb Moshe calmly insisted that he be allowed to speak with the woman. The angry father finally conceded and allowed the group to enter. Reb Moshe calmly and clearly explained to the woman what a tragic mistake she was making. She agreed to accept the *get,* whereupon the *shaliach* gave it to her and they left.

As they were walking down the steps, the *talmid* said, "Please forgive me, but when the *Rosh Yeshivah* presides over such cases doesn't he represent the Jewish court? Is it proper that he should belittle himself so by trekking up flights of steps to take such abuse? The *Rosh Yeshivah* is a *gadol b'Yisrael* — it is not fitting for him ... "

"What?" Reb Moshe countered forcefully. "In such situations I should be concerned not to belittle myself? What about the honor of *Hashem?* What if the woman would, G-d forbid, have found a new husband without having accepted a *get?* The honor of Heaven would have been cast into shame! Can there be a greater disgrace than that?"

In a responsum, Reb Moshe writes, "I literally have no free time, even for a short while, because I must respond to those who ask in practical matters. Nevertheless, since his honor has raised a challenge to my words ... I must respond, and may *Hashem* help me to clarify matters."

How much Reb Moshe did to merit that divine assistance!

CHAPTER SIX

Leader of His People

Rabbi Meir said: Whoever engages in Torah study for its own sake merits many things ... from him people enjoy counsel and wisdom, understanding and strength ... (Avos 6:1)

FOR MANY PEOPLE, one of the greatest expressions of honor for Torah they ever witnessed was the sight of Reb Moshe entering a crowded auditorium to take his seat. He would rush to his **Greeting the Shechinah** place, with concentration etched on his face and his body bent forward. As soon as his presence was noticed, there would be total silence and people would jump up from their seats, lean, push, stand on chairs and contort their bodies to get a glimpse of him. To some, it was reminiscent of the accounts of the *Chofetz Chaim* entering the *K'nessiah Gedolah* hall in Vienna in 1923, causing a hush to come over the crowd as people strained to see him.

Attending the annual Agudath Israel convention each year was a man who did not attend meetings featuring Yiddish addresses, for he did not understand the language. But whenever Reb Moshe — who spoke a quick, heavily accented Yiddish — would be on the program, the man would come early to get a front seat. When asked why, he explained, "I can't understand what Reb Moshe says, but when he speaks, I feel that the *Shechinah* is coming to us from him through his throat."

Indeed, the Jewish soul has an instinct that enables it to recognize its *gedolim*, to sense the throat through which the voice of the *Shechinah* comes to earth. In Reb Moshe, the nation recognized its living Torah scroll.

WHEN ASKED IF HE COULD COMMENT on his father's wisdom in practical matters, Rabbi Reuven Feinstein said, "In the family, once

A Heavenly Ring

we brought a question before him and he offered his counsel, the matter was settled. We had no further doubts about what to do."

Reb Moshe's family knew that his ability to solve any given problem was in no way limited to matters of *Halachah*. In the Torah — of which it is said, *Delve into it and continue to delve into it, for everything is in it (Avos 5:6)* — lies the solution to all problems, the guidance to all matters. Not everyone has the vision to see all this in the Torah, but it is there nonetheless. Reb Moshe's total immersion in Torah study, along with his many other attributes, earned him the wisdom and necessary Heavenly assistance to advise people from all walks of life in all sorts of matters.

A widow was having difficulty with her daughter, who was an older girl. Someone arranged for the two of them to meet with Reb Moshe in his home. When the meeting was over, the widow said, "Reb Moshe did more for my daughter than the greatest psychologist in the world could have done. He spoke to her as a father would to a daughter. She is a changed person."

A young man once came before Reb Moshe deeply troubled by some unpleasant news. He had been in poor health for a long time and had finally gone to a specialist to try to find the cause of his troubles. The doctor ran a series of tests and had just called with the results. He told the young man that he was suffering from a physical abnormality that could not be corrected; nothing could be done for him.

Reb Moshe listened as the young man continued to speak for a while longer and then said decisively, "The doctor is wrong. *Chazal* speak of the type of abnormality that the doctor claims you have. According to them, a person affected by this problem should have certain symptoms. I have observed you for the past few minutes and you have none of the signs mentioned by our Sages. The doctor is wrong. You have nothing to be concerned about. You will get better."

Reb Moshe was right — the young man recovered in due time.

HIS ABSOLUTE CONVICTION in the truth of every word of the Oral and Written Torah was apparent time and again, as was his firm **Everything in the Torah** belief in the supremacy of Torah above all else and the teaching that, "There is not a thing which is not alluded to in the Torah."

To a *talmid* whose wife had given birth to a baby boy, Reb Moshe wrote that in wanting to express his wishes to the parents many blessings came to mind. However, our Sages have established a standard blessing for such an occasion: "Just as he has entered the *bris* so may he enter into the Torah, the marriage canopy, and good deeds." We can be sure, Reb Moshe went on, that if these particular blessings were chosen by our Sages, then there cannot be a blessing in the world that they do not represent.

As the years passed, more and more people would seek Reb Moshe's advice. He received them all with great respect and sincere warmth. Sometimes the questions were rather unusual. A young *kollel* scholar once asked Reb Moshe if it was proper for him to do janitorial work in his yeshivah in his spare time. The money he earned would help him make ends meet and could prolong his stay in *kollel*. Reb Moshe replied, "If you are concerned that such work might be degrading to the Torah's honor, you have nothing to worry about. It is no disgrace to do physical work for the sake of Torah study. However, your wife may be upset if you do such work. Do not undertake it without her consent."

Once, a man came to Reb Moshe complaining that his young son was very ashamed because he was quite short for his age. This was making the boy unhappy and the father could not find a way to pacify him. Reb Moshe, who was not well at that time, wanted to speak to the boy personally. In the meantime, he told the father, "Tell your son that Moshe Feinstein said that he knows some short people who can learn quite well!" Saying this, Reb Moshe, who was a very short man, broke into a huge grin.

REB MOSHE POSSESSED THE WISDOM to know not only what to advise, but also when it was proper to advise it.

A Time and a Place While a Purim *seudah* was in progress in his home, two men came in to wish him well. Surrounded by family and friends, Reb Moshe greeted the visitors warmly. Before leaving, the two asked Reb Moshe's advice on a matter affecting a friend of theirs. Reb Moshe refused to talk about it, saying, "I do not discuss someone's private matters in public."

Yet, on another Purim, his reaction in a similar setting was totally different. After the *Megillah* reading, Reb Moshe's home was filled with family, friends and *talmidim*, one of whom was experiencing difficult personal problems. Reb Moshe motioned to the young man to come into his study. "How are things?" Reb Moshe asked as soon as they were alone. While moved by Reb Moshe's genuine concern, the young man said that he did not want to take up the *Rosh Yeshivah's* time while his apartment was filled with guests. Reb Moshe answered, "I have time for my guests later; you have a problem now."

In a similar case, he once wrote a *teshuvah* clarifying the *halachah* regarding someone's very delicate personal problem. Later, he gave his only copy of the *teshuvah* to the person involved, saying, "If this remains in my files, someone may read it someday. It is very private and no one should know about it but you."

IN A WELL-KNOWN ADDRESS, he lamented the fact that people rarely come to seek guidance in the areas of giving *tzedakah* and **Tzedakah** Torah education of their children. With regard to **and** *tzedakah*, Reb Moshe said that times being what they are, people should not be satisfied with **Education** contributing one tenth or even one fifth of their earnings for the benefit of Torah institutions.

"In our days, this is not simply a matter of *tzedakah*. When one gives to strengthen Torah study, he is actually giving for his own sake and for the satisfaction he hopes to reap from his offspring. With regard to *chinuch* of one's own children, there is no limit (as to how much one should give) …

"It goes without saying, of course, that one must not only consult the *halachah* with regard to how he should distribute his funds, but also in the way he goes about earning this money. A Jew must honor all laws pertaining to honesty, being careful to avoid all prohibitions against cheating and thievery."

A man once came to Reb Moshe and presented him with a generous donation for his yeshivah, which at the time was experiencing financial difficulties. Knowing the donor to be a man of means, Reb Moshe asked that he increase the donation to a specific sum. The donor replied that he would increase his contribution, but was unable to contribute as much as the *Rosh*

Yeshivah had requested. He promptly wrote out a new check and handed it to Reb Moshe.

Some time later the Internal Revenue Service conducted a tax audit on the man's business. After negotiations between the IRS and the company's accountants, a settlement was reached requiring the man to pay a specific amount in back taxes. The amount was the exact difference between what the man had donated to Tifereth Jerusalem and what Reb Moshe had requested of him.

The above incident is reminiscent of a story recorded in the Talmud (*Bava Basra* 10a). Rabbi Yochanan ben Zakkai once dreamt that his nephews would suffer a loss of seven hundred *dinarim* in the coming year. Throughout that year, Rabbi Yochanan coaxed his nephews into contributing to the poor. By years' end, they had contributed a total of 683 *dinarim*. On *Erev Yom Kippur* the Roman government imposed upon them a tax of seventeen *dinarim*. Rabbi Yochanan reassured them, "Do not fear; they will take only seventeen *dinarim* from you," meaning that there would be no further tax. "How do you know?" they asked him. Rabbi Yochanan related his dream to them. They complained, "Why didn't you inform us of this [so that we would have contributed the full amount to the needy]?" Rabbi Yochanan replied, "I felt that it would be better for you to give *tzedakah* only for the sake of a *mitzvah!*"

THE FIRST ORGANIZATIONAL LEADERSHIP that Reb Moshe assumed was the presidency of his own yeshivah. Along with this
Raising Funds title came the tiresome and often thankless burden of fund-raising. Reb Moshe's angelic personality shone through even in his solicitations for funds. A man recalled one such encounter.

"One evening I answered the doorbell and there stood Reb Moshe and his assistant Rabbi Moshe Rivlin. We shook hands and I then escorted them upstairs to my dining room. My wife brought in glasses of tea and we began to talk. Reb Moshe had come to ask that I become a supporter of his yeshivah, and our discussion went on for some time.

"Finally, Reb Moshe rose to leave. It was then that my two young sons came over and asked Reb Moshe if he would pose with them for a picture. I was embarrassed and told them that it was wrong to ask such a thing of the *Rosh Yeshivah*, but he interjected, "No, no, there is nothing wrong at all. I would be happy to pose with them." I went and got my camera and Reb Moshe put one arm

At a fund-raising function in Miami, Florida

around each of my sons for the picture. He then wished me well and left.

"A few minutes later the doorbell rang again. I opened the door and was shocked to find Reb Moshe and Rabbi Rivlin standing there again. Reb Moshe explained that he had forgotten to thank my wife for the tea. He and Rabbi Rivlin climbed the stairs again (Reb Moshe was seventy-four at the time), thanked her and then left."

☙   ☙   ☙

In 1957, severe financial problems threatened to permanently shut down the Lower East Side's *mikveh*. At an emergency meeting it was declared an obligation upon all to help raise the necessary funds. Reb Moshe, accompanied by Reb Nissan Alpert, went knocking on doors soliciting donations. More often than not their efforts were rewarded with only a token contribution. One day, after completing their door-to-door rounds, they went to solicit at a *shul* where a board meeting was in progress. While acknowledging Reb Moshe's presence, the board members had the audacity to continue with their agenda until its completion before permitting Reb Moshe to address them. After he spoke, they presented him with a pitifully small contribution on behalf of their community.

As he left the *shul*, Reb Moshe noticed Reb Nissan's dejected look. He said, "Yechezkel *haNavi* was called *ben* (son of) Buzi, for he was willing to suffer disgrace for the sake of the Torah. [The *Midrash* derives בּוּזִי, Buzi, from the word בּוּז, *shame*.] The disgrace we have suffered is in itself a benefit!"

> Someone once spent the good part of a day accompanying Reb Moshe on a fund-raising mission. As the day wore on, the man noticed Reb Moshe growing weary. He suggested that they return home, but Reb Moshe wanted to press on until they had accomplished more. Feeling that the strain would be too much for Reb Moshe, the man searched for some way to convince him to stop.
>
> Suddenly, he hit upon the perfect argument. "The *Rosh Yeshivah* has not had much time to learn today. Perhaps we should go home now ..."
>
> Reb Moshe replied, "In the *Shema*, we are commanded to love *Hashem* with all our heart, soul, and resources. Our Sages teach that the intent of these words is that we are to serve *Hashem* with such devotion that we would sacrifice for Him whatever is most precious to us. My greatest love is learning Torah. I must sacrifice even this when my service to *Klal Yisrael* requires it."

The word "responsibility" is one of the keys to understanding Reb Moshe and his career. By nature, Reb Moshe was not a public man. He shunned the limelight, leadership, and controversy. His loves were Torah, teaching and defining the *Halachah*, and committing his Torah thoughts to writing. Nevertheless, when he felt that his responsibility to *Klal Yisrael* required that he assume a public role, he did so.

Reb Moshe's selfless dedication to the spreading of Torah, and to *Klal Yisrael* in general, was apparent throughout his forty-nine years as a Torah leader in America. After World War II had ended, a handful of great survivors formed the *Moetzes Gedolei HaTorah* (Council of Torah Sages) of Agudath Israel of America. The first chairman of the Council, Rabbi Reuven Grozovsky, and his colleague Rabbi Aharon Kotler called on Reb Moshe to serve. In this way, he became involved in formulating a Torah approach for, and making major decisions on, matters affecting Jews the world over.

The authority of the *Moetzes Gedolei HaTorah* was based on

Chairing a meeting of the Moetzes Gedolei HaTorah attended by (left to right) Rabbi Nachum Perlow (Novominsker Rav); Rabbi Moshe Horowitz (Bostoner Rebbe); Reb Moshe; Rabbi Yitzchak Hutner; (to the extreme right) Rabbi Boruch Sorotzkin (Telshe Rosh Yeshivah); and (second from right) יבל״ח Rabbi Yaakov Yitzchak Ruderman

the fundamental principle that Jews must follow the directives of Torah leaders even with regard to politics and other areas not mentioned specifically in the *Shulchan Aruch*. Reb Moshe explained the concept this way: "There are people who maintain that *talmidei chachamim* are not qualified to decide political matters, that *gedolei Yisrael* should limit themselves to Torah and *Halachah*. Such people cannot be considered within the Torah camp. One might well say that ignoring the advice of a *talmid chacham* is far worse than violating a commandment. One who violates a commandment because he is too weak to resist temptation at least knows that his action is wrong. By contrast, one who ignores the advice of a *talmid chacham* denies that a Torah scholar's wisdom is superior. This is a far more serious breach."

WHEN REB MOSHE CAME TO THE EAST SIDE, he became the neighbor of a remarkable man and a remarkable organization. *Ezras*

Rabbi Henkin and Ezras Torah *Torah* was founded by the *Agudath HaRabbanim* during World War I, at the urgent request of the *Chofetz Chaim* and Rabbi Chaim Ozer Grodzenski. Its task was to provide for poor Torah scholars and their families and for the great

Rabbi Yosef Eliyahu Henkin (right) with יבל"ח *Rabbi Moshe A. Margolin*

yeshivos everywhere in the world. Several years after it was founded, *Ezras Torah* came under the guidance of Rabbi Yosef Eliyahu Henkin, a rare *gaon* and *tzaddik*. Seldom has a *tzedakah* institution been under the full-time supervision of one of the greatest rabbis in the world. Throughout his very long lifetime, Rabbi Henkin was respected as one of the leading *poskim* in the United States.

Though Rabbi Henkin was much older than Reb Moshe, it was natural for them to become close friends. They often consulted one another on halachic questions. Not always did they agree, but there was always great love and respect between them. In a *teshuvah* Reb Moshe wrote how he and Rabbi Henkin had disagreed about the matter in question and written to one another, each attempting to disprove the other's points. The respect with which Reb Moshe writes about his great contemporary is a classic example of the love *tzaddikim* feel for one another.

Of Rabbi Henkin, Reb Moshe once said, "This man has not benefited an iota from the pleasures of this world."

Rabbi Henkin often asked Reb Moshe to make appeals for *Ezras Torah*, sometimes involving long walks on a Shabbos or *Yom Tov*. Reb Moshe never refused, out of respect for the holy cause of

Ezras Torah and the great *gaon* who led it. Rabbi Henkin was at the head of *Ezras Torah* for nearly fifty years, until he passed away in his nineties. He used to keep a record of the time that he was busy responding to Torah questions while in his office — that was time that he "owed" to *Ezras Torah*, and he always stayed at his desk extra hours to make it up. He often refused to accept raises in salary, because he felt that the needy were more entitled to *Ezras Torah's* funds than he was. Even when he became blind in his old age, he continued to study Torah by heart and with others who read the *Gemara* aloud, and he continued to run the affairs of *Ezras Torah*. In these ways, he and Reb Moshe were very similar: they put *Klal Yisrael* and service to *Hashem* ahead of everything.

Once, Rabbi Moshe A. Margolin, a chief lieutenant of Rabbi Henkin, came to Reb Moshe's apartment at Rabbi Henkin's request, at a time when he was ill. The *Rebbetzin* was visibly upset that Reb Moshe was not permitted to rest. Rabbi Margolin waited as Reb Moshe rushed into the kitchen and calmed her, "The *gaon* Rabbi Henkin called about *Ezras Torah*. How can I refuse him?"

After Rabbi Henkin's death, *Ezras Torah's* work was carried on in his tradition by Rabbi Margolin and the late Rabbi Moshe Roginsky, who had served under him and learned from his ways.

IT IS REMARKABLE that two names come to mind when one thinks of the main leaders of the American yeshivah world from 1940-

Go to Meet Moshe

1986: Rabbi Aharon Kotler and Rabbi Moshe Feinstein. They first came to know each other in Slutzk, where Reb Moshe studied and Reb Aharon was the son-in-law of Rabbi Isser Zalman Meltzer, but it seems that *Hashem* wanted to bring them together to replant Torah Judaism in America.

When Rabbi Aharon Kotler was in Japan in 1940 along with other *roshei yeshivah* and their students who had escaped from German-occupied Europe, he debated whether to come to America or join his father-in-law, Reb Isser Zalman, in *Eretz Yisrael*. His goals were to save as many European Jews as possible and to replant Torah — in which continent should he work? As he frequently did where major decisions were involved, he cast the *goral haGra*, the method taught by the Vilna Gaon to find a Scriptural verse that would indicate what someone should do in a crisis. The indicated verse was, וַיֹּאמֶר ה' אֶל אַהֲרֹן לֵךְ לִקְרַאת מֹשֶׁה הַמִּדְבָּרָה, *Hashem said to Aharon, go toward Moshe to the wilderness (Exodus 4:27).*

With Rabbi Aharon Kotler

To Reb Aharon, this was a clear indication that he was to join the Moshe *par excellence* of this generation, Reb Moshe Feinstein, in the spiritual "wilderness," the term that was characteristically used to describe the United States in those years.

The two leaders had enormous respect for one another, but they had different personalities and each had a role in which he was preeminent. It was as if they had divided the responsibilities for the future of Torah life. Reb Aharon was the dynamic, charismatic teacher and builder of Torah, who brought to America the concept that our most talented young men should devote themselves exclusively to Torah study. Reb Moshe shunned the limelight, channeling his prodigious energies to serve as tireless leader of his own yeshivah and foremost *posek* of the nation. Reb Aharon was, so to speak, the *Rosh Yeshivah* of *Klal Yisrael*, while Reb Moshe was its *posek*.

As with Torah leaders of all generations, the idea of competition with each other in role or popularity did not exist between these two *gaonim* and *tzaddikim*. A Torah scholar does not become a recognized leader through opinion polls or elections. His greatness in Torah, zeal for every *mitzvah*, genuine concern for his people, combined with true humility and a revulsion for honor, catapult him into a position of leadership, often against his will.

A good example of the difference between Torah leaders and statesmen is the manner in which these two Torah giants traveled from place to place. For years, Reb Moshe would walk the mile-or-so distance from his home to the yeshivah. Only in later years was he always driven to yeshivah and accompanied wherever he went. Similarly, Reb Aharon could often be found traveling alone on a subway train or bus as he shuttled between his yeshivah in Lakewood, New Jersey and his apartment in the Boro Park section of Brooklyn.

THE LOVE AND REVERENCE the two *gedolim* felt for one another is an inspiring lesson. Once, a student of Reb Moshe met Reb Aharon

Mutual Respect sitting on a train, recording his *chiddushei Torah* in a notebook. The two discussed a topic which the young man was studying, after which Reb Aharon asked his companion to relate some of Reb Moshe's recent halachic rulings. To one *p'sak*, Reb Aharon said, "This is a *chiddush* (original idea) and a correct one. The *halachah* is as Reb Moshe has said." The next day the *talmid* repeated the conversation to Reb Moshe. He beamed upon hearing that Reb Aharon agreed with his ruling.

It was rare that Reb Aharon conferred *semichah* upon a *talmid*. Those of his *talmidim* who sought to be ordained, he usually sent to Reb Moshe, who would accord special honor to these young men, for they were Reb Aharon's *talmidim*.

Once a *talmid* came to Reb Moshe with a glowing letter of recommendation from Reb Aharon. Reb Moshe told the young man that since Reb Aharon thought so highly of him, he would be given *semichah* [ordination] without a test; no test was necessary. The young man was taken aback, because he had mastered the *semichah* curriculum and would feel slighted to be ordained as a mere formality. Realizing that the young man was hurt, Reb Moshe suggested that he and the *semichah* candidate become study partners in the yeshivah for several weeks, and in that way he could prove his mettle. So it was.

One day the young man overslept and rushed to the yeshivah without eating breakfast. Reb Moshe noticed that he seemed a bit weak. Had he eaten? No. Reb Moshe took him downstairs to the

At a wedding ceremony

kitchen for breakfast. It happened again several days later. This time the kitchen was locked — and Reb Moshe insisted that the young man come home with him. That morning he ate a breakfast prepared by Reb Moshe himself — and he never overslept again.

As Reb Aharon once prepared to leave for a visit to Israel, his *talmidim* were making plans to escort him to the airport. When Reb Aharon learned of this he let it be known that he would much prefer that everyone remain in the *beis midrash* rather than close their *gemaras* to see him off. The *talmidim* appointed a representative to call Reb Moshe and ask him what to do. He replied unequivocally, "Escort the *Rosh Yeshivah*. To honor Reb Aharon is to honor the Torah itself."

Reb Moshe visited Lakewood a number of times to visit his relatives there and participate in family celebrations. On these occasions, he was invited by Reb Aharon to deliver *shiurim* in the yeshivah's *beis midrash*. Those who were there still recall the sight of Reb Moshe giving the *shiur* while Reb Aharon sat to the right of the *Aron HaKodesh* concentrating intently on Reb Moshe's every word. They also recall that some of Reb Moshe's *chiddushim* were identical to some that Reb Aharon had said in previous *shiurim*.

❧　❧　❧

It happened once that a *chassan* was confronted with an interesting problem. He had studied for a number of years under Reb Moshe at Tifereth Jerusalem and then moved on to Beth Medrash Govoha in Lakewood, where he studied for a relatively short time before becoming engaged. Whom should he honor with officiating at his wedding, Reb Aharon or Reb Moshe?

He consulted the sons of his two *rebbeim*, Rabbi Shneur Kotler and Rabbi David Feinstein. Both agreed that since the *chassan* was then studying in Lakewood it would be appropriate to ask Reb Aharon to officiate. The *chassan* followed the recommendation.

The wedding night arrived. Under the *chupah*, Reb Aharon said to the *chassan*, "You presented me with the honor of being *mesader kiddushin* and I accepted. Now that the honor is mine I hereby transfer it to the *posek hador*, Rabbi Moshe Feinstein!" With the room filled with guests waiting for the start of the ceremony, Reb Moshe had no choice but to accept.

AFTER REB AHARON PASSED AWAY IN 1962, Reb Moshe was drafted by his colleagues to assume the helm of *Klal Yisrael*.

New Role Leadership meant a major change in Reb Moshe's life; indeed, it forced upon him roles that he had previously avoided. Why had he become chairman of the *Nesius* (Presidium) of Agudath Israel, and so involved in day-to-day affairs of Agudath Israel? And then, why did he accept the chairmanship of the *Moetzes Gedolei HaTorah* on top of that, as well as the presidency of the *Agudath HaRabbanim*, *Chinuch Atzmai* [Torah Schools for Israel], and *Ezras Torah*, a leadership role in Torah Umesorah and so forth?

The turning point can be summarized in an almost unknown incident that was witnessed by Rabbi Meir Zlotowitz, who was standing only a foot away from Reb Moshe when it took place. Reb Aharon was in the hospital during his final illness, and Reb Moshe and his students were reciting *Tehillim* in the *beis midrash* of Mesivtha Tifereth Jerusalem. Suddenly someone entered the room with the tragic news that Reb Aharon was gone, and he motioned to indicate that it was no longer necessary to recite *Tehillim*.

Reb Moshe looked across the room at the bearer of the news and asked quietly, "Is it all over?" The head nodded yes.

At a meeting of the Moetzes Gedolei HaTorah: (counter-clockwise around table) Reb Moshe, Boyaner Rebbe, Sadigerer Rebbe, Novominsker Rebbe, Reb Yaakov Kamenetzky, and יבל״ח Rabbi Yaakov Yitzchak Ruderman; (extreme left) Bluzhover Rebbe; (standing) Rabbi Yechezkel Besser and Rabbi Moshe Sherer

Reb Moshe stood stone still with shock and disbelief on his face. He mumbled these words to himself:

"It can't be.

"But, if it is true, it is the Will of the Creator.

"This is how it must be.

"If so, then it must be good."

He repeated this monologue twice as if in a trance.

In retrospect it seems as if he could have been evaluating both the tragedy and his new responsibilities: *It can't be! But if this is Hashem's will, then it must be good and we must accept it.* On the one hand, his personal struggle constituted *tzidok hadin*, an acceptance of the Divine judgment. But those who were close to Reb Moshe saw in it also that he was grappling with the Heavenly decree that would cast upon *him* much of the burden of leadership and responsibility that had been borne by Reb Aharon up to then. It was regarding this decree, too, that Reb Moshe could have said, "If this is *Hashem's* will then it must be good and we must accept it."

ANOTHER MAJOR TORAH FIGURE with whom Reb Moshe had a special relationship was Rabbi Yaakov Kamenetzky, *Rosh Yeshivah*

With Rabbi Yaakov Kamenetzky

Reb Moshe and Reb Yaakov of Mesivta Torah Vodaath. After the passing of Reb Aharon, there were knowledgeable people who urged that the various positions of leadership be divided between Reb Moshe and Reb Yaakov, but Reb Yaakov would not hear of it. He insisted that Reb Moshe alone must lead *Klal Yisrael* in America. Many years later, a friend suggested to Reb Yaakov that he would have been better suited than Reb Moshe for a particular post. With typical modesty, Reb Yaakov responded, "But my colleagues voted for Reb Moshe, not for me." A close disciple of Reb Yaakov explained why he said that. Reb Yaakov did not want anyone to think that it was up to *him* to decide whether or not Reb Moshe should be selected for a role, therefore he said simply that it was the unanimous decision of the *gedolei Yisrael* that Reb Moshe should lead them. As Reb Yaakov once told his son, "Whenever Reb Moshe is present among other *gedolim*, only he can be referred to as THE *Rosh Yeshivah.*"

❀ ❀ ❀

For twenty-three years following Reb Aharon's passing Reb Moshe and Reb Yaakov worked closely and tirelessly in guiding the

With his son Reb Reuven during a visit
from Rabbi Yaakov Kamenetzky and his Rebbetzin

course of *Klal Yisrael*. Our generation viewed them as our two wise
fathers, who always put their children's concerns ahead of their
own.

Their love for each other was deep. Reb Moshe himself once
said, "I love Reb Yaakov and I am certain that he loves me as well;
כַּמַּיִם הַפָּנִים לַפָּנִים כֵּן לֵב הָאָדָם לָאָדָם. (*As a face sees its reflection in the
water, so does one man's heart reflect another's feelings [Proverbs
27:19]*)." When these words were repeated to Reb Yaakov, he
beamed with obvious pleasure.

When speaking before a group, Reb Yaakov once said, "When
I was a five-year-old boy, everyone in my town envied an old man
of about ninety, who at age five had shaken the hand of Reb Chaim
Volozhiner. I assure you that in years to come your grandchildren
will boast that they had the privilege of meeting Reb Moshe
Feinstein."

When illness gradually confined Reb Moshe to his home, Reb
Yaakov was still quite active, even speaking in public on numerous
occasions. Reb Yaakov visited Reb Moshe regularly, until his own
illness prevented him from doing so. During one of his last visits,
Reb Yaakov said, "Reb Moshe, you must protect your health. We
are two of the last ones left, and the young people need us."

During another visit, Reb Moshe bemoaned the fact that his weakened condition was forcing him to sleep more than he had for most of his life. He remarked that, often, older people are able to manage on less sleep than they had in their younger years, but with himself the opposite was true. Reb Yaakov attempted to console Reb Moshe. He said, "People who sleep less in their old age can do so because their life styles slow down when they grow old. They strain their bodies less, so they need less sleep. But, you, Reb Moshe, have always engaged in mental strain more than physical strain. Even now you continue to strain your mind in study as you always did. You have not slowed down, so you need more sleep."

In the summer of 1984, after having partially recovered from a stroke, Reb Yaakov visited Reb Moshe. The next day, Reb Moshe remarked to someone how upset he felt at seeing Reb Yaakov not well.

❀　❀　❀

One day, Reb Moshe received word that Reb Yaakov's condition had worsened. At his *minyan's* Torah reading, he instructed the *gabbai* to recite a *mi shebeirach* for him. However, no one present could recall the name of Reb Yaakov's mother (which is always used when praying for the sick). Reb Moshe then told the *gabbai*, "It is enough to say 'Reb Yaakov' — the *Ribbono shel Olam* knows who Reb Yaakov is!"

BEGINNING WITH 1983, an annual testimonial dinner was held in Reb Moshe's honor, with the proceeds of the affair going to Tifereth Jerusalem. In 1983 and again in 1984, Reb Moshe came a few hours before the dinner and received visitors in a private suite. It was a physical strain for him, but he considered it his duty to honor supporters of Torah who went to the effort of coming to help his yeshivah. Guests at the dinners treasure the unforgettable moments when he entered the ballroom or rose to speak, though it was clearly very difficult for him. Nearly a thousand people shot to their feet in silent reverence in an inspiring display of honor for Torah and the *gadol hador*. In 1985, despite his strong desire to come, he was unable to do so.

In Reb Moshe's Honor

Each of those years, Reb Yaakov came to the dinner. In 1983 he spoke and paid a moving tribute to Reb Moshe. He quoted the teaching of the Sages that if we are like mortals, then the earlier Sages are like angels compared to us. We should realize, Reb Yaakov told the audience, that Reb Moshe is equal to the great *gaonim* and *tzaddikim* of earlier generations.

In 1985, Reb Yaakov was very weak after a stroke, and his family pleaded with him not to go, but he insisted that he must attend in Reb Moshe's honor, especially since Reb Moshe himself was unwell. As Reb Yaakov made his way from the elevator to the dais, he was forced to stop every fifteen or so steps and sit. He made a brief speech and left shortly thereafter, again pausing to rest frequently on his way out. On the way home, he sat slumped in the car, barely able to sit up. Reb Yaakov's coming had been an extreme sacrifice, for the honor of the man with whom he had shepherded the nation for twenty-three years.

They passed away but two weeks apart. It seemed incredible, yet to some it magnified what they had both meant to *Klal Yisrael*

(Above) Reb Yaakov arriving at Mesivtha Tifereth Jerusalem dinner
(Facing page) Reb Moshe, escorted by יבל״ח *Alexander Hasenfeld (l.) and Dov Levy; greeting Reb Yaakov; and receiving a scroll from Zalman Margulies (l.), Allen Zelinger (partially obscured) and Joseph S. Gruss*

during these last decades — they who were "beloved and pleasant in their lifetime and in their deaths were not parted."

BEFORE REB AHARON'S PASSING, Reb Moshe headed the presidium of Agudath Israel, while serving as a member of the *Moetzes*

For Klal Yisrael

*Gedolei HaTorah.** When Reb Aharon passed away and Reb Moshe was appointed to succeed him as the *Moetzes* head, the Agudah leadership requested that he remain at the presidium's helm as well, surely a strain on his precious time and energy. As Rabbi Moshe Sherer, President of Agudath Israel of America recalls, Reb Moshe responded, "If you feel that it is important for the Agudah, then I will remain." This is but one illustration of Reb Moshe's enormous sense of responsibility toward *Klal Yisrael*. When meeting with people involved in such work he would often ask, "How can I help?" His time, every second of it, was so precious, but if it was used for *Klal Yisrael's* sake, then it was being spent wisely.

One year, on the fast of *Tzom Gedaliah*, Reb Moshe sat at a phone, placing call after call to inform key people of a development in an important matter. After a few hours of calls, he wearily leaned his head on the palms of his hands. Someone said, "The *Rosh Yeshivah* appears very tired; perhaps he should rest a bit." Reb Moshe responded, "Whom else should we call?"

In the mid-1970's, an urgent meeting was held in New York to discuss a renewed threat of compulsory conscription of women in Israel. Knowing that Reb Moshe was not well, Rabbi Moshe Sternbuch (who was in America at the time) visited him to request only that he write a letter to be read at the meeting. Reb Moshe said, "I am ill only when my own needs are concerned, not with regard to the *Klal's* needs — especially a matter as serious as this." Reb Moshe attended the meeting.

---

* Simply put, the *Moetzes* charts the course of Agudath Israel, through formulating policies according to Torah, while the presidium guides the diversified activities of Agudath Israel for the benefit of Jews throughout the world.

(Top) *At Agudath Israel convention in 1958: (left to right) Rabbi Yehudah Altusky, Rabbi Mendel Chodorow, Novominsker Rav, Reb Moshe, Boyaner Rebbe, Rabbi Eliezer Silver, Kapitshnitzer Rebbe, Rabbi Binyamin Zev Hendles, Rabbi Meir Schwartzman, Rabbi A.B. Silberberg*

(Bottom) *At a meeting of Rabbinical leaders listening to a report by* **Rabbi Moshe Sherer**; *at the head of the table are Reb Moshe, Reb Yaakov and* יבל״ח **Rabbi Yaakov Yitzchak Ruderman**; *at the right are* **Rabbi Gedaliah Schorr** *and* יבל״ח **Rabbi Shraga Grosbard**; *at the left is* **Rabbi Boruch Sorotzkin**

Reb Moshe's dedication to the needs of Jews everywhere was obvious from the way he went about raising funds for institutions other than his own yeshivah. Sometimes he would approach a wealthy person for a contribution to *Chinuch Atzmai,* knowing that this would make the donor less likely to contribute to Tifereth Jerusalem. That did not bother him for an instant. Jewish children everywhere needed a Torah education. What difference did it make if the money was going to support Torah on the East Side, Jerusalem, or elsewhere?

❀   ❀   ❀

He never allowed his commitment to one organization to conflict with his obligation to another. He once called the office of a well-known benefactor to request a donation for *Chinuch Atzmai,* only to be told that the man was not in at the time. That night the man greeted Reb Moshe at the annual Torah Umesorah dinner. "I understand that the *Rosh Yeshivah* called today. Is there some way that I can be of help to the *Rosh Yeshivah?*"

"I am sorry," replied Reb Moshe, "but we are here for the benefit of Torah Umesorah. I will call you again tomorrow about the other matter." The man was amazed by Reb Moshe's words. The next day, the two did speak, with the result being a $50,000 donation for *Chinuch Atzmai.*

This sense of responsibility prevented him from ever undertaking tasks that he could not carry out properly. Many organizations involved in very important work for Jewry sought to have Reb Moshe as their leader, but he refused. He endorsed their work, always made himself available for guidance and decision-making, but would not serve as their president or chairman. To serve in such capacities meant assuming responsibility for all that went on within an organization. Reb Moshe knew that his previous obligations would not allow him the necessary time to assume yet another such role. To assume such a position and *not* meet the responsibilities that came with it were out of the question, as far as Reb Moshe was concerned.

ONE OF THE POSITIONS thrust upon Reb Moshe after the passing of Rabbi Aharon Kotler was the presidency of *Chinuch Atzmai*,

Chinuch Atzmai Torah Schools for Israel, the network of more than two hundred yeshivos in *Eretz Yisrael*. When Reb Moshe became president, it was a time of crisis for *Chinuch Atzmai*. Energetically, he reorganized the entire organization, recruiting all the major *roshei yeshivah* to become actively involved. There were regular meetings, all of which he attended. He supervised policy-making, fund-raising, and the budget. Not a day went by that he was not in personal contact with Rabbi Henoch Cohen, *Chinuch Atzmai's* executive director, and Rabbi Yosef Tannenbaum, his chief colleague. He wanted information about activities in *Eretz Yisrael*, American fund-raising, the day's mail, the bank balance, plans for the annual dinner and mail campaigns — everything!

He devoted countless days and nights to personal visits to raise funds for *Chinuch Atzmai*, and he personally guaranteed bank and private loans even though he knew that this would jeopardize the campaigns of Tifereth Jerusalem. To Reb Moshe, the cause of Torah was higher than that of any individual institution, even his own. In the case of *Chinuch Atzmai*, this was even more true, because Reb Moshe, like Reb Aharon before him, felt that the future of Torah Jewry in *Eretz Yisrael* depended on the health of *Chinuch Atzmai*. In May 1967, when Egypt and its Arab allies threatened to invade Israel, the *roshei yeshivah* proclaimed a day of fast and *tefillah*. The fast day was a few days before the *Chinuch Atzmai* dinner, and immediately after *Minchah*, Reb Moshe and Reb Yaakov went to visit people to help insure the success of the dinner — even though

*Greeting Rabbi Aharon Kotler at a Chinuch Atzmai dinner;
in the center is יבל"ח Rabbi Yosef Dov Soloveitchik,
Rosh Yeshivah of Yeshivas Rabbi Yitzchak Elchonon*

both men were in their seventies and still fasting.

As the head of *Chinuch Atzmai*, Reb Moshe was loyal to its employees and encouraged them to use their own initiative. As he told Rabbi Cohen, who requested authorization for an office expense, "That is your job. If you feel it is necessary, buy it."

When Reb Aharon first asked Rabbi Cohen to work for *Chinuch Atzmai* full-time, he had doubts. He had a lucrative business opportunity and felt that it might be better to become a businessman who would be an active volunteer in community affairs. He consulted Reb Moshe, who said, "Henoch, in the time of the *Gemara*, people were so great that they could be *roshei yeshivah* and still support themselves by some occupation. For example, Reb Yitzchak gave *shiurim* even though he was a blacksmith. But nowadays, we can't do both. If someone wants to serve *Klal Yisrael* in the most effective way, he must give it his full concentration. If you truly want to serve our nation, you should do it full-time. *But,*" Reb Moshe concluded, "you must make a living. You have the right to request a proper salary."

He gave similar advice to Rabbi Tannenbaum when another institution tried to hire him away from *Chinuch Atzmai* at a much higher salary. Rabbi Tannenbaum consulted Reb Moshe, who felt that it was not right for him to be approached by others. However, Reb Moshe urged him to request that *Chinuch Atzmai* grant him an increase. To their great credit, however, neither Rabbi Cohen nor Rabbi Tannenbaum requested anything close to what they could earn elsewhere. One who lives in proximity to people like Reb Aharon, Reb Moshe, and Reb Yaakov, realizes that there are far more important goals in life than the size of a paycheck.

HIS RESPECT FOR OTHER Torah leaders sometimes caused him to abstain from offering his view on a matter. As a rule, Reb Moshe

Deference to Torah Sages

would not render decisions on issues and events that concerned the Torah community of *Eretz Yisrael.* He insisted that such decisions were to be made only by the Torah leadership of that land.

Rabbi Eliezer Menachem Shach

Once, when Reb Moshe was asked to participate in a meeting whose outcome could have had a bearing on matters in *Eretz Yisrael,* Reb Moshe phoned Rabbi Eliezer Shach, the senior *Rosh Yeshivah* in Eretz Yisrael, to be sure Rabbi Shach would not object.

Often, Rabbi Shach would call Reb Moshe before making a statement on an important issue, to be sure that Reb Moshe did not oppose his view.

In a *teshuvah,* Reb Moshe writes, "My outlook is based only on knowledge of Torah whose ways are truth, without any influence of secular knowledge" *(Even HaEzer* 2:1). Torah leaders are referred to in Scriptures as "the eyes of the nation." They, with their clear Torah perception of everything, often have a much different view of matters than do others. Those who benefited from

Reb Moshe's guidance in their own work for *Klal Yisrael* often saw this for themselves.

With (left to right) Novominsker Rav, Boyaner Rebbe, Kapitshnitzer Rebbe, Stuchiner Rebbe and יבל״ח Bobover Rav

With Kapitshnitzer Rebbe (left) and Boyaner Rebbe (center)

On following page (clockwise from upper left): With Rabbi Avraham Yoffen; יבל״ח the Satmar Rebbe (Rabbi Moshe Teitelbaum), Rabbi Mordechai Gifter, Rabbi Henoch Leibowitz, the Bluzhover Rebbe, and Rabbi Ovadia Yosef

TWO MEN HAD WORKED together on an important project and had achieved much success. Then a time came when they did not see

Overlook Your Differences

eye to eye on certain things, and one of them suggested that the partnership had come to an end. A few days later the man who had initiated the break-up received a call from Reb Moshe, who had learned of what had transpired. After hearing the man's feelings on the matter, Reb Moshe said, "I understand what is bothering you. Certainly you have a valid point, but you must weigh the consequences of your decision. The two of you have accomplished so much for *Klal Yisrael* and there is so much more that you can still accomplish *together*. There is no doubt in my mind that you are much more effective as a team than as individuals. For the sake of *Klal Yisrael*, I think you should overlook your differences and continue working together."

The man heeded Reb Moshe's advice, and with his partner went on to new achievements.

> Once, a dilemma faced a man who had successfully represented Torah organizations in places of government. He had been granted a meeting with a group of United States senators, in Washington, D.C., to discuss a matter of prime importance to the Torah community in *Eretz Yisrael*. The meeting had been scheduled for *Erev Rosh Hashanah* and there was a real possibility that he would not have enough time to return home for *Yom Tov*. Should he cancel the meeting?
>
> Again, it was Reb Moshe who placed a call, after being informed of the man's doubts. "I *pasken* (rule) that you *must* attend that meeting, even if you will have to remain in Washington over *Yom Tov*. You will be going there for the sake of *Hashem*, the Torah and *Klal Yisrael*, and your personal considerations should not deter you from going."

IN 1965, PRESIDENT LYNDON JOHNSON was seeking the passage of his Elementary and Secondary Education Act, which would have

Mordechai's Mission

provided federal funds to all elementary and secondary schools, including parochial schools. American yeshivos sent Mr. Reuven Green* to

---

* The gentleman involved asked that his real name not be used.

Washington to lobby for the bill, which would have provided desperately needed help for yeshivos and day schools around the country. In the course of his meetings with Catholic lobbyists for the bill, Mr. Green learned of an astounding development. Catholic divinity schools were being recognized as colleges, and it might be possible to obtain the same recognition for yeshivos. This would mean millions of dollars in Federal aid for Torah institutions.

For this dream to have any hope of becoming a reality, Mr. Green would need the cooperation and backing of certain Church leaders, and favors would have to be done for them in return. Did the *Halachah* forbid such association with Catholic religious leaders for even so lofty a purpose? Mr. Green took his case to Reb Moshe, who was very excited by the information.

Reb Moshe ruled that collaboration with the Church was permitted under carefully defined guidelines, which he outlined to Green. In the months that followed, Mr. Green became almost a member of Reb Moshe's household. As the project progressed from stage to stage, careful planning was required and new questions of *Halachah* arose. Reb Moshe was always ready to offer his *p'sak*, advice and encouragement in a long and often frustrating affair. Finally, the entire plan was worked out. It had Reb Moshe's full approval and blessing. Now came the hardest part — winning the government's agreement to accredit yeshivos.

There was no doubt in Green's mind that the key man in achieving success was Dr. Samuel Halperin, an official at the Department of Health, Education and Welfare. Green arranged for a Sunday afternoon meeting at Halperin's home. Reb Moshe's instructions to Green in dealing with government people still ring in his ears. "You are going on a mission for the sake of *Hashem*. Go with truth. Speak truth, and *Hashem* will be with you."

The meeting on that Sunday afternoon lasted four hours. Green presented his case well, but Halperin, though sympathetic, said he could not hope to help Green; perhaps in a few months ...

"Go with truth. Speak truth and Hashem will be with you."

"Do you know what Purim is about?" Green suddenly asked. A Reform Jew all his life, Halperin had not the slightest idea. Green proceeded to explain how Mordechai told Esther that she had been made queen *only* so that she could help her people. Mordechai had warned, *'If you persist in keeping silent at a time like this, relief and deliverance will come to the Jews from another place, while you and your father's house will perish. And who knows whether it was just for such a time as this that you have attained a royal position'* (*Esther* 4:14). Because Esther accepted the challenge, the Jewish people was saved.

Green now stared at his host. "Dr. Halperin, in all your years in government, this is probably the first time that you've been given an opportunity to do something for the eternity of the Jewish people. And this may be the very reason that you were placed where you are. G-d will find another way if you refuse to help. But the loss, Dr. Halperin, will be yours."

With those words, Green rose to leave for an appointment with the Israeli Ambassador. An obviously moved Dr. Halperin rose with him and insisted on driving him to the appointment. Green reluctantly accepted the offer, on the condition that they not discuss the project any further. As the two parted from each other, Halperin said, "I'll never forget Mordechai."

The next day Halperin phoned Mr. Green. He had been unable to sleep the entire night. He would do anything necessary to gain recognition for the yeshivos.

Green then met with Rep. James H. Scheuer of New York, powerful chairman of the sub-committee that would deal with a law recognizing the yeshivos. He was one of the most respected men on Capitol Hill. The conversation did not go well. Rep. Scheuer objected to the proposal on philosophical and constitutional grounds, but he was an intelligent and open-minded person who was willing to listen. Again, Green combined logic with passion and Scheuer became a powerful ally. Thanks to his support, Halperin was able to convince the Office of Education to recognize the yeshivos.

From that time on, Mr. Green made a point of sending a gift to Dr. Halperin before every *yom. tov.* He sent hand-baked *matzah* before Pesach, *shalach manos* for Purim, a *menorah* for Chanukah, and so on. The thank-you notes he received were all signed, 'Mordechai.'

Two years later, Mr. Green received a phone call from Dr. Halperin. He said, "I've made a decision that I want you to know about. For the last two years my conscience has bothered me. I've made a contribution toward the eternity of my people, but my own life has no real connection with eternity. Now, I'm finally doing something to change this. I'm taking my son out of public school and enrolling him in a yeshivah."

On the day of Reb Moshe's passing, Green called Halperin and

informed him of the tragic news. Halperin then revealed for the first time that he had received a warm letter of thanks from Reb Moshe for his efforts on behalf of Torah institutions. "Now I will treasure that letter more than ever," he said.

The result of the above story has been many millions of dollars in government aid to yeshivos over the last twenty years. Green makes it clear that all this could never have happened without the guidance and encouragement of Reb Moshe.

CHAPTER SEVEN

The Beauty of His Ways

A Jew should study Scripture and Mishnah, serve Torah scholars, deal honestly in business, and speak pleasantly to his fellow creatures. What will his fellow creatures say of him? "Fortunate is his father who taught him Torah! Fortunate is his teacher who taught him Torah! Woe to those who do not study Torah! He who studies Torah — how beautiful are his ways and how proper are his deeds." To him the verse applies: And He said to me: You are My servant Israel, through whom I will be glorified [Isaiah 49:3]. (Yoma 86a)

SOMEONE ONCE ASKED Reb Moshe in what merit he had become so revered by all. He replied, "All my life I never knowingly caused hurt to another human being."

Respect for Everyone Reb Moshe possessed all the wonderful attributes that the Torah seeks in a person and his every word and deed was governed by the Torah. His behavior toward all with whom he came in contact is but one example of this. It is such behavior that can bring others to declare, "Praiseworthy is his father who taught him Torah! ... He who has learned Torah — how beautiful are his ways and how proper are his deeds."

Someone who knew Reb Moshe for many years remarked, "I never met another man who could make people feel so important simply by the way he looked at them."

He greeted everyone with respect and good cheer. One man recalled how Reb Moshe had once failed to notice him and walked by without greeting him. About ten steps later, Reb Moshe turned around and came back, greeted the man and then, to make up for his oversight, spent some time conversing with him.

Rabbi Ephraim Greenblatt recalls walking Reb Moshe to *shul* in the morning when he visited Memphis, Tennessee. He wished good morning to every man, woman and child whom he passed on the way. As he was walking down the street, a youngster ran in front of him to take a picture. One of Reb Moshe's escorts told the "photographer" not to annoy the *Rosh Yeshivah*, to which Reb Moshe responded, "Let him take the picture. He enjoys it, so let me give him some pleasure."

❀　　❀　　❀

One day, as Reb Moshe walked through the lobby of his apartment building, a woman held the front door open for him. The next day, Reb Moshe was in the lobby and noticed the woman coming toward the door. This time he rushed over to hold the door for *her*. "No, no!" she protested, but to no avail.

When Rabbi Michel Barenbaum assumed the position of *mashgiach* in Tifereth Jerusalem some forty years ago, he gave his first *shmuess* (ethical discourse) in a classroom. When Reb Moshe learned of this he told Reb Michel, "Next time you will speak in the *beis midrash* and you will stand at my place!" Reb Michel agreed to the first part of the request but under no circumstances would he stand in the *Rosh Yeshivah's* place. Instead, he had his lectern set up on the side of the *beis midrash* opposite where Reb Moshe's place was. Reb Moshe made a point of attending the *mashgiach's* addresses [which were intended for the students] and would listen intently to every word.

REB MOSHE PROTECTED the honor of young and old alike.

Avoiding Embarrassment

Mr. Louis M. Friedman was a generous supporter of Mesivtha Tifereth Jerusalem. In addition to the money which he donated, Mr. Friedman would outfit the yeshivah's neediest students each year before Pesach. At that time, a large truck would pull up in front of the yeshivah building, loaded with new, first-quality suits, shoes, shirts, ties, caps, socks, underwear, and *tzitzis* to make some one hundred children happy.

One year, to honor Mr. Friedman for his clothes distribution, the yeshivah's administration organized an assembly in its *beis midrash* which was to be followed by a dinner in the lunchroom. The *beis midrash* was crowded with Jews from the Lower East Side. The poorer boys, who were to be outfitted, sat in a section to the left, women sat in the ladies section to the right, while the center was filled with the Board of Directors, members, parents and local people. In the back were tables heaped high with the clothing that Mr. Friedman had donated.

The president of the yeshivah spoke, praising Mr. Friedman profusely. Before ending, he turned to the boys and suggested that they show their appreciation by rising in honor of Mr. Friedman. The boys looked at one another sheepishly, embarrassed to stand up in front of so many people and thereby acknowledge their poverty.

Their embarrassment lasted for but a moment. Sensing the boys' discomfort, Reb Moshe instantly stood up. Some men, seeing the *Rosh Yeshivah* stand up, stood up as well. The Board of Directors stood up. The women stood up. Everyone else stood up. The boys, now having nothing to feel ashamed of, all stood up, too. Even Mr. Friedman, who was a modest man, felt embarrassed at being the only one left sitting. He too stood up, giving the impression that everyone was rising in honor of some other Mr. Friedman.

REB MOSHE ONCE sat at his desk in the front of the *beis midrash*, while a middle-aged scholar sat in the back studying alone. The door

Honor for Scholars of the *beis midrash* swung open and in walked a stranger, looking for a way to pass the time. Noticing the man studying on the back bench, the stranger attempted to "quiz" him on what he was learning, challenging him to explain the *Gemara's* questions and answers. In a flash, Reb Moshe was there. "Excuse me," he said "but I can assure you that this man is a great *talmid chacham;* there is no need to test him."

He once listened as someone made a disparaging remark about a certain *talmid chacham*. Reb Moshe's normally calm demeanor underwent a sudden change. He looked straight at the speaker and said with barely suppressed anger, "I am prepared to testify that [for making such remarks] one is *pasul l'eidus* [unfit to serve as a court witness]!"

After concluding an address to a gathering on the East Side, Reb Moshe quickly made his way toward the exit. As he neared the door, the chairman of the gathering introduced the next speaker — a respected *Rav* of an East Side congregation. Reb Moshe feared that some might misinterpret his exit as a lack of regard for the *Rav*, which was certainly not his intention. The honor of another man was more important than his other affairs of the moment. Reb Moshe returned to his seat and sat through the *Rav's* address. On other occasions, if he arrived at an affair while someone else was speaking, he would wait outside until the speaker was done, in order not to interrupt him.

❈　　❈　　❈

Reb Moshe once visited Baltimore to attend a family wedding. Some local supporters of Tifereth Jerusalem took advantage of Reb Moshe's visit to hold a fund-raising meeting that was graced with his presence. Attending the meeting was Rabbi Yaakov Yitzchak Ruderman, *Rosh Yeshivah* of Ner Israel Rabbinical College in Baltimore, and one of the generation's senior Torah sages. Rabbi Ruderman had taken time from his own schedule to attend, primarily in tribute to Reb Moshe and, indeed, Reb Moshe was accorded great honor throughout the course of the meeting. It was obvious to everyone that Reb Moshe felt very uncomfortable at receiving such honor in the presence of Rabbi Ruderman. Reb Moshe began his address by saying, "I do not understand why I am being accorded so much honor. Surely it is not me as a person to whom this honor is being shown. Perhaps it is because I have learned some Torah ..."

❈　　❈　　❈

One year, a *Melaveh Malkah* was held for the benefit of Tifereth Jerusalem in a Manhattan neighborhood. The event was a dismal failure, with less than twenty people in attendance, although Reb Moshe was scheduled to address the gathering. Some suggested that since almost no one was there his talk should be cancelled. However, to Reb Moshe, it made no difference whether twenty people or two hundred people were present. Every Jew was important in his own right. Incredibly, Reb Moshe opened his address by excusing all those who had failed to attend, saying that the lateness of the hour coupled with other factors had made it difficult for them to come. He then delivered a *d'var Torah* with the fire and enthusiasm expected of one standing before a huge crowd.

HIS RESPECT FOR OTHERS sometimes took on a more subtle form. When *Rebbetzin* Feinstein would bring women guests to the dining-

Gracious Host

room table while Reb Moshe was sitting there studying, he would immediately acknowledge the guests and close his *sefer*, so that no one would feel ignored by him. He would not necessarily join the conversation, but the *sefer* would remained closed nonetheless. His son Reb Reuven recalled his father saying that it is good for one to memorize a portion of *Mishnah* or *Gemara*, so that he will be able to study from memory at times when it is inappropriate or impossible to study from a *sefer*. When one studies from a *sefer* he is, in effect, ignoring everyone and everything present. However, when one reviews Torah in his mind, it is not obvious to anyone. No one who ever sat at Reb Moshe's table ever felt a reluctance on Reb Moshe's part to converse. In this way, no one was ever slighted.

An aged *talmid chacham* whom Reb Moshe knew for many years once came to visit him. Reb Moshe began a conversation, but soon noticed that his visitor was not well enough to respond. Reb Moshe stopped speaking and sat in silence with his long-time friend. Seeing an opportunity to discuss Torah with Reb Moshe, a young man who had accompanied the visitor began asking questions in *Halachah*. However, Reb Moshe did not acknowledge the questions and continued to sit in silence. He felt it disrespectful to discuss Torah in front of his visitor, who, unfortunately, could not take part in the conversation.

On the morning of April 8, 1981, Jews all over the world gathered to recite *Bircas HaChamah*, a blessing for the sun that is recited but once every twenty-eight years. The preferred time to recite the blessing is at sunrise, and so, early that morning, scores of Jews converged on FDR Drive, so that they could fulfill this unique *mitzvah* together with Reb Moshe. Rabbi Aharon Felder, a *Rav* in Philadelphia and a former *talmid* of Reb Moshe, drove to the East Side for the event and was waiting outside Reb Moshe's apartment door at 4:00 a.m., together with his young son. Rabbi Felder dared not knock at that hour (though Reb Moshe usually rose around that time), but someone in the apartment opened the door for some reason, and, seeing Rabbi Felder, ushered him inside. Reb Moshe warmly greeted his *talmid,* invited him and his son into his dining room, and had a glass of tea brought for his guest. Then Reb Moshe disappeared into the kitchen and as Rabbi Felder sipped his tea, he could hear the repeated sounds of cabinet doors being opened and closed. After a few minutes, Reb Moshe returned to the dining room with some sugar cubes in his hand which he presented to Rabbi Felder's son. "I am sorry," he said, "but the *Rebbetzin* is not up yet and I can't find the candies. I hope you will like these cubes."

THROUGH HIS OWN CONDUCT, Reb Moshe taught that the mentally ill must also be treated with dignity. One day, his *shiur* in **Everyone** Tifereth Jerusalem was interrupted by a man who sat reviewing the *Sidrah* in a loud voice. A student went **Counts** over to the man and told him that he was disturbing the *Rosh Yeshivah's shiur.* However, the man, seemingly oblivious to what he had been told, continued his chanting just as before. A couple of students then suggested to Reb Moshe that they escort the man out of the *beis midrash.* "No," came the reply. "He doesn't know what he is doing. I will speak louder." And so the *shiur* continued, with Reb Moshe speaking as loud as he could, while the man went on with his chanting, undisturbed.

Nor was his respect for people limited to Jews only. There was an old Russian who worked as a janitor in Tifereth Jerusalem. He spoke little English and no one paid much attention to him. One day he suffered from a toothache and walked around with a kerchief tied around his cheeks. When Reb Moshe met the janitor in the hallway he stopped and spoke to him in Russian for a few minutes. When the conversation ended, the janitor walked away with the biggest smile that anyone could ever remember seeing on him.

Rabbi Chaim Twersky, a distinguished Boro Park *rav* and the Chaplain at Maimonides Medical Center in New York, once addressed a group of nurses and in the course of his remarks mentioned Reb Moshe's name. "Oh!" exclaimed a black nurse, named Shirley. "I know Rabbi Feinstein. He's a *real* rabbi!"

Rabbi Twersky could not imagine how the woman could know Reb Moshe and told her that she must be confusing him with someone else. No, Shirley insisted, there was no mistake. She was speaking of the famous Rabbi Feinstein. She had been the house-nurse for one of Reb Moshe's newborn great-grandsons, at whose *bris* Reb Moshe had served as *sandak*. As he was being wheeled out following the *bris*, Reb Moshe made a point of turning around in his wheelchair to say good-bye to the nurse. This show of respect had made an indelible impression on her.

This same nurse called Reb Moshe's family after his passing to express her condolences. "I remember how the Rabbi smiled and wished me a good day," she recalled. "I could see that in his eyes I was important."

❧   ❧   ❧

During the last few years of his life, a police escort would accompany him to *Tashlich*. One year, the sergeant asked him for a blessing, saying, "My mother taught me always to ask for a blessing from holy people." The other officers, too, asked for blessings, and Reb Moshe obliged. Then they asked for permission to take a picture with him, to which he again agreed.

❧   ❧   ❧

Once, someone who was to take *Rebbetzin* Feinstein to the doctor rang the doorbell to announce his arrival. Reb Moshe opened the door and greeted the man, upon which the driver joked, "In Europe they would say, 'The wagon-driver is here.' In America we say, 'The car is waiting!' " Reb Moshe made no comment and went to call the *Rebbetzin*. He returned and led the driver to his study, while they waited for the *Rebbetzin* to get ready. Reb Moshe said, "Your comment illustrates a sad fact about this country. In Europe, no one would ever say, 'The wagon is here.' It was always 'The *wagon driver* is here.' The emphasis was on the person. But, here in America, it is 'The *car* is here.' An individual is not given the respect he deserves."

❧   ❧   ❧

After concluding a meeting, Reb Moshe and Reb Yaakov Kamenetzky stood outside a waiting car discussing who would sit in front next to the driver (the preferred seat) and who would sit alone in the back seat. Reb Yaakov took the front seat. After Reb Moshe alighted from the car, Reb Yaakov explained to the driver, "We were discussing who would be getting off first. That person, we decided, should sit in the back. Would he sit in the front, you would be left alone in that seat when he left the car, with your remaining passenger in the back. It would have looked as if you were nothing more than a chauffeur."

MANY YEARS AGO, a prominent *Rav* gave a weekly course in homiletics to students of Tifereth Jerusalem. One evening, he

Apologies and Deference

walked into the *beis midrash* before going up to the third floor where the class was held. He noticed Reb Moshe sitting in his usual seat up front and quickly hurried over to greet him. In his haste, the *Rav* failed to notice that *Ma'ariv* was in progress and Reb Moshe was in the middle of reciting the *Shema*. When the *Rav* realized his error, he turned around hurriedly, and went up to his class.

A short while later there was a knock on his classroom door. It was Reb Moshe. He apologized profusely to the *Rav* for not responding to his greeting. He explained that although the *halachah* does permit such a response, he could not break the accepted custom of not answering greetings while reciting *Shema*. Now, Reb Moshe greeted the *Rav* warmly and spent several minutes speaking with him before leaving.

A similiar story occurred with a young boy who greeted Reb Moshe in the house of a mourner during the *shivah* period. Reb Moshe did not acknowledge the greeting. Later, after leaving the house, Reb Moshe asked someone to go back inside and find the boy. When the child came outside, Reb Moshe extended his hand and warmly greeted him. "I'm sorry that I could not greet you before, but this is not permitted in a mourner's house."

One snowy evening, a young man was loading his family into a car on an East Side street, when he noticed Reb Moshe trudging through the snow on his way to a meeting in Tifereth Jerusalem. The man quickly hurried over and offered Reb Moshe a ride, which he graciously accepted.

The car was crowded and at one point a three-year-old girl sitting in the back with Reb Moshe cried out, "I'm being squished!" When the car pulled up in front of the yeshivah, Reb Moshe thanked the young man, then turned to the three-year-old and said "Excuse me for 'squishing' you."

In his last years, his weakened health confined him to his home, and a daily *minyan* was held in the dining room of his small apartment. At one point, the *minyan* was also convened on Friday nights. In another wing of the building lived a Chassidic *rebbe*, who for a long time had a Friday night *minyan* in his home. Reb Moshe became aware that his own *minyan* was drawing people away from that of the *rebbe*, so he disbanded it. When Pesach arrived, the *rebbe* transported his *minyan* to Reb Moshe's apartment so that he could daven with a *minyan* on the *Seder* night. Though it was not Reb Moshe's custom to recite *Hallel* at Ma'ariv on the first night of Pesach, he insisted that it be done, in deference to the *rebbe*, who observed the custom.

REB MOSHE FULFILLED THE DICTUM "and he [a husband] should honor her [his wife] more than himself" in its fullest sense. A year

Concern for the Rebbetzin

before his passing, when hospitalized with an illness that had caused him to drift in and out of a coma, Reb Moshe was informed by a grandchild that he would soon be going home, where a male nurse would administer necessary treatments.

"The *Bobbeh* must give her consent," Reb Moshe responded, knowing that the presence of a stranger in the apartment would inconvenience her. While his own weakened condition required the most delicate medical care, this did not allow his wife's feelings to be ignored. For her part, where Reb Moshe's health was concerned, *Rebbetzin* Feinstein would do whatever the situation warranted, even things that seemed out of character for a woman of her stature.

It was Reb Moshe's practice to deliver an address on the *yahrtzeit* of his beloved son-in-law, Rabbi Eliyahu Moshe Shisgal. One year, when Reb Moshe's weakened heart was regulated by a pacemaker, his address had been going on for quite some time, when the door of the *beis midrash* opened and in walked the *Rebbetzin*, to insist that he had spoken long enough. He motioned to her that he was nearly finished, and brought his talk to a prompt conclusion.

❀   ❀   ❀

For a time, some of the fund-raising for Mesivtha Tifereth Jerusalem was done by people making telephone calls from Reb Moshe's small apartment. The reason for this novel arrangement was that often the solicitor felt that Reb Moshe should express his appreciation and blessings to the donor on the other end of the line, and if the solicitor had easier access to Reb Moshe, much time would be saved and much more could be accomplished. The caller had only to take a few steps to Reb Moshe's study, and briefly interrupt his learning to have him pick up the phone and speak for but a few moments.

Reb Moshe appreciated the reasoning behind this arrangement, but he put a halt to it soon after it was begun. Reb Moshe was concerned for his *rebbetzin*, for he felt that she had become a prisoner in her own home. With the yeshivah occupying her living room and with her husband at his desk in the study, the *Rebbetzin* was confined to her kitchen and bedroom. This Reb Moshe would not permit. Instead, a private line was installed in the yeshivah through which the solicitor could contact Reb Moshe at home to express his good wishes to a donor any time.

> As with every *mitzvah*, Reb Moshe was extremely meticulous in reviewing the weekly *Sidrah* twice with *Targum*, as prescribed by *Halachah*. Even during a period in his later years, when weakened eyesight forced him to study with the aid of a magnifying glass, he would strain to review the *Sidrah*, often repeating the same word two or three times to be certain he had pronounced it correctly.

> One Friday night, as Reb Moshe was reviewing the *Sidrah*, the *Rebbetzin* announced that the *Seudas Shabbos* was ready to begin. Reb Moshe closed his *Chumash* in the middle of a *pasuk*, so as not to keep her waiting even for a moment.

Despite his *Rebbetzin's* desire that he not involve himself in the mundane household matters, Reb Moshe would come to her aid in these affairs whenever necessary. When they first arrived in America and she found it an ordeal to shop in a strange land with an equally strange language, it was not beneath Reb Moshe's dignity to accompany her to the grocery or fruit market.

WHEN ALREADY ADVANCED IN AGE, Reb Moshe was once found in his kitchen washing the mealtime dishes. He explained, "The

Considerate Husband

Rebbetzin is not feeling well and I know it upsets her to have the dishes dirty and not put away."

His grandson, Rabbi Mordechai Tendler, who was almost inseparable from Reb Moshe in his final years, relates that Reb Moshe would urge him to return his wife's phone calls at the earliest possible time. Reb Moshe would also not allow his grandson to remain with him past the time he was expected back home, saying,

"It is more important that you be home when your wife expects you, than for you to remain here with me."

To a young man who complained that his wife became upset if he did not call her during the day, Reb Moshe responded with amazement, "But of course you should call her during the day. I always call the *Rebbetzin*."

Like any couple, Reb Moshe and his *Rebbetzin* had their light moments together. Someone recalled being present on a *Motza'ei Shabbos* as Reb Moshe and *Rebbetzin* Feinstein prepared to leave for a *Melaveh Malkah*. "You must change your shirt, Rabbi Feinstein," the *Rebbetzin* said, referring to her husband by last name, as she always did when anyone but relatives was present.

"Change my shirt?" Reb Moshe responded. "Whatever for? The Shabbos shirt that I am wearing is nice and clean." With a twinkle in his eye, Reb Moshe turned to the man who was to drive them to the affair. "Tell me," he said. "Does one normally change his shirt before attending a *Melaveh Malkah* or not?"

Not sure how to reply, the person said, "At times yes and at times not!"

Reb Moshe laughed and went to change his shirt.

Before leaving for a wedding, the *Rebbetzin* could often be heard to remark, "Rabbi Feinstein, your frock is simply sparkling!"

On one occasion, Reb Moshe seemed in an unusual hurry to leave for a wedding. "'What is the rush, Rabbi Feinstein?" the *Rebbetzin* asked. "Enough pictures of you have already been taken!"

❧ ❧ ❧

In the summertime, when they would spend a few weeks enjoying the refreshing mountain climate in New York's Catskill Mountains, Reb Moshe would have with him the *Tanach* that he carried with him everywhere he went. When either he or his wife had something to discuss, Reb Moshe would keep the *Tanach* closed, with his finger at the place he was up to, and speak with his *Rebbetzin* for any length of time. When the conversation had run its course, Reb Moshe would open the *Tanach* and study, until *Rebbetzin* Feinstein had to speak to him again, upon which the *Tanach* would be closed ...

Rabbi Isaac Small   *Rabbi Nechemiah Katz*

Brothers-in-law of Reb Moshe

This perhaps best sums up the relationship of this very unique couple. The *Rebbetzin* was her husband's willing helpmate in assuring that every moment of his life revolved around his Torah study; and Reb Moshe, while being the most diligent Torah scholar imaginable, was sincerely sensitive to his wife's feelings and needs at all times.

Reb Moshe's Sister

REB MOSHE HAD only one surviving sibling in the United States, his sister *Rebbetzin* Chana Small of Chicago. They were very close personally, and they shared many character traits, as well. Her respect for him was boundless; she used to refer to him as "my brother, the *tzaddik*," and her husband, Rabbi Isaac Small, had an extremely warm relationship with Reb Moshe. She always went out of her way to judge people favorably, even when they did not seem to deserve such sympathy. When she was not well, and particularly during her terminal illness, she used to say that she was suffering becase of this or that shortcoming of which she had been guilty, the same sort of self-searching that was so pronounced in Reb Moshe.

When *Rebbetzin* Small was suffering for five years with a lingering, very painful illness, Reb Moshe made it a point to call her regularly.

THE BEAUTY OF HIS WAYS / *161*

With his sister Rebbetzin Chana Small (standing) and יבל״ח *his rebbetzin*

During one of these calls, a grandchild overheard her say,
"Moshe, pray for me." She listened to his response and then said,
"Moshe, since we were young we all knew that the One above
listens to your prayers."

Toward the end of her life, *Rebbetzin* Small slipped into a
coma. When she had been comatose for four days, her doctors
suggested to the family that they "pull the plug." There was
virtually no hope that she would ever be conscious again, they
argued, and even if she were to come out of the coma briefly, her
brain could no longer function. The Small children asked Reb David
and Reb Reuven to consult Reb Moshe on what they should do. Reb
Moshe was in very delicate health and his sons felt that it would be
dangerous to give him such tragic news, but they told the Small
family that he had never permitted such a procedure.

Soon after that call, Reb Moshe was reminiscing about his

Family portrait of Reb Moshe with (counterclockwise) his son-in-law Rabbi Eliyahu Moshe Shisgal; and יבל"ח his son Reb David and his wife; his daughter Sifra (Tendler); his Rebbetzin; his daughter Faya (Shisgal); his son Reb Reuven and his wife; his son-in-law Rabbi Moshe David Tendler

siblings and he mentioned the names of those who were no longer living; "אבער חנה לעבט נאך" (but Chana is still alive), he said. That very day, she revived from her coma and became completely lucid. Her children and grandchildren visited and carried on conversations with her. For the first time she was able to meet a grandson's new bride. For the next seven days she was completely conscious, and then she died.

Her son says of her, "She was a Feinstein. She suffered terribly, but she always tried to act cheerful and keep us from knowing how much pain she was in."

Yes, she was a Feinstein.

AS INVOLVED as Reb Moshe was with the needs of *Klal Yisrael*, he never neglected his obligations to his own children. Rabbi Reuven

Father and Grandfather

Feinstein recalled that as the youngest in the family, he was always seated next to his father at mealtime. The children were taught both through word and example that the needs of others came before their own. Yet, no matter how many guests joined the Feinsteins at their table, Reb Moshe always kept his young son next to him.

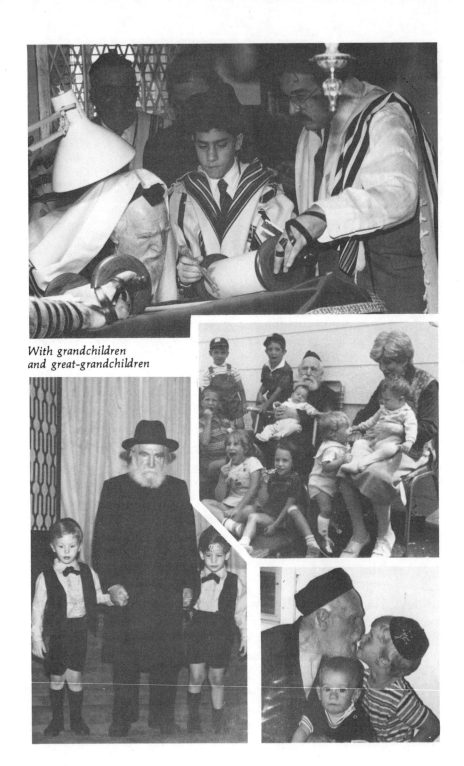

With grandchildren
and great-grandchildren

There was not a more loving grandfather. He would cuddle his grandchildren and play with them. They adored him and loved to sit on his lap or roll a ball back and forth with him. On *Yom Tov*, he would take his young grandsons under his *tallis* for *Bircas Kohanim* and would move his *siddur* over so that they could follow along. When *Zeidy* was around the grandchildren were calm and happy, even after a long and cramped automobile trip. Reb Moshe's family and others who were close to him say that it was difficult to feel awestruck in his presence because his manner of doing things was so plain and simple. He never gave the slightest impression that he was different from anyone else. Nevertheless, even a very young great-granddaughter, while feeling quite content sitting on her great-grandfather's lap, would refer to him as "our *Tzaddik*." And, his children recall feeling even as youngsters that there could be no one better to emulate than their father.

He would call and ask how a grandchild was faring in school, or how well he or she was recovering from a cold.

When a nine-year-old great-grandson began to study *Gemara*, his parents encouraged him to call Reb Moshe and read some *Gemara* for him. The boy felt somewhat shy about doing this but was finally convinced to place the call. Then, the child thought of a problem. "How will *Zeidy* be able to follow what I'm saying without a *gemara* in front of him?" His parents laughed and convinced the young scholar that it would not be a problem.

The boy called and told Reb Moshe the exciting news. Reb Moshe congratulated his great-grandson and then the boy proceeded to read from a *gemara*. After a couple of lines, he stopped to take a breath. Thinking that the boy had gotten stuck on a word or two, Reb Moshe continued the *Gemara* for him. When he hung up the phone, the boy exclaimed with astonishment, "*Zeidy* knew it by heart!"

All the children, grandchildren, and great-grandchildren were called by Reb Moshe and the *Rebbetzin* on their birthdays. The family would reciprocate by calling Reb Moshe every seventh of Adar to wish him well on his birthday. Those who lived in the New York area would come to the East Side to do this in person. This was so accepted a practice in the Feinstein family, that when one grandchild was once unable to get through on the phone, she received a call that night from Reb Moshe, who was concerned that something was amiss. The family emphasizes, however, that these were not simply 'Happy Birthday' calls, but opportunities for them to express their fervent hopes and blessings that their father and grandfather merit another year of life in good health, and receive his blessing in return.*

Tolerance for All

FOLLOWING REB MOSHE'S PASSING, a noted *Rosh Yeshivah* expressed concern that he had caused anguish to Reb Moshe by resisting his counsel in a personal matter. Rabbi David Feinstein replied, "My father never felt hurt by such things. He considered everyone as if he were his own child. A parent makes allowance for his children's short-comings."

❧　　❧　　❧

A gentleman from northern New Jersey started to become observant when he was past the age of sixty. He told a friend that he felt despondent because, when his time was over, he would have to face the Heavenly Court without having amassed any Torah knowledge. The friend suggested that he drive to the Yeshivah of Staten Island from time to time — surely one of the students would be glad to teach him. So it was. He went to the yeshivah once a week for an hour of learning. It came very hard to him, because he had no Torah background and was not of an intellectual bent; however, after four years he glowed with pride at having mastered his first *"blatt gemara."*

One of the students told the story to Reb Moshe, who said that for this man, a single *blatt* was as much of an accomplishment as for a scholar to complete an entire tractate. The *Rosh Yeshivah* asked the *talmidim* to celebrate the occasion with a *seudas mitzvah*, which he, too, would attend. The *seudah* was festive indeed, with Reb Moshe adding his own words of blessing and congratulation. With tears in his eyes, the "guest of honor" rose to thank everyone for making his life so much more meaningful. He said, "Now I am not afraid to die."

---

* Some of Reb Moshe's other "children," namely his *talmidim*, had their own way of marking his birthday. For a number of years, a group of students from Yeshivah of Staten Island would travel to the East Side on the seventh of Adar to present Reb Moshe with a looseleaf containing *chiddushei Torah* written by the yeshivah's *talmidim*. Reb Moshe would glowingly accept this unique gift and leaf through the entire collection in the presence of the *talmidim*.

Aron HaKodesh in the Beis Midrash of Yeshiva of Staten Island

In his *Igros Moshe*, Reb Moshe writes forcefully and unequivocally against the doctrines and practices of those segments of Judaism that are unfaithful to Torah, going so far as to declare it forbidden even to enter their places of worship. His opinions on these matters were motivated to a large degree by his deep love for every Jew, which caused him to overcome his humility and express vehemently his opposition to such practices. It pained Reb Moshe to see so many of his fellow Jews being led astray from the path of truth, and he saw it as his obligation to rule on any question involving a breach in *Halachah*. But this in no way diminished his love for individuals who blindly engaged in the practices he condemned.

One *Erev Yom Kippur*, a few years before his passing, Reb Moshe was wheeled into an elevator of his apartment building, in front of which stood a car that was to take him to the Yeshivah of Staten Island, where he would observe the fast. In the elevator stood a Jew whose head was bare. The man bent down towards Reb Moshe and with a touch of hesitation said, "A happy new year, Rabbi." Reb Moshe looked up and with genuine warmth wished the man the same. Reb Moshe's sincerity moved the man to bend down again and say, "And a healthy year, too, Rabbi." With his sparkling eyes, Reb Moshe looked back at the man and said, "May you also be blessed with a healthy year, one filled with success and *nachas* from your children. And may you live to witness *Mashiach's* arrival."

The man was moved by Reb Moshe's words. As Reb Moshe was wheeled to the car, he turned to *Rebbetzin* Sheila Feinstein (wife of Reb Reuven) and said, "It is obvious that I am not religious — my head is not even covered — yet, to the Rabbi I am a 'Somebody'!"

When they were in the car, Reb Moshe's daughter-in-law related what the man had said. Reb Moshe explained his show of warmth to the man in one short sentence — "אבער ער איז א איד" (But he is a Jew).

With his genuine love for every Jew and deep understanding of the importance of peace, Reb Moshe, throughout his long life, remained above the disputes and strife that unfortunately plague the Orthodox community. It made no difference to Reb Moshe if someone was a *chassid, misnagid, Sefardi* or *Ashkenazi* — if the person was a Jew he had Reb Moshe's love and concern. Everyone was welcome at his door and as a result, his name is revered wherever true Torah values are respected.

❀   ❀   ❀

On a *Motza'ei Shabbos* in 1968, minutes after Shabbos had ended, the phone rang in Reb Moshe's apartment. It was a representative of the Satmar community calling to ask Reb Moshe to pray for the recovery of Rabbi Yoel Teitelbaum, the late Satmar *Rebbe*, who earlier that day had suffered a crippling stroke.

❀   ❀   ❀

Because Reb Moshe was removed from all pettiness and strife, he was often asked to mediate in disputes between quarrelling parties. He once stayed up throughout the night in an attempt to resolve an angry dispute — despite the fact that some of the people involved were treating him with less than the full respect he deserved.

❖   ❖   ❖

Someone once began to complain about the practices of certain zealots who were in the habit of making known their displeasure with others in an ugly manner. The person had only started to speak when he noticed tears in Reb Moshe's eyes. He abruptly changed the subject.

> Reb Moshe once said, "*Chazal* tell us 'The *yetzer hara*, the evil eye and a hatred of people can take a person from this world.' Now, isn't 'hatred of people' included in '*yetzer hara*'? What else can cause baseless hatred of others?
>
> "This, however, is precisely the point that *Chazal* are making. Often, one develops a hatred for someone else, mistakenly thinking that his feelings stem from the *yetzer tov!* The other person's customs or opinions differ from his own, and this — he thinks — is sufficient grounds for hatred. Beware — it is not! One need not agree with everything that others do or even *understand* everything that others do, but he must respect them nonetheless. Receive every person with a cheerful face and give others the benefit of the doubt — this should be a Jew's path in life."

When, on another occasion, Reb Moshe spoke on a similar theme, someone asked, "But isn't it hard to be like that?"

Reb Moshe replied, "With regard to sin, *Chazal* say, 'Once he has sinned and repeated it (the sin), it becomes to him like something permissible' (*Yoma* 77a). Habit has a powerful effect. The same is true with proper behavior. The more a person does that which is correct, the easier it becomes."

Following Reb Moshe's passing, Rabbi Reuven Feinstein said, "My father's deepest desire was to bring peace to Jewish life. If he could speak to us now, that is what he would tell us."

How wonderful it would be if his desire were realized.

CHAPTER EIGHT
A Giant of Thoughtfulness

"A distinguished Rav once asked me, 'Why does the Rosh Yeshivah give a personal letter of recommendation to every person who asks him for one? It cheapens the value of his signature! People pay little attention to these letters. It is not fitting for him!'

" ... It seems to me that this was the Rosh Yeshivah's basic approach to matters: If a Jew comes asking for something, one must respond first with chesed — a desire to help him and grant him whatever he seeks ... "

(Rabbi Nissan Alpert, at the funeral of Reb Moshe.)

REB MOSHE'S DEDICATION to anyone who came in contact with him is the subject of countless stories. He rarely declined to officiate at a wedding ceremony or to serve as *sandak* at a

Always Available

bris milah. It is customary for a father not to honor the same person as *sandak* twice, unless he is a person of exceptional stature. Often, Reb Moshe was asked to be *sandak* for every son in a family, but in such cases he would sometimes refuse if he felt the honor belonged to a grandfather. When he once accepted a second such invitation, his humility caused him to remark to the father in jest, "Being *sandak* is a *segulah* for wealth, which is why one who has already had this honor should give others a chance at gaining good fortune. Well, my being *sandak* at your first child's *bris* did not make me wealthy. So I guess it is all right for me to be *sandak* again."

❧　❧　❧

As sandak

At times, he would officiate at three weddings on the same night. Rabbi Nissan Alpert once escorted Reb Moshe on one such night. He recalled how taxing the evening was on the *Rosh Yeshivah*; still, Reb Moshe never entertained the thought of cutting down on such excursions. He once told someone, "I don't know why people feel it is so important that I attend their *simchos*, but if they feel this way, then I cannot refuse them."

THE WEDDINGS OF HIS *TALMIDIM* were of particular importance to him. One Friday morning, someone met him in New York's Port **Special** Authority Bus Terminal, waiting with Rabbi **Weddings** Moshe Rivlin to board a bus for the annual convention of Agudath Israel. The person could not believe that a car had not been provided to take the *Rosh Yeshivah* to the convention. Rabbi Rivlin explained, "Certainly a

Dancing at a talmid's wedding

car was provided. The *Rosh Yeshivah* was to be driven to the convention last night, following the *chupah* at a *talmid's* wedding. The car was there waiting after the ceremony had ended, but the *Rosh Yeshivah* said, 'How can I leave without dancing with the *chassan?'* He insisted that the car, which was to pick up other *roshei yeshivah*, not wait for him; he would find other means of transportation."

One did not have to be close to Reb Moshe to merit his presence at a wedding. One young man — a total stranger to Reb Moshe — asked that he attend his wedding to insure that the *kesubah* be written in accordance with *Halachah.* He came.

A *Rav* who had been designated as *mesader kiddushin* at one particular wedding was shocked when he saw Reb Moshe there. The *Rav* could not imagine how *he* could officiate in the presence of the *Rosh Yeshivah.* He inquired of the father, "How could you ask me to officiate when you knew that Reb Moshe was coming to the wedding?" The father replied honestly that he was unaware that Reb Moshe was going to attend and, in fact, was still not sure why he had come.

The *Rav* then asked Reb Moshe why he had come. "This morning," Reb Moshe said, "in the elevator of my apartment building I met a neighbor who told me that his granddaughter was getting married tonight and it would mean a lot to him if I would attend. That is why I am here."

> He was always scrupulous to bring joy to orphans. Seldom would he stay to the end of a wedding, but he would almost always stay late at the wedding of an orphan.
>
> Rabbi Moshe Rivlin once asked Reb Moshe to accompany him to visit a wealthy man, on behalf of Tifereth Jerusalem. Reb Moshe replied that the time of the appointment coincided with the wedding of an orphan girl to which he had been invited. "I don't know the girl, but she came to me the other day and said that she would be grateful if I came to her wedding. You will have to visit that man alone."

Reb Moshe did not ask to be paid for officiating at weddings, writing *gittin*, or deciding matters of *Halachah*, though he was certainly entitled to. Many people gave him money anyway, often very large sums. Over the years, tens of thousands of such dollars passed through his hands, but he always turned it over to Tifereth Jerusalem or another *tzedakah.* He supported his family with his modest salary as *Rosh Yeshivah*.

HE FOUNDED HIS OWN PRIVATE CHARITY FUND, which he called *'Tzor'chei Am'cha'* (The Needs of Your People), and kept a

Distributing Charity
ledger with an exact accounting of where each dollar went. Someone who used to watch Reb Moshe apportion his funds said that it was done with the same consideration and forethought as when he ruled on halachic matters.

❀   ❀   ❀

Often, he would sit with a pile of charity envelopes that had come in the mail and place a specific amount in each. Always, he would refer to his ledger to see how much his last donation to that particular organization had been. Among the organizations Reb Moshe sent to were American institutions for the physically handicapped and mentally ill. He felt it an obligation to respond to such requests to show that religious Jews — and rabbis in particular — respected the work of these causes.

In Reb Moshe's home was a large jar filled with quarters. Before leaving for a public function the *Rebbetzin* would reach into the jar and give her husband a handful of coins so that he would be able to give something to every solicitor he would meet at the door. In general, Reb Moshe never refused a request for *tzedakah*. Even if a number of children would solicit for the same cause in *shul*, Reb Moshe would give them all something. This he did for *chinuch*, so that children learn not to refuse the requests of others when they grow older and are in a position to give.

When a needy individual would ask him for a donation, Reb Moshe would listen to the person's story with complete attention. Then, he would turn around, so that the supplicant would not see him counting out the money. Along with the donation came something that meant more to many than the money — Reb Moshe's warm smile and good wishes.

❀   ❀   ❀

Reb Moshe and the *Rebbetzin* lived frugally on his small salary. Not only were their needs so simple that they managed quite well, but they even contributed very generously to *tzedakah* causes.

So large were Reb Moshe's contributions in proportion to his income, that the Internal Revenue Service questioned his income tax return regularly. Virtually every year, he, his accountant or a member of the yeshivah staff would appear at an IRS office audit to show proof of Reb Moshe's contributions.

ONCE, HE WAS supposed to attend his first meeting as chairman of the *Moetzes Gedolei HaTorah,* and the meeting was scheduled right

The Essence of Charity after his *shiur* and *Minchah* in Tifereth Jerusalem. A car was waiting for him outside the yeshivah and as soon as *Minchah* ended, the students surrounded their *Rosh Yeshivah* to escort him out without a second's delay, since many of the other members of the *Moetzes* would already be there waiting for him. As he was about to get into the car, a poor man asked him for charity. Reb Moshe reached into his pocket and gave the man a few coins, but the beggar wasn't finished yet. He began a conversation with Reb Moshe, while the waiting driver and students became more and more impatient. A few attempted to tell the poor man that Reb Moshe was in a hurry, but Reb Moshe waved to them to go away. After ten minutes, Reb Moshe excused himself, shook hands with the beggar and finally got into the car.

One of the students was brave enough to ask his *rebbi* why he had not simply given the man the money and said he had no time to talk.

Reb Moshe said, "You must understand that to that man the conversation meant more than the money. My *mitzvah* of *tzedakah* included showing him that I care about what he thinks and that I am not too busy to speak to him."

> Reb Moshe's older son, Reb David, remarked about him, "My father never wasted a minute, but if a poor or troubled person — or even a *nudnik* — took an hour to pour out his heart, my father could spare an hour."

His younger son, Reb Reuven, recalled that *chesed* was an integral part of his parents' home. When he was a five-year-old, Reb Reuven would regularly help an old woman carry firewood up the stairs to her tenement apartment. No one ever told him; it was simply the natural thing to do because he had always seen his parents and older siblings performing such acts as a matter of course. Reb Moshe and the *Rebbetzin* knew that the most effective way to teach was by example. *

There were always guests at the Shabbos table. For many years, an elderly widow was a steady guest at Reb Moshe's *Seder*. One year she did not come, and Reb Moshe would not start the *Seder* until Reb Reuven and his wife went to the woman's home to see what the problem was. When they returned with her, the *Seder* began.

❊   ❊   ❊

Helping others was so natural a part of their parents' home that it is difficult for the Feinstein children to recall stories that left an impression. People tend to recall unusual events, not everyday occurrences. One incident, though, stands out in Reb Reuven's mind.

When already *Rosh Yeshivah* at Yeshivah of Staten Island, Reb Reuven came to Tifereth Jerusalem to discuss a pressing yeshivah matter with his father. Before he had a chance to begin, a well-dressed woman entered Reb Moshe's office and began to pour out her troubles. It soon became apparent that the woman was somewhat deranged. She imagined that "aliens" were chasing her and she wanted Reb Moshe to hear her "harrowing experiences." She went on speaking for half an hour. At that point, Reb Reuven — for his father's sake — was going to tell the woman that the *Rosh Yeshivah* now understood her plight well. Reb Moshe stopped him, saying, "זי האָט קײנעם נישט איהר אויס צוהערען אַזעלכיבע זאַכען" (She has no one who will listen to her tell of such things)."

The woman continued speaking *for another hour and a half!* She finally left, only because nightfall had come "and that was when the aliens came out."

A certain woman used to call Reb Moshe a few times a day with halachic questions. Often she would call two or three times just to be sure that she had heard the answer correctly the first time. Someone was tempted to take the

---

* In commenting on the Torah's account of Rebecca giving water to Eliezer's camels, Reb Moshe notes that when she responded to Eliezer's entreaty, she did not *offer* to water the camels, but watered them anyway. This was in contradiction both to his prayer, which mentioned an explicit response on her part, and to Eliezer's repetition of the incident. Reb Moshe explains that Rebecca's kindness was so great that she took it for granted that another's needs should be provided for, whatever they were. That his camels had to be watered was so obvious to her that it was unnecessary for her to announce her intention to do so (*Igros Moshe, Orach Chaim II* responsa 52).

phone and explain to her that she was wasting the *Rosh Yeshivah's* precious time. "No," insisted Reb Moshe. "She is a nervous woman and cannot help herself."

Mr. Daniel Sukenik recalls that concerned men and women from the East Side used to tell Reb Moshe about their dreams and ask him to interpret them and convene a *beis din* for *Hatavas Chalom* [Amelioration of Dreams] to counteract possible ill effects. Even though he might have felt that their fears were groundless, he would listen patiently and discuss the dreams with them because no one else cared to be bothered.

❂ ❂ ❂

People would sometimes ask him to purchase a *lulav* and *esrog* for them. Though he had no time to spare, he never refused such requests. When asked why, he replied, "How can one refuse a Jew who seeks a favor?"

A woman once appeared at Reb Moshe's door, asking to speak to the *Rosh Yeshivah*. When told that the *Rosh Yeshivah* was busy, the woman insisted that she needed Reb Moshe to translate a letter she had received from her sister in Russia. The man at the door was stunned. "The *Rosh Yeshivah* cannot be bothered with such things!"

"What do you mean?" retorted the woman. "He has been translating my letters for twenty years!"

❂ ❂ ❂

Rabbi Chaim Twersky recalls that he once drove Reb Moshe from New York to his vacation spot in the Catskills. The trip was exhausting, and Rabbi Twersky stopped off at his own bungalow first so that Reb Moshe could rest before completing the trip. As usual, the first thing he did was call the *Rebbetzin* to tell her his schedule and make sure she was all right. Word spread quickly that Reb Moshe was there, and people came to pay their respects. A few people from a neighboring bungalow colony asked if he would be willing to check their *eruv*, a sometimes strenuous task in a sprawling bungalow colony. As was his nature, the tired Reb Moshe agreed, but his host Rabbi Twersky put his foot down and would not permit it.

REB MOSHE DID NOT WAIT to be asked when he saw that his help was needed. Once, the old *shamash* in Tifereth Jerusalem needed

Without Being Asked help in placing the *s'chach* on the yeshivah's *succah*, and asked if the *Rosh Yeshivah* could send a few students to assist him. Instead of honoring the request, Reb Moshe climbed onto a ladder and put the *s'chach* up himself.

❈   ❈   ❈

Rebbetzin Malka Feinstein, wife of Reb David, recalls that she first came to know Reb Moshe when she was a child. At that time, she knew him and the *Rebbetzin* as friends of her parents, and had no idea that he was a great man, too. One day, when she was thirteen years old, and living in the Williamsburg section of Brooklyn, she came home from school for lunch. The door was unlocked — not unusual in those days — but her mother was not home. She took her own lunch and then noticed a note saying that if the key was not in its usual place, she should not go back to school in the afternoon. She was puzzled, so she tried to call her brother, who was studying in Mesivta Torah Vodaath. He could not be found, but a friend of his came to the phone and told her that her mother and brother had gone somewhere together.

By now she was frightened and she felt she had to call for help and advice. The family had dozens of close friends, but somehow, instinctively, the person she thought of to call was Reb Moshe. Even a young teen-ager felt that sort of closeness to him. He calmed her and told her to stay home until she heard from him. Before long, she looked out the window and saw Reb Moshe and the *Rebbetzin* coming down the street. He had called the slaughterhouse where her father was a *shochet*, and learned that he had suffered a heart attack at work and had not survived the trip to the hospital. Immediately, Reb Moshe and the *Rebbetzin* crossed the Williamsburg Bridge and went to stay with the worried child in her time of fear and tragedy. Later, he left to take part in her late father's *taharah* [cleansing and preparation for burial].

❈   ❈   ❈

She recalls another incident — a very minor one — that illustrates his thoughtfulness. The second summer after her marriage, she and her husband were in the city for the summer while Reb Moshe was in the Catskill mountains, where summer bungalows did not have telephones. One day she received a post card from Reb Moshe telling her that he had been in New York for a day, but had not had an opportunity to call her. He was therefore writing to apologize.

❈   ❈   ❈

One *Erev Yom Kippur* after *Minchah*, as the *beis midrash* of Tifereth Jerusalem was quickly emptying out, Rabbi Nathan Lomner observed an interesting sight. In the back of the room sat Reb Moshe and the old *shamash*, emptying *tzedakah* plates (that are customarily placed in *shuls* on that day) into envelopes, so that the monies could later be distributed to the various organizations for which they were intended. When Reb Moshe noticed Rabbi Lomner watching him, he said, "He (referring to the *shamash*) also must go home and eat before the fast."

Another *Erev Yom Kippur* after *Minchah*, Reb Moshe and Rabbi Lomner were walking home together when Reb Moshe suddenly said, "Let's visit the old *Rav* of Boyan (not to be confused with the late *Rebbe* of Boyan) who is ill and bedridden. It's *Erev Yom Kippur* and probably no one has time to visit him today." Sure enough, when they entered the *Rav's* bedroom they found him lying in bed with no one at his side. Reb Moshe sat down and chatted with him as if he had all the time in the world. Finally, he rose and blessed the now smiling *Rav* with a complete recovery and a good year, and then left.

For a time, he would detour on his way home from *davening* on Shabbos mornings to visit a chronically ill man. He once commented to someone walking with him that this *mitzvah* was especially important, for people who are ill for a long time tend to become forgotten as time passes.

A man was once hospitalized at Beth Israel Hospital in New York when he received the surprise of his life. In walked Reb Moshe, whom he did not know personally, to visit. In explanation, Reb Moshe said that earlier that day he had been told that an old Jewish man, who was also a patient at Beth Israel, had no visitors. Once Reb Moshe had come to see that man he decided to visit other patients as well.

WHEN RABBI ALPERT was still a student, Reb Moshe asked him for a favor. He had received a letter from a needy person asking for **Doing It Right** financial help before Pesach, but he had misplaced the letter. All he remembered was that the sender was a Belzer *chassid* who lived on Rivington Street.

"Nissan, come with me to Rivington Street and let's try to find him." They went, but failed; Rivington Street was crowded with Jews of all sorts in those days. Reb Moshe was distressed but there was nothing he could do. On *Erev Pesach*, Reb Moshe came to the Alpert apartment and asked for Nissan. He had found the letter and wanted to deliver the money immediately; a poor family's *Yom Tov* would be much more festive if they knew there was some cash on hand. Would Nissan accompany him?

The two went to the Rivington Street address and delivered the money. On their way back, it started to rain. Reb Moshe told Nissan to hurry home; he, Reb Moshe, had to make a detour to buy a newspaper. Nissan wanted to go along, but Reb Moshe insisted that he not walk unnecessarily in the rain. It seemed strange to Nissan that his *Rosh Yeshivah* should want to read a paper on *Erev Pesach*, and to walk two blocks in the rain to buy one, but he did not dare ask why.

Several weeks later, Nissan found an opportunity to satisfy his curiosity. He told Reb Moshe that he had been wondering about the newspaper and thought he had solved the mystery. Reb Moshe asked to hear the solution. "The *Rebbetzin* probably would not have wanted the *Rosh Yeshivah* to deliver the money himself on such a busy day; so the *Rosh Yeshivah* said he was buying a newspaper. In order not to break his word, the *Rosh Yeshivah* had to go for a paper even though it was raining." Reb Moshe smiled and nodded.

❈   ❈   ❈

Reb Moshe would not allow his deep humility to stand in the way of a kindness. Mr. Joseph Friedenson, editor of *Dos Yiddishe Vort*, Agudath Israel's Yiddish-language monthly, related how some twenty years ago, he had called Reb Moshe for a favor. The *Rosh Yeshivah's* Shabbos address at that year's Agudah Convention had been transcribed after Shabbos by someone who had not been well that weekend. The transcript was short and lacking in content. Could the *Rosh Yeshivah* give Mr. Friedenson some details of what he had said?

Reb Moshe did not understand the request. "What is wrong if my *drashah* is short? I did not say anything new ... It is sufficient to write that I exhorted the gathering to strengthen themselves in Torah learning, *tzedakah*, ..."

Mr. Friedenson explained that his readers would consider it an affront on his part if he were to publish only a short synopsis of Reb

Reb Moshe's manuscript
of a convention address

Moshe's address alongside much lengthier transcripts of other speeches. Upon hearing this, Reb Moshe's attitude immediately changed. Of course he would help. No, it would not be necessary for Mr. Friedenson to come see him. He would write out the address and mail it to Mr. Friedenson.

Mr. Friedenson said that it would be sufficient for Reb Moshe to send him a few notes in Hebrew, and Friedenson would write the article.

"No," Reb Moshe said, "I'll write it in Yiddish, just as I used to write my mother, and send it to you."

Reb Moshe's three-page, closely written address arrived the next day. Mr. Friedenson called to thank him and said he would publish it word for word if Reb Moshe wished.

Reb Moshe would not hear of it. He said, "I wrote it out to help you, but you should print whatever you see fit. You are an editor and you know better."

In his last years, Reb Moshe would *daven* the latter part of *Neilah* outside the *beis midrash* at Yeshivah of Staten Island, because he was too weak to stand as the fast neared its end and he would not sit in a *beis midrash* while the *Aron HaKodesh* was open, as is the custom during *Neilah*. On one Yom Kippur, he was joined in the hallway by a fifteen-year-old student who felt so weak that he sat with his head resting on his arms.

Then, during those awesome moments, when the fate of every Jew is sealed for the coming year, Reb Moshe went over to the boy, put his hand on his shoulder and said, "Don't worry, only a little while longer."

AT TIMES, REB MOSHE'S *CHESED* was done so subtly that it could go almost unnoticed. Some twenty years ago, a young man entered **Subtle** the *beis midrash* of Tifereth Jerusalem seeking to discuss an urgent matter with him. To his dismay, he **Chesed** was told that Reb Moshe was at his apartment, preparing to leave the city for a few days, but if he would hurry, he might meet the *Rosh Yeshivah* on his way out.

The young man ran the three-quarters of a mile to Reb Moshe's house at top speed. He was met at the apartment's door by two students carrying out some of Reb Moshe's luggage. No, it was impossible to see the *Rosh Yeshivah* now; he would be leaving in a matter of moments.

Just then Reb Moshe noticed the young man, still panting to catch his breath. He invited his visitor to have a seat in his study, while he busied himself gathering some *sefarim* to take along on his trip.

For the next few minutes, Reb Moshe spoke to the young man in idle conversation, without pausing to allow his visitor to speak. "I'm going away for a few days ... it's good to get away once in a while ... I'll have more time to learn than I usually do ..."

Only after the young man had fully recovered from his dash to the apartment did Reb Moshe ask him why he had come.

> While he was quick to help others, Reb Moshe always sought not to inconvenience anyone. For many years, he spent Succos in the home of his daughter Sifra and his son-in-law, Rabbi Moshe David Tendler. (Rabbi Tendler is a *rosh yeshivah* at Yeshivas Rabbi Yitzchak Elchonon and rabbi of the Monsey Community Synagogue.) Reb Moshe would sleep in the *succah* and get up to learn before dawn, as he did all year long.

During her father's later years, *Rebbetzin* Tendler used to arrange a line of chairs so that he could support himself on them as he walked from his bed to get his morning coffee and to go to the room where he learned. Every morning, the family found the chairs neatly placed around the table, and everyone thought that some other family member had done it. The "family member" was Reb Moshe himself, who wanted to spare everyone else the bother of putting the chairs back where they belonged.*

During the last several summers of Reb Moshe's life, his daughter-in-law תבל״ח, *Rebbetzin* Sheila Feinstein, wife of Reb Reuven, helped care for Reb Moshe in Camp Staten Island. He would sit and learn at a table on the lawn and she would sit nearby in case she was needed. From time to time he would ask how she was or ask about the children or something else. She realized that he was interrupting his learning only so that she should not feel ignored, and it made her uncomfortable that she was interfering with his concentration. She wanted to serve him but she did not want him to stop learning because of her. So she said, "It makes me happy just to watch you learn."

"And it makes me happy that you want to sit nearby to help me," he responded.

Then she hit on a plan. She set up an intercom between his table and her bungalow so that he could have his privacy, while she would be available at a moment's notice. But he never called for her, for fear that she was busy and he would be disturbing her.

Early every Shabbos morning in camp, he would sit on his porch and chant the weekly Torah reading with the *trop* [cantillation]. She remarked to her friends that she loved to listen to her father-in-law chanting the *sidra*. The next Shabbos morning, he was not on the porch. Alarmed, she ran to his bungalow to find out if anything was wrong. He was reviewing the *sidra* at the kitchen table. Why was he not on the porch as usual? He explained that he had overheard her telling her friend that she used to hear him every Shabbos morning. Apparently the sound of his voice was waking her up, and she was entitled to sleep later on Shabbos. With

---

* One Succos there was a severe windstorm in Monsey on the first night of Succos, and many *succahs* and much *s'chach* were blown down. Most of the *s'chach* in Rabbi Tendler's large *succah* was blown down, but all the *s'chach* over Reb Moshe's bed remained in place.

difficulty she convinced Reb Moshe that she was always up anyway, and that he would be doing her a favor by chanting the *sidra* on the porch, where she could enjoy listening to him.

HIS APPRECIATION toward those who assisted him in any way knew no bounds. His grandson Rabbi Mordechai Tendler was with

Appreciation him for many years as a *talmid*, companion, and protector, at a time when Reb Moshe's strength had to be conserved and his generous openness to all had to be curbed. Reb Mordechai became *S'gan Rosh Kollel* of Beth Medrash L'Torah V'Horoah in Tifereth Jerusalem, and continues the task of preparing Reb Moshe's voluminous writings for publication. He distinguished himself for his single-minded devotion to his grandparents and he undertook the unpopular but essential task of protecting Reb Moshe from the incessant demands upon his time and strength. Those close to Reb Moshe often noted his special appreciation for his grandson's efforts.

Other grandchildren helped as well in caring for Reb Moshe in his last years, as did *talmidim* of Tifereth Jerusalem and other local yeshivah *bachurim*. Often, he would fondly kiss those who came to his aid and would occasionally present them with one of his *sefarim* — personally inscribed — as a token of appreciation.

In the summertime, when his younger assistants would leave for summer camps, Reb Moshe would be sure to send them personal regards at every opportunity. Once, he noticed one of his "boys" in a crowd of people that surged forward to greet him. Unable to get near the *bachur*, Reb Moshe smiled and waved at him.

When one of his attendants was hospitalized with appendicitis, Reb Moshe telephoned him every day.

❀   ❀   ❀

He felt a deep appreciation for all who served his yeshivah in any capacity. This included the yeshivah's cooks, Mr. and Mrs. Jaeger, who performed their chores with true dedication. Someone once answered the public telephone in the hallway of Yeshivah of Staten Island. The caller was none other than Reb Moshe, asking to speak to the Jaegers. The yeshivah's annual Chanukah celebration had taken place the night before and by the time it was over, the Jaegers had left. He was calling to thank them for having made the *simchah* so beautiful.

Mr. and Mrs. Jaeger were very devoted to the students of the yeshivah in general, but their dedication to the *Rosh Yeshivah* was boundless. During the summer they made a special arrangement with a fisherman to bring them fresh-caught fish, which they prepared for Reb Moshe's Shabbos meals. He, in turn, showed his gratitude in many ways. He once wrote them a personal letter of appreciation, which was mounted on a plaque and which they will always treasure. A few weeks before his passing he asked to see them. Although his doctors did not want him to shake hands with anyone, he insisted on shaking hands with Mr. Jaeger, as he thanked and blessed the Jaegers for the last time.

It is remarkable that Rabbi Aharon Kotler and Rabbi Reuven Grozovsky also went out of their way to show their respect and gratitude for the cooks of their yeshivos. Our truly great people do not categorize people according to wealth or position, but according to personal worth.

As a rule, Reb Moshe personally supervised the baking of his Pesach *matzos*. He would emphasize that he came to perform the *mitzvah*, and not because he questioned the *kashrus* of the bakery. There were some who urged him to change to a larger, newer, more efficient bakery, but he always refused, explaining that people might take such a change as an aspersion on the *kashrus* of the older bakery. Those who accompanied Reb Moshe to the *matzah* bakery recall his zealousness in performing this *mitzvah* and his joy when the finished *matzos* were taken from the oven. To someone who was overzealous in rejecting *matzos*, he gave the gentle, humorous rebuke, "Rabbi Akiva would eat our *matzos*, but we would not eat his." The same person was in the habit of breaking off parts of many *matzos* because he maintained that they were not well baked. Reb Moshe opposed this practice. He told the gentleman that he should pay for the complete *matzos* because the breakage was unnecessary.

One year, he asked someone to bring some of these *matzos* to a man who had made a number of appeals for funds on behalf of Tifereth Jerusalem. Reb Moshe knew that the man sought nothing in return for his efforts, but was hopeful that the very personal gift he was now sending would be accepted as a token of his appreciation.

WHEN RABBI REUVEN FEINSTEIN was a child, a student of the yeshivah offered to treat him to an ice cream. The youngster said no,

They're All His Children

he could not accept a treat unless his friends got one, too. Years later, his "benefactor" told him about the ice cream he was never given. Reb Reuven did not remember the story, but said that in his parents' household they were brought up that way by example; it was perfectly normal that no one accepted a favor or a treat that was not available to others.

Indeed, that was an old Feinstein tradition. In Luban, as well as in many European cities, it was customary that weddings took place on Friday afternoons. On the Friday that Reb Moshe and his *Rebbetzin* were married, there were two other weddings. Luban's only Jewish fiddler came to the *Rav* and proudly told him that he would play only at *his* wedding, and do so free of charge. Reb Moshe shook his head and said that he could not permit the fiddler

to play at his wedding unless he played at the other weddings, too.

One Shabbos afternoon, two of Reb Moshe's grandchildren were playing with one of their friends in the lunchroom of Tifereth Jerusalem where Reb Moshe and some others had gathered for *Shalosh Seudos*. In the midst of their playing, the grandchildren ran to their grandfather, with their little friend tagging along behind them. Reb Moshe gave each of his grandchildren a hug and a kiss and without a moment's hesitation hugged and kissed the other child as well.

Similarly, when an older grandson visited Reb Moshe before leaving for *Eretz Yisrael* and brought with him a friend who would be accompanying him, Reb Moshe wished them both well and kissed them both goodbye.

✾ ✾ ✾

One summer day some thirty years ago, Reb Moshe sat in the lobby of a Catskill Mountains hotel, when a five-year-old child wandered in. Seeing no one but strangers in the room, the child tottered over to the small man, with the greyish-white beard and friendly look, hopped onto his lap and announced, "You are my *Zeidy!*" Reb Moshe put his arms around his little friend and they began an animated conversation. A few minutes later, the boy's father entered the lobby in search of his son, only to find him on Reb Moshe's lap, a very content look on his small face. Before the father could apologize, Reb Moshe said, "Oh, what a shame you weren't here! Your son had so many clever things to tell me!"

❃ ❃ ❃

A little boy once entered the *beis midrash* of Tifereth Jerusalem crying profusely. When someone asked him what was wrong, he explained that his *rebbi* had refused to allow him into class because he had forgotten to bring a quarter for a notebook. Before anyone else could make a move, Reb Moshe was there, having heard the boy's tale from his place in front of the room. He held out a quarter for the boy and told him to take the money and return to class. When Reb Moshe saw the boy's reluctance to accept the gift, he gently took him by the hand, led him up the three flights of stairs to his classroom, handed the *rebbi* the quarter and left.

HIS EXTREME SENSITIVITY toward the feelings and needs of others went far beyond open acts of kindness.

Deflecting Criticism There is a well-known story about someone driving Reb Moshe to yeshivah who accidentally slammed the car door shut on the *Rosh Yeshivah's* fingers. Reb Moshe clenched his injured fingers with his other hand, bit his lips against the excruciating pain and walked into the yeshivah building without uttering a sound. Several *talmidim* who had witnessed the incident later asked Reb Moshe why he had restrained himself so. He answered quietly, "The young man was kind enough to drive me to the yeshivah. Could I hurt his feelings by letting him know something was wrong?"

Shortly after World War II, the Shulsinger Brothers Publishing Company published a beautiful *Shas*. It was the first *Shas* of such quality ever published in the United States and Reb Moshe purchased one as soon as it became available. Once he left his desk briefly and, while he was out, one of his *talmidim* accidentally tipped over a bottle of ink on the brand new *Shas gemara*.

The culprit was deeply chagrined and the others in the room were horrified as well. Just then Reb Moshe returned. Seeing what had happened, he broke out in a pleasant smile and said that blue was his favorite color and that the *gemara* looked even more beautiful than before. With that, he went back to his writing as if nothing unusual had happened.

※   ※   ※

Driving along a highway one rainy afternoon, Reb Moshe's driver missed an exit sign and was forced to make a lengthy detour. Someone else in the car criticized the driver for not being alert. For about fifteen minutes Reb Moshe did not say a word. Then, he remarked, "My, what a foggy afternoon it is! It is difficult for me to read the road signs ... "

On another occasion, a driver got off the highway at the wrong exit, whereupon one of the passengers complained, "Oh, he is lost." The driver tried to mollify the passenger with humor, but not to much avail. A few moments later, Reb Moshe began commenting on the heavy clouds and poor visibility. "It is a miracle that anyone can drive in such bad weather." Only much later did the driver realize that the *Rosh Yeshivah's* intention was to deflect the criticism of his driving.

※   ※   ※

Another *rosh yeshivah* had come to discuss something with Reb Moshe. While being ushered in, the visitor was told that Reb Moshe had been lying down, for he was ill. Later, Reb Moshe told his visitor the source of his illness. "I was compelled to say something that caused anguish to another Jew," he said painfully.

As much as he respected Reb Moshe as a man of truth, the visitor found this difficult to believe — until Reb Moshe explained himself: He had been judging a dispute and had stated his opinion. The party he had ruled against could not accept Reb Moshe's decision and continued to adamantly defend his position. Finally, Reb Moshe was forced to remark, "You must realize that it is difficult for a person to see things objectively when he has a personal interest in a matter."

Reb Moshe feared that the man may have felt hurt by this comment. It was this that had caused him to become physically sick.

Once, a childless woman, a talented artist, came to Reb Moshe for a blessing that she have a child. When the blessing was fulfilled, the woman brought Reb Moshe a painting as a sign of gratitude, which the *Rebbetzin* hung in the dining room. When the woman's new baby was old enough to travel without difficulty, she gratefully brought him to visit the Feinstein family and show Reb Moshe the fruit of his blessing. As she left the apartment and was waiting at the elevator, Reb Moshe himself came rushing out into the hall. He remembered that her painting was no longer hanging on the dining-room wall and feared that she might feel slighted. Reb Moshe explained to the woman that the dining room had been converted into a *shul* for a morning *minyan*, so it was not proper for the painting to hang there. The *Rebbetzin* had hung the picture in the bedroom.

HE ONCE RECEIVED a letter of apology from someone whom he had never met. The writer told of how he and a friend had become

Offering Reassurance

involved in a heated halachic discussion. The friend had cited a statement of Reb Moshe's to back up his opinion, to which the writer had responded with a remark to the effect that the proof was of little meaning to him. Later, when the discussion had ended, the man realized that his manner of dismissing the proof was in fact a slight to Reb Moshe's honor. In the letter he wrote how this was troubling him day and night to the point that he had difficulty sleeping. He humbly begged Reb Moshe's forgiveness.

Reb Moshe, who more than once remarked that he had never held a grudge against anyone, forgave the man. However, this was not sufficient — as far as he was concerned. The man was troubled by what he had done and his mind had to be put at ease. It would not be enough to write the man a letter; it could take two or three days for a letter to arrive and what about the man's feelings until then?

Reb Moshe did what, to him, was the natural thing to do. Using the address on the envelope, he obtained the man's phone number, called him immediately, and put his worries to rest.

❧　　❧　　❧

On his way to the elevator after a *chupah* ceremony, Reb Moshe was surrounded by well-wishers. When the elevator had deposited them on the building's ground floor, Reb Moshe told Rabbi Rivlin, his companion, that they would have to go back up again. He had been unable to shake a man's hand which was extended as the elevator door closed. They returned to the floor of the wedding, Reb Moshe found the man, shook his hand and then left.

At the wedding of Rabbi Chaim Twersky's daughter, Reb Moshe arrived unexpectedly. He had been sent an invitation, but Rabbi Twersky had not invited him personally in order not to tax his strength. Both fathers asked Reb Moshe to be *mesader kiddushin*, but said that they would like him to leave right after the *chupah*, in view of his need to rest. Reb Moshe thanked them for their concern, but he stayed to dance with the *chassan* before leaving. When his car was nearly at the Manhattan Bridge, he asked the driver to go back to the hall. In the commotion of the wedding, he had forgotten to wish Rabbi Twersky *mazal tov* before leaving.

❁   ❁   ❁

He once visited someone's home on *Yom Tov*. So enthralled was the family by Reb Moshe's presence that they remained oblivious to a baby crying in a playpen. Reb Moshe interrupted the conversation to say, "For the baby it is also *Yom Tov!*"

❁   ❁   ❁

Once a few students of the yeshivah were playing basketball and an errant rebound hit another boy in the face, breaking his glasses. Later the boys came to Reb Moshe to inquire whether they were halachically liable to pay for the glasses. They were in the middle of a series of arguments regarding their responsibility when Reb Moshe cut them off. First, he wanted to know if the victim had been hurt and how he was.

❁   ❁   ❁

When he developed a painful leg infection, the doctor recommended that the leg be kept raised to ease the pain. Reb Moshe would not permit a milk crate to be brought into his *beis midrash* for his leg to be placed on, for fear that this would cause concern among his *talmidim*.

DURING THAT TIME, he was once driven home from Yeshivah of Staten Island by Rabbi Gershon Weiss, *Menahel* of the yeshivah.

For the Sake of a Child One of Rabbi Weiss' children was crying in the car and because of this, Rabbi Weiss could not escort Reb Moshe to his apartment. Instead, another passenger, a *talmid* in the yeshivah, went along while Rabbi Weiss waited in the car with the child. The high-rise apartment buildings on FDR Drive have separate elevators for even and odd floors. Reb Moshe, who lived on the second floor, missed his elevator as it began its ascent. Knowing that the *talmid* would not leave until Reb Moshe was at his apartment door and not wanting to deny the crying child from going home, he took the odd-elevator to the third floor and, limping on his infected leg, walked down the flight of steps to his apartment.

❈ ❈ ❈

Rabbi Weiss related another anecdote that reveals yet another aspect of Reb Moshe's unusual sensitivity toward others. In the summer camp of Yeshivah of Staten Island, it was the responsibility of a particular student to bring meals from the camp kitchen to Reb Moshe and his *Rebbetzin* in their bungalow. One day, the waiter had not arrived in time, and Rabbi Weiss' young son, who happened to be near Reb Moshe's bungalow, was asked to bring the *Rebbetzin* a container of milk. The boy excitedly raced to the camp kitchen, but when he got there he saw the waiter bringing lunch, including milk, for the *Rosh Yeshivah's* family. Not one to easily give up a chance to serve Reb Moshe and his wife, the child clutched the milk container and raced to the bungalow — but he was too late. The student had already arrived with the lunch.

Someone who happened to be in the bungalow at the time told the boy to return the milk to the camp kitchen. Overhearing this, Reb Moshe said to the crestfallen child, "No, don't return it. We need it! We can use it tomorrow!" Reb Moshe then asked the boy to sit down, while the *Rebbetzin* went to get him some candy. He asked the boy his age and which *masechta* he was learning at the time. Hearing that he was eleven years old and studying *Bava Metzia*, Reb Moshe smilingly exclaimed, "Oh, when I was eleven years old I also learned *Bava Metzia!* In fact I memorized the entire *masechta* that year. May *Hashem* help you to do the same."

Instead of being sent away with the container of milk, the child went away with candy from the *Rebbetzin* and the even sweeter memory of a warm encounter with the giant of the generation.

CHAPTER NINE

Faith and Zealousness

The lighting of the Chanukah menorah for eight days commemorates the victory of the Chashmonaim over the Syrian-Greeks, after which a flask of oil bearing the Kohein Gadol's seal was found in the Beis HaMikdash. The flask contained a one-day supply of oil for the menorah, but, miraculously, the oil lasted for eight days.

For centuries, commentators have grappled with an obvious question: Should not Chanukah be celebrated for only seven days, since there was enough oil for one day?

Reb Moshe explained that herein lies a fundamental lesson of faith. In decreeing that the festival be celebrated for eight days, Chazal were implying that every occurrence in this world is, in essence, a miracle. Oil burns because it is the will of Hashem that this particular liquid serve mankind as a fuel. If Hashem so willed, vinegar could also burn, as it did for Rabbi Chanina ben Dosa. We light the Chanukah menorah for eight days, instead of seven, to demonstrate the common denominator between natural and supernatural occurrences — both occur only because Hashem wills them to ("Kol Rom" [Bastion of Faith], Rabbi Avraham Fishelis).

REB MOSHE'S FAITH AND TRUST in *Hashem* were rare and sublime. His firm belief that all is from *Hashem* and that nothing is beyond His power was apparent time and time again. Of

Nothing By Chance course, one must be worthy to have his faith rewarded, as Reb Moshe's was so often. Then again, such faith in itself is justification for it to be rewarded.

Some years ago, he received a phone call from a man whose doctor had told him that he was suffering from an incurable ailment and had but a few weeks to live. The man was calling to discuss an item which he planned to include in his will. Reb Moshe refused to discuss the matter. He said that the man should not be so quick to accept the doctor's word as fact, as doctors are only human and can make mistakes. He instructed him to seek the opinion of a second doctor and assured him that *Hashem* would help him.

The caller followed Reb Moshe's advice. A subsequent series of tests showed that, indeed, the first doctor had erred. The man was indeed ill, but his ailment was not terminal as the first doctor had said, and the ominous prediction did not come true.

※　　※　　※

Rabbi Elimelech Bluth (presently *Av Beis Din* of the *Vaad HaRabbanim* of Flatbush) was one of Reb Moshe's closest *talmidim* and attended him for many years. He recalls that a man once gave

Reb Moshe the gift of a fountain pen, which he uncharacteristically accepted. The man explained that his wife had given birth to a healthy child after receiving Reb Moshe's blessing, and the gift was their token of appreciation. Noting Rabbi Bluth's surprise at his acceptance of the gift, Reb Moshe explained, "This is 'my' child."

What happened was that the mother had several children with birth defects — and then had developed a disabling condition. As a result, it was considered impossible for her to bear more children. This complication was to her benefit, since her condition made pregnancy a life-threatening matter. When the "impossible" happened and she became pregnant again, her doctor said that it was a matter of life and death to end the pregnancy. Reb Moshe was consulted and he startled the parents by telling them that the pregnancy was a miracle and that they should have faith that *Hashem* would not let it happen unless mother and child would be healthy. The miracle *did* end happily. She had no ill effects and the newborn infant was completely normal.

A MAN ONCE CAME before Reb Moshe with a dilemma. His father was quite advanced in years and his children had delicately

With Perfect Faith
suggested that he indicate where he desired to be buried. The father had refused to discuss the matter, and his son now asked Reb Moshe what the family should do next.

Reb Moshe replied, "Let the matter rest! Perhaps your father does not want to discuss it because he believes that he will live until the time of the Redemption. And with such faith he may yet live to see *Mashiach!*"

His grandson Rabbi Mordechai Tendler once expressed the wish that he, Reb Moshe, would officiate at the weddings of his great-granddaughters (for which he would have had to live past his one hundredth year). Reb Moshe answered *Amen*, adding that one was obligated to do so, for had not *Hashem* found fault with eighty-nine-year-old Sarah for laughing when the angels (who were disguised as wayfarers) foretold the birth of a son? Indeed, Reb Moshe had commented that Abraham, too, was at fault for not having inculcated unquestioning faith in his household. Nothing is beyond *Hashem*'s power.

"Blessed is the man who trusts in *Hashem*" (*Jeremiah* 17:7), for with proper trust one can live a life free of worry and fear. Additionally, the stronger a person's trust, the more he will benefit from Heavenly compassion, as King David said, "And he who trusts in *Hashem* will be surrounded with kindness" *(Psalms* 32:10).

Someone once submitted to Reb Moshe the name of an expectant woman who was experiencing difficulties, asking that he offer his blessings that all be well with both mother and child. After Reb Moshe had granted this request, the person said, "The woman is worried over what will happen." One would have thought that Reb Moshe, whose heart overflowed with concern for every Jew, would offer words of compassion and comfort for the woman. Instead, he said simply, "Of what help is it to worry?" Reb Moshe's message was that to have faith could do more for the woman than hours of compassionate talk.

An elderly native of Radin who knew the *Chofetz Chaim* as a neighbor explained the difference between him and everyone else. He said, "The *Chofetz Chaim* believed in the World to Come and *we* believe in the World to Come. But to us, the World to Come is a matter of faith, while to the *Chofetz Chaim* it was as real as the room next door."

The same could have been said about Reb Moshe. The World to Come, reward and punishment, the coming of *Mashiach* — to him anything mentioned in the Torah was as real as something we can touch, smell, and see.

One year, at the beginning of the month of Iyar, someone heard a sigh escape Reb Moshe's lips. When asked what was the matter, he explained, "*Chazal* have said, 'In Nissan they were redeemed (from Egypt) and in Nissan they will be redeemed.' Now, another Nissan has passed, and we were still not worthy to greet *Mashiach*."

THE BIRTH OF A *PARAH ADUMAH* (completely red cow) in *Eretz Yisrael* some years ago caused great excitement. All Jews today are **Ready** considered to be in a state of *tumas meis* (ritual **for** defilement brought about through contact with a corpse) and as such are not permitted to enter the **Mashiach** Temple area, nor would they be permitted to partake of sacrifices were the *Beis HaMikdash* to be in existence. The Torah prescribes that only by means of a ritual involving a *Parah Adumah* can people be cleansed of this defilement. Many saw the rare birth of a red cow as a sign that the redemption was not far off.

Reb Moshe, however, was not moved by the news. "The cow must be at least two years old for its ashes to be fit for this service. What if *Mashiach* were to arrive tomorrow? Would we have to wait two years in order to become *tahor*? They will have to discover a red cow somewhere that is older than the one just born!" Subsequently Reb Moshe's skepticism was vindicated, because some hairs on the cow's hide later changed color, rendering it unfit for a *Parah Adumah*.

For a time, Reb Moshe contemplated the idea of writing a code of law on the *Kodashim* section of the Talmud which deals with the Temple service. Such a work, he felt, would help familiarize *Kohanim* and scholars with laws they would need to know at the time of the Redemption. He decided, however, that in light of the fact that the *Aruch HaShulchan HeAsid* (by Rabbi Yechiel Michel Epstein) and *Likutei Halachos* (by the *Chofetz Chaim)* already dealt with these subjects, he would devote his time and energy to other areas.

❀   ❀   ❀

On *Yamim Tovim*, as he would shake the hand of each *Kohein* at the conclusion of *Bircas Kohanim*, he would say to him, "May you merit to perform the service in the *Beis HaMikdash.*"

When he needed a cardiac pacemaker inserted in his chest, he asked his son-in-law, Rabbi Moshe David Tendler, to detail the surgical procedure to him. Then he asked Rabbi Tendler to review the procedure, once and then again, something very uncharacteristic of Reb Moshe. Rabbi Tendler asked Reb Moshe what troubled him. Reb Moshe said, "I know that I am not worthy to be a member of the *Sanhedrin*, but in this generation, I may be one of those selected when *Mashiach* comes. I fear that the surgery will make me a *ba'al mum*, thus disqualifying me." Only when he had ascertained to his satisfaction that the medical procedure would not have that effect did Reb Moshe consent to the operation.

WHEN REB MOSHE UNDERWENT SURGERY for the repair of the pacemaker he engaged in some soul-searching, trying to discover the

Before Hashem sin that had caused his suffering. He was sure that his pain must be a punishment for having hurt someone else's feelings — but he could not recall having done so. He reviewed in his mind all the years of his life until he came to his childhood days. There, he found the source of his affliction. As a young *cheder* child he and a classmate had both offered an answer to their *rebbi's* question. Reb Moshe recalled feeling a sense of pride when the *rebbi* found his reasoning superior to that of his friend. While he had not actually done his friend any harm, still it was wrong for him to feel uplifted by an incident that had embarrassed someone else. Reb Moshe viewed his mistake as an indirect form of מַלְבִּין פְּנֵי חֲבֵירוֹ, *shaming one's friend*, for which the surgery he was to undergo was a proper punishment.

Once, while he was being driven along an icy road, the car skidded and his head bumped against the dashboard. Fortunately, he was not seriously hurt, but upon arriving at his destination, he said that he needed a few minutes to contemplate what possible sin could have caused the mishap to occur. As the Talmud teaches, whenever suffering befalls a person, he should examine his deeds, because nothing is coincidental. After a few minutes of intense thought, Reb Moshe resumed his studies.

❀   ❀   ❀

In the opening paragraph of *Shulchan Aruch*, *Rama* writes that the verse שִׁוִּיתִי ה׳ לְנֶגְדִּי תָמִיד (I envision *Hashem* before me always; *Psalms* 16:8), is a great concept in Torah and in the attributes of *tzaddikim*. Anyone who was privileged to meet Reb Moshe could see this concept etched upon his features, and it found obvious expression in his *tefillah*.

Reb Moshe was extremely zealous in all aspects of *tefillah*. Our Sages attach great significance to being among the first ten men who comprise a *minyan*. Throughout the many years that he was healthy enough to walk to the yeshivah alone, he was usually the first person present for *Shacharis*.

He said every word from a *siddur* and during the time when he had trouble seeing, his family made oversized photostats of *siddur* pages for him. At *Modim*, he would bow so deeply — even when suffering from sciatica — that a yeshivah *bachur* who had once observed this as a youth, recalled vividly thirteen years later the impression it had made on him. During the repetition of *Shemoneh*

Esrei he would stand, following the *chazzan's* every word from a *siddur*.

He would recite pages of *Tehillim* every day. Years ago, when he would go to a hotel for a brief summer vacation, he would walk along a country road or sit on the porch at 6:00 a.m. praying from a *Tehillim* which he held open before him. People would often gather to gaze at the devotion with which he prayed. One man later remarked that it had been worth his trip to the hotel just to watch Reb Moshe recite *Tehillim*.

Reb Moshe always enunciated his prayers clearly and distinctly. His *Pesukei D'Zimrah*, as its name implies, was a song of praise in a real sense. His *Shema* — which he recited with the most careful enunciation, using the melody of the *trop* (cantillation) as if reading in the Torah — was the epitome of *Kabbalas Ol Malchus Shamayim*, the acceptance of *Hashem's* sovereignty. Most of us find it difficult to sense *Hashem's* Presence as keenly as we should when praying the *Shemoneh Esrei*, but anyone who watched Reb Moshe pray could almost feel it.

He would stand motionless during *Shemoneh Esrei*, except when bowing. In explanation, he related that when the Communists brought him in for interrogation in Luban, he had been forced to stand at attention as a guard stood watch. Never had he felt so subservient. From then on he decided that he would demonstrate his subservience to the true Ruler by standing this way during *Shemoneh Esrei*.

One day he received very distressing news. Before *Minchah*, he instructed the *chazzan* in Tifereth Jerusalem not to wait for him to finish *Shemoneh Esrei*. That afternoon, it took Reb Moshe almost an hour to recite *Shemoneh Esrei*, as he beseeched his Creator to come to the aid of those in distress.

A grandchild once became quite ill, but the family did not tell Reb Moshe in order not to disturb him. However, when the child took a turn for the worse and had to be rushed to the hospital, Reb Moshe was told and asked to pray. "Why was I not told earlier?" he asked with annoyance. He grabbed a *Tehillim*, and, standing near a window in his dining room, began to pray, as tears streamed down his cheeks.

A few minutes later the phone rang in the Feinstein home. Reb Moshe looked up from his *Tehillim*. "Are they calling from the hospital?" he asked anxiously. Told that the call was not from the hospital, Reb Moshe went back to reciting *Tehillim.* This same scene was repeated a few more times, as other calls came in. Finally, the phone rang and after a few moments, *Rebbetzin* Feinstein called to her husband, "They're calling from the hospital — *Baruch Hashem,* everything is fine. The child was given a new medication and is responding beautifully."

"*Baruch Hashem,*" Reb Moshe sighed, as he closed his *Tehillim,* beads of perspiration visible on his forehead. Slowly, he made his way to the bedroom where he collapsed into bed and fell into an exhausted sleep.

A young couple once asked Reb Moshe for some practical advice on child rearing. Reb Moshe told them to follow the example of Chanah (*I Samuel* ch.1 and 2), who prayed both before and after her son Shmuel was born that her aspirations for him be realized.

AFTER MOVING TO FDR DRIVE, where he lived until the end of his life, Reb Moshe remarked to a visitor, "*Baruch Hashem,* I have

Zeal for a Mitzvah

moved to a new apartment." The visitor asked, "Is the *Rosh Yeshivah's* new apartment that much better than his old one?" Replied Reb Moshe, "Oh, no! A dwelling is a dwelling — the advantages of one over the other are insignificant to me. I am happy, though, that I now live further from the yeshivah than before. I will be able to earn more *s'char halichah* (the reward for traveling or walking to perform a mitzvah)!"

His zealousness was apparent in many other ways. He would escort his visitors out the door (as required), usually walking them until the elevator. When an older person would come to see him, he would escort him to the lobby of his building until the front door. In his last years, he once attempted to escort a former *talmid* to the elevator. Seeing how weak he was, the *talmid* insisted that he not accompany him. Reb Moshe would not agree to this without begging forgiveness of the *talmid.*

Reb Moshe followed the opinion of the *Vilna Gaon* not to carry anything in his pockets on Shabbos while in a private domain for fear that he might mistakenly carry it to a public domain. At the

Selecting haddasim

At tashlich

Shlugging Kapparos

During Succos

On Chanukah

Covering the blood of the Kapparos chicken that had been slaughtered in his apartment in fulfillment of the mitzvah of kisui hadam

Shabbos meal he would sing *zemiros* and invite others to sing as well. Only a few weeks before his passing, he taught a young great-grandchild a tune for *Mizmor L'David*, customarily sung at the *Shalosh Seudos* meal. Occasionally, he would discuss the contents of the *zemiros* and would offer possible reasons why certain *zemiros* had become more popular than others.

In his last years, when his diet had to be watched, he refrained from eating white bread. However, in honor of Rosh Chodesh he would have *challah*.

While fulfilling the *mitzvah* of *arba'ah minim*, Reb Moshe had a unique way of vibrating his hands to make the leaves of the *lulav* rustle. Someone tried to emulate this practice, but found that his hands hurt too much and gave it up.

A *talmid* once accompanied him on a *shivah* call. When they entered the house, they saw that the widow was grief stricken. As Reb Moshe offered his words of consolation, the *talmid* watched as the woman's distraught expression changed before his eyes. When they rose to leave, her face reflected hope and appreciation.

As they left the house, Reb Moshe whispered to his *talmid*, "I hope that I fulfilled the *mitzvah* of *nichum aveilim* properly." Surprised, the *talmid* responded, "But of course! Surely the *Rosh Yeshivah* saw how her mood was transformed by his words."

"Yes," replied Reb Moshe, "I did notice it. But can one be sure of what she was feeling in her heart?"

When they reached the subway station for the return trip home, Reb Moshe insisted on paying the *talmid's* fare. "You did not know the woman's family. You came to accompany me. It is only proper that I pay your fare."

The *talmid* said, "If the *Rosh Yeshivah* insists on doing this, then it must be in accordance with a *halachah* in *Shulchan Aruch*."

"No," replied Reb Moshe, "I am simply doing what is proper."

In 1969, a seventy-four-year-old Reb Moshe vacationed at a cottage some three miles from Camp Yeshivah, the summer home of Yeshivah Ch'sam Sofer. One of the older students was assigned the task of driving Reb Moshe to the camp each morning for *davening* and then back home later in the day. One day, due to a misunderstanding, the student did not come to pick him up for *Shacharis*. When Reb Moshe realized that the student would not be coming, he started to walk. A good part of the three-mile journey was uphill, but this did not deter him, despite his age. As the camp's *minyan* was about to begin the Torah reading, the door of the *beis midrash* opened and in walked Reb Moshe. Everyone was shocked, while the student who had not fulfilled his duty was devastated.

When *davening* ended, the students crowded around Reb Moshe. Someone asked why the *Rosh Yeshivah* had found it necessary to strain himself so, when he knew that he would miss most of *davening*. Besides, under the circumstances, he was clearly excused from joining the *minyan*. Reb Moshe said, "Should I miss *Krias HaTorah?"*

While taking him home, the driver begged Reb Moshe forgiveness for what had happened. Reb Moshe told the student that he need not be concerned, for there was nothing to forgive. The walk, he said, was healthy, and besides, he had earned much *s'char halichah!*

❀ ❀ ❀

One evening, when still robust but in his eighties, Reb Moshe was about to rush out of his apartment with Rabbi Bluth, when the *Rebbetzin* protested. "Don't run. You are always running! It will affect your health."

Reb Moshe stood straight and still, and answered firmly, "לְבָךְ נוֹצַרְתִּי", *for this have I been created*. The Torah says that our days will be increased if we perform *Hashem's mitzvos*. This will *improve* my health, not harm it!"

WHEN THE JEWS entered *Eretz Yisrael* they traveled to the mountains of *Gerizim* and *Eival*, where they heard the blessings and curses listed in *Sidra Ki Savo* (Deuteronomy 27).

Rejoicing in Judgment

Mount *Gerizim* was designated as the mountain of blessing, while Mount *Eival* served as the opposite. The Jews were also commanded to erect an altar upon Mount *Eival* upon which they would bring peace-offerings and "rejoice before *Hashem"* (ibid. vs. 5-7).

Reb Moshe asked: Why were the Jews commanded to rejoice upon the mountain reserved for the curses? Would it not have been more appropriate to bring offerings and celebrate upon Mount *Gerizim*, the place of blessing?

From here, said Reb Moshe, we can learn a basic principle of faith — "All that *Hashem* does, He does for the good" (*Berachos* 60b). When *Hashem* causes tragedy to befall a Jew, G-d forbid, He does so with the person's *benefit* in mind. *As a man chastises his son, so does* Hashem, *your G-d, chastise you (Deuteronomy 8:5).* Though it pains a father to inflict punishment upon a child, it is sometimes necessary, in order that the child not stray from the proper path. *Hashem* is sometimes forced to deal with His children in this same way.

The peace offerings and rejoicing on Mount *Eival* were an expression by *Klal Yisrael* that even the curses of the Torah are for our benefit. As such, they are cause for rejoicing (*Kol Rom*).

This teaching was basic to Reb Moshe's life. He accepted hardship and suffering with perfect faith, never once questioning the Divine will.

In the summer of 1973, the Feinstein family suffered a tragic loss with the passing of Rabbi Eliyahu Moshe Shisgal, husband of Reb Moshe's eldest child, Faya.

To appreciate the strength of Reb Moshe's faith in accepting the loss of his son-in-law in the way that he did, we must attempt to understand the greatness of Rabbi Eliyahu Moshe Shisgal.

CHAPTER TEN
An American-bred Gadol

R ABBI ELIYAHU MOSHE SHISGAL, Reb Moshe's elder son-in-law, was a rare *gaon* and *tzaddik*, without a doubt among the most outstanding of his generation, one who seemed certain to emerge as a *gadol* of world stature. To someone who expressed his condolences over Reb Eliyahu Moshe's passing, Reb Moshe said, "You have come to console me? You must console the entire world; you do not know what he was."

Rabbi Yaakov Kamenetzky once asked a son-in-law of Reb Eliyahu Moshe if he had had the opportunity to become well acquainted with his father-in-law before his passing. After the young man replied that he hadn't, Reb Yaakov remarked wistfully, "No one *really* knew him," meaning that no one had plumbed the depths of his greatness. On another occasion, Reb Yaakov said, "He belonged in an earlier generation."

HE WAS BORN IN THE CITY OF SLUTZK, White Russia, in the year 1921. Rabbi Isser Zalman Meltzer, who headed the city's yeshivah,

Growing Up
was *sandak* at Eliyahu Moshe's *bris milah*. In later years, Reb Eliyahu Moshe would remark with great feeling how fortunate he was that Reb Isser Zalman held him and blessed him that he become great in Torah.

His father, Rabbi Avraham Yitzchak Shisgal, had studied in

the Slobodka Yeshivah together with Rabbi Yaakov Kamenetzky and other well-known personalities, and then became the *Rav* of Rostov, White Russia. In 1925, when Eliyahu Moshe was four years old, his family emigrated to the United States. Rabbi Shisgal entered the American rabbinate in Pawtucket, Rhode Island, where he served until 1933. Young Eliyahu Moshe attended public school in Pawtucket until 1932. Then, when he was eleven years old, his parents sent him to study in the Yeshivah Torah Vodaath in the Williamsburg section of Brooklyn, where he boarded with a local family. A year later, his father found a position in Williamsburg. Still later, he became a rabbi on the Lower East Side.

Eliyahu Moshe was a pleasant, friendly, athletic child, but even as a schoolboy, he was remarkable. When his friends were given a few cents to spend, they would run to the store for ice cream or candy, but he would save his money until he had enough to buy a *sefer.*

Upon completing elementary yeshivah, Eliyahu Moshe was enrolled at Mesivta Torah Vodaath, then one of the very few secondary yeshivos in America. When he first came to Torah Vodaath, his background had been somewhat poor and he was placed in a class with younger boys. Not for long though. He made great strides quickly and before long he had established himself as a Torah prodigy, complementing a brilliant mind with diligence. At a relatively young age, Eliyahu Moshe was promoted to the yeshivah's highest *shiur,* that of its *Rosh Yeshivah,* Rabbi Shlomo Heiman.

Reb Shlomo had gained renown in Europe as a *gaon* and master teacher of Torah, and, at the suggestion of Reb Chaim Ozer Grodzenski, had been brought to America to serve as head of Torah Vodaath. Eliyahu Moshe quickly became the apple of his *Rosh Yeshivah's* eye. "Where is Shisgal?" Reb Shlomo would ask whenever his prize *talmid* was not present at the start of a *shiur.* Only after Eliyahu Moshe had been seated would Reb Shlomo begin. Often when Eliyahu Moshe asked a question during the *shiur,* Reb Shlomo would say, "Shisgal asks like a *lamdan!"*

Rosh Yeshivah and *talmid* became exceptionally close. Reb Shlomo fell ill and passed away at a relatively young age, while still in his prime. At his funeral, Eliyahu Moshe wept so uncontrollably that it interfered with the eulogies. Some of the rabbis were annoyed with him, but one of them said, "Let him be. His is the greatest eulogy."

ELIYAHU MOSHE'S STUDY-PARTNER from those years and lifelong friend יבל"ח Rabbi Eliyahu Simcha Schustal is presently **Thirst** *Rosh Yeshivah* of Yeshivah Bais Binyamin, in **for** Stamford, Connecticut. Throughout their lives, whenever they met it seemed as though they were **Learning** returning to an incessant, heated discussion of Torah subjects, as two brilliant minds honed one another in an unending quest for the truth of *Hashem's* word.

In his thirst for learning, Eliyahu Moshe would seek out the greatest Torah minds to discuss his studies. At the age of twenty-one, while spending his summer at Camp Mesivta in Ferndale, New York, he traveled to nearby Woodridge to "speak in learning" with Reb Moshe, who was vacationing there. Reb Moshe was impressed with Eliyahu Moshe's Torah knowledge, as well as his shining personality. Shortly thereafter, Eliyahu Moshe and Reb Moshe's daughter Faya were engaged and married.

Not long after his marriage, Reb Eliyahu Moshe was appointed to deliver the *shiur* to the first-year *beis midrash* (i.e., post-high school) class of Torah Vodaath. This seems incredible, considering his young age; but it is understandable when one realizes how exceptional a young man he was. From then on in Torah Vodaath he became known simply as Rav Shisgal.

Rabbi Avraham Yaakov Pam, *Rosh Yeshivah* at Mesivta Torah Vodaath, was a colleague and close friend of Rav Shisgal and compares him to the great men of generations past. Wherever he was, at any time of day or night, he was involved in *Hashem's* service. He never went anywhere without a *sefer*. On dimly lit subway platforms or under incandescent street lamps, he would strain to read the words of his pocket-size *gemara* or volume of *Rambam*. When he arrived at a wedding, he would be discussing Torah even before his coat was off. He would scan the banquet hall in search of a *chavrusa* [study partner] — a yeshivah student, *kollel* fellow, layman or *rosh yeshivah* — someone, *anyone*, to discuss Torah with. He would pause in his discussion to fulfill the *mitzvah* of dancing before the bride and groom — only to resume exactly where he left off as soon as the dancing ended.

In those years, Torah Vodaath was located in the Williamsburg section of Brooklyn. On Friday afternoons, when classes were dismissed early, Rav Shisgal and Rabbi Pam would walk together to the Bridge Plaza — discussing

Reb Moshe with יבל"ח *(left to right) Rabbi Avraham Yaakov Pam,*
Rabbi Mordechai Tendler and Rabbi Moshe Sherer

Torah. At the plaza they were to part, Rabbi Pam to continue
on to the subway station and Rav Shisgal to take the bus
over the Williamsburg Bridge to the Lower East Side.
However, rather than see their discussion end, they would
walk one another back and forth, from Bridge Plaza to the
subway station, until the advancing hour left them no choice
but to go home.

After Rav Shisgal passed away, Rabbi Pam paid a consolation
call to his family. He asked to be shown the room in which his
beloved *chaver* had usually studied, a room whose walls were
saturated with a never-ending stream of Torah thought. Rabbi Pam
stood silently in the room for a few minutes, as if in the presence of
the *Shechinah*, then left.

The speed of Rav Shisgal's thought process was one of the
most remarkable in his generation, but his *talmidim* could never
have known this from his *shiurim*. His delivery was slow and
deliberate, so that every *talmid* could grasp each point. He chose
each word carefully to convey the intended meaning. Each change of
tone was an explanation in itself. He had no desire to compose

Rav Shisgal discussing Torah with Reb Aharon;
in the background is Reb Moshe's mechutan, Rabbi Yitzchak Tendler,
a rosh yeshivah in Yeshivah Rabbi Jacob Joseph

dazzling *chiddushim*, weaving together concepts from a variety of sources. Instead, he sought to reveal the treasures that lay buried in every word of *Gemara, Rashi* and *Tosafos.* Often, he would point out a difficulty or a proof from a word or sentence that others might have glanced over. He would often exclaim, "Oh — to understand but a morsel of Torah!" As Rabbi Pam expresses it, Rav Shisgal amassed many such morsels in becoming one of the *gaonim* of his generation.

His search for truth in Torah was such that he would cancel a scheduled *shiur* if he felt that the subject matter was not perfectly clear to him.

NOWHERE WAS HIS GENIUS MORE APPARENT than in his discussions with Rabbi Aharon Kotler, whose own lightning-quick

With Reb Aharon mind was legendary. Rav Shisgal sought out every opportunity to discuss Torah with Reb Aharon. When Reb Aharon attended a wedding in New York, Rav Shisgal would be there. Reb Aharon delivered a weekly *shiur* in *Seder Zeraim* on the Lower East Side, which Rav Shisgal never missed (though the *shiur* was officially for laymen).

Few who observed the two discuss Torah could follow the pace of their machine-gun-like conversation. Reb Aharon spoke almost as quickly as his mind worked, and when speaking with him, Rav Shisgal spoke in a very similiar way!

When Rav Shisgal was thirty-two years old, he traveled to Lakewood, New Jersey, for the annual convention of Agudath Israel. The Shabbos services of the convention were held at Beth Medrash Govoha, Reb Aharon's yeshivah. When Rav Shisgal went to wish Reb Aharon a *Gut Shabbos* at the conclusion of the Friday night *tefillos*, he was told, "Tonight you will be my guest at the *seudah!*" Of course, Rav Shisgal did not decline the offer, which, in essence, was an invitation to discuss Torah with Reb Aharon.

The next morning, prior to the Torah reading, Reb Aharon discussed the distribution of the *aliyos* with the *gabbai*. Although many *rabbanim* and *roshei yeshivah* were in attendance no *hosafos* were made. Nevertheless, Reb Aharon motioned toward Rav Shisgal and said, "He must be given an *aliyah*. He is young, but a *gadol b'Torah*."

At Reb Aharon's funeral in 1962, Reb Eliyahu Moshe wept uncontrollably, until Rabbi Yitzchak Hutner, who also knew Rav Shisgal well, succeeded in calming him.

THERE WAS MUCH that Reb Eliyahu Moshe's *talmidim* learned from him, aside from his superlative method of study. His zeal in

Dimensions of Teaching

Torah was obvious in that *he* was always the first one seated in the classroom at the start of a *shiur*, with his *gemara* open to the correct page, ready to begin. He would not begin the *shiur* until everyone had found the place, but the *talmidim* knew that they were expected to find it quickly, for their *rebbi* could not bear to see precious seconds go to waste.

During a *shiur*, a *talmid* disputed Reb Eliyahu Moshe's interpretation of the *Gemara*. The contention seemed so ludicrous that the class burst into laughter. Reb Eliyahu Moshe chastised his students, "Why do you laugh? Is this the proper way? Besides, how can one be sure that what he suggested is wrong? Perhaps it is we who are in error? It is possible, you know, for one man to arrive at the truth, while the majority's thinking is wrong."

Having spoken, he excused himself and left the room, returning in a few minutes with a *gemara* that he had climbed two flights of stairs to get. From it, he read the text of a *Rashi* aloud and said, "It is apparent from *Rashi* that our explanation is the correct one."

One day, some students requested of him that he no longer allow questions to be asked during the *shiur*. The class wanted to hear what the *rebbi* had to say; any difficulties a *talmid* might have could be clarified after the *shiur*. Reb Eliyahu Moshe responded with typical humility. "What do you mean? There is no *rebbi* here, nor are there *talmidim!* We are all studying together and we need one another. This is the way to acquire a true understanding of Torah, through discussion among those who study it."

❦   ❦   ❦

When a *talmid* approached him, he would rise in respect. If ever he saw *talmidim* engage in idle chatter while sitting before an open *gemara*, he would walk over, and gently and respectfully steer the conversation toward learning.

Once, in Torah Vodaath, he was engaged in a Torah discussion with a student of the post-graduate Beth Medrash Elyon in Upstate New York. The student excused himself, saying he had to get to Washington Heights to meet the person who would drive him back home. Undeterred, Rav Shisgal accompanied him for the hour-and-a-half trip to Washington Heights to continue their discussion.

A legendary Torah figure on the Lower East Side was Rabbi Yaakov Safsal, known as the Vishker Iluy, who was famous as one of the great Torah geniuses of the century. He studied Torah all day, alone in a *beis midrash*. Rav Shisgal used to visit him regularly to discuss Torah with him. Rav Safsal looked forward to these sessions, and he would say to the much junior scholar, "Tell me — when can I come to you to speak in learning?"

After more than twenty years on the staff of Torah Vodaath, Rav Shisgal accepted a position as *rosh yeshivah* in Mesivta Be'er Shmuel. He explained to Rabbi Schustal that in Torah Vodaath he could have a student for only one year, and he felt that he could accomplish more if he could teach the same students year after year. Later, Rav Shisgal became a *rosh yeshivah* in the Yeshivah of Staten Island, which afforded him the same opportunity.

One of Rav Shisgal's students in Torah Vodaath described the impact Rav Shisgal had on his *talmidim:* "A student who entered his class still, in essence, a 'kid,' would leave it a full-fledged yeshivah *bachur* and a mature young man."*

He would never trouble a *talmid* to bring him a *sefer.* Yet, when he was at home, he would sometimes ask one of his daughters to come from another room to fetch him a *sefer* that was not far from where he sat. One of the girls asked why he did this, and he replied, "So that you can fulfill the *mitzvah* of *kibud av.*" His brother-in-law, Reb Reuven, maintains that he also did this to maintain a personal relationship with his daughters.

Mitzvos and Kindness

TO HIM EVERY *MITZVAH* was a priceless gem. He recited blessings with such intense concentration that even scholars many years his senior were inspired by him. Before partaking of food at the *seudas Shabbos,* he would say with feeling, "In honor of the holy *Shabbos.*" On Purim, he would hear the *Megillah* reading in *shul* and then read it aloud at home, for fear of having missed a word due to the banging and other disturbances at the mention of Haman's name. A number of neighborhood women made a point of attending Rav Shisgal's private reading, for they felt inspired by it.

❀   ❀   ❀

Those who knew Rav Shisgal canno · forget his way of prayer.

---

* From a fictional story by Mr. Wolf Karfiol (*Jewish Observer*, June 1979), in which one of the characters was modeled after Rav Shisgal. In a subsequent issue (October, 1979), the following appeared:

To the Editor:

Reading Wolf Karfiol's article "The Thirty-Year Trip" (June '79) enabled me to make my own personal trip back to the year I spent in Rabbi Shisgal's class, in the first year *Beis Midrash.* A raw young man from the Midwest was inspired and helped along to develop an appreciation for Torah and the yeshivah way of life.

Rabbi Shisgal was one of those truly special and unique *rebbis* who by his very nature was able to serve as a model and to inspire his *talmidim.* The evenings we spent in his house on the East Side are still very real in my mind, and his *hasmadah* in the *Beis Midrash* in the late afternoon hours still serves as an incentive to me to study and learn.

There is so much more one could say about Rabbi Shisgal. Certainly Karfiol's description is true for him, as well as it is for me. Hopefully all of our children will at one time or another experience such a *rebbi.*

St. Louis, Mo.   Alan Green

He pronounced each word slowly, meaningfully. One could easily tell from watching his lips where he was up to in the *tefillah*. Even the slow swaying of his body was full of meaning. He was usually the last person in the *beis midrash* to complete the *Shemoneh Esrei*, and it usually left him drained of energy. Often, he would mop his brow after finishing.

He distributed *tzedakah* far out of proportion to his modest earnings. He gave until his pockets were literally empty. There were beggars on the Lower East Side who, knowing Rav Shisgal's generosity, would wait for him each morning along the route he took to *shul*. Often he would give away every cent he had so that he had no money left for carfare. Finally, he began using one pocket exclusively for carfare and not for anything else.

Like his father-in-law, Rav Shisgal's insatiable thirst for Torah did not prevent him from performing countless acts of kindness. Each week, he visited an old-age home to brighten the lives of its residents with his warm words and genuine concern. On *Erev Shabbos*, he would purchase *challos* for an impoverished widow and hand-deliver them (something which even his own family did not know of until after his death). Often he would give immeasurable encouragement to unfortunate people by asking them for advice. They felt uplifted by the fact that he considered them important and wise.

❋   ❋   ❋

After his father died, Rav Shisgal succeeded him as *Rav* of his small Lower East Side *shul*. It was not a position he sought, especially since he continued to serve as a *rosh yeshivah*, but he took on the responsibility because the *shul* was his mother's source of income. The *shul's* members were, for the most part, ordinary people, who would recite *Tehillim* when the *Rav* was not teaching them *Chumash* or *Mishnayos*. Rav Shisgal served his congregants more like a *shamash* than a *Rav*, accommodating them in every way possible. One frigid winter evening, as the hour approached midnight, he walked the few blocks from his home to *shul* to turn on the heat, so that those who would come early for *Shacharis* the next morning would not be cold.

An elderly man who lived in Staten Island once gave Rav Shisgal a sum of money to purchase a *lulav* and *esrog* for him.

Finding an *esrog* for the man was a relatively simple task, in light of the fact that he paid more than the man had given him. However, when it came to selecting a *lulav*, he had difficulty finding one to his satisfaction. When he finally found one that appeared to be kosher, though not of the best quality, he asked a second person for an opinion. The man, who knew Rav Shisgal well, asked, "Are you buying it for yourself?"

"I am buying it for someone I know," Rav Shisgal replied.

"Well," the man said, "For a man like yourself I would not recommend such a *lulav*, but for an average Jew it is good."

When the man was out of earshot, Rav Shisgal turned to a *talmid*, and said incredulously, "I do not understand what he meant. Why am I different than any other Jew? Either the *lulav* is good or it is not!"

Rav Shisgal decided that the *lulav* was kosher and took it for *himself*, and to Staten Island he took the superior *lulav* that he had bought for himself. He explained to his *talmid* that the middle leaf of the new *lulav* could easily split if shaken too hard, which could render it unfit for use. *He* would take care to shake it gently so that this should not happen; the elderly man might not be capable of this.

Rav Shisgal then set out for Staten Island where the elderly man lived. Though he had already spent a good part of the day performing a kindness for the man, he did not hurry home after delivering his purchases. Instead, he asked quite innocently if he could see the man's *succah*. While the man thought that this request was made out of curiosity, Rav Shisgal was, in fact, concerned that the *succah* be halachically valid. After inspecting the *succah*, he wished the man a *Gut Yom Tov* and left.

ON THE LOWER EAST SIDE, there lived an odd Jew known as "the Professor." The Professor imagined himself to be both a medical **"The** genius and a high-ranking army official. Attired in **Professor"** a long army coat, he would walk into hospitals and bark orders that were either laughed at or ignored. He was a harmless fellow and most people paid little attention to him. Rav Shisgal befriended this man as he did other unfortunate souls, and the Professor became a familiar face in the Shisgal home. He would join the family for meals and they would often prepare food for him to take along wherever he might be going.

Rabbi Peretz Steinberg, *Rav* of the Young Israel of Queens

Valley in Flushing, New York and a prime disciple of Rav Shisgal, was privileged to remain close to him until his passing. He once visited Rav Shisgal's home and found that his *rebbi* had company.

"Allow me to introduce you to the Professor," Rav Shisgal said to him. So that his *talmid* should not think that he was making fun of the poor fellow, Rav Shisgal quickly added, "I call him the Professor, because that is how he wants to be called."

The Professor had brought along a transistor radio, which he was proudly showing off. He turned the radio to its highest volume and proceeded to switch from station to station — over and over again. The Professor was enjoying himself immensely and he assumed that the others were enjoying themselves as well. Rav Shisgal did not have the heart to dampen the man's spirits by asking him to turn the radio off.

Suddenly, Rav Shisgal had an idea. He put his ear to the radio and said, "Professor, are these military secrets that I hear?"

"Yes!" the Professor shouted excitedly. "This is a military radio and it carries military secrets!"

"Well," said Rav Shisgal, "As you know, I am not a member of the military. I probably should not be hearing these things."

"You are right," the Professor replied, and promptly turned off the radio.

Rav Shisgal was once walking with someone when he noticed a drunkard stagger and fall. Quickly, he rushed over and helped the man to his feet. Noticing his companion's look of surprise, Rav Shisgal said, "He is also a *tzelem Elokim.*"

Sage Counsel

HE WAS EXCEPTIONALLY WISE and perceptive; he could see through to the root of any problem and offer counsel that would set matters straight and uplift one's spirits. As he lay perilously ill only weeks before he passed away, the phone rang frequently in his hospital room. People whom his family never knew were calling to ask his advice. When one caller was told that Rav Shisgal was too ill to speak with him, the person exclaimed, "Please! You must let me speak with Rabbi Shisgal — just for two minutes! He will save my life!"

Following Rav Shisgal's passing, *Rebbetzin* Shisgal received a letter from a man who was a total stranger to her. He wrote:

Dear Mrs. Shisgal,

With tears coming down my face, I must relate how your husband saved my family from much pain. It was six years ago — your husband came to my store — I can't even remember for what. Anyway the way he looked at me I knew that I had to run out from behind the counter and tell him of my problem. My son announced that he wanted to marry an Italian girl in a few months — her family gave their approval for this match. I could not mix in — after all, he was twenty-four and had a mind of his own and how could I, of all people, object if I attended a synagogue only twice a year.

Your husband agreed to see my son in a week. He came by and took him around the block for a walk, returning fifteen minutes later. At first, my son said nothing, but the next morning he said to me, "Father, dear, if we have such a man as part of our people I can't marry her."

So you see that your husband saved many people from heartache.

Of course my son married a nice Jewish girl and just last week he told me that he had registered his daughter in an Orthodox day school.

Let me say that we lost a good public relations man for Judaism.

Who can replace him ... ?

Mr. S.

REB MOSHE AND HIS SON-IN-LAW had a deep love and respect for one another. Reb Moshe would rise whenever Rav Shisgal entered a

Special Relationship room, while Rav Shisgal, even in the last pain-racked weeks of his life, would force himself out of bed, adjust his robe and put on his slippers whenever speaking with Reb Moshe over the phone. The only other callers for whom he was observed doing this were his mother and Rabbi Yaakov Kamenetzky.

Whenever the two were together, they engaged in the delight of their lives — Torah discussion. At gatherings held in the Yeshivah of Staten Island, Reb Moshe and Rav Shisgal could be seen sitting at the head table, involved in lively discussion, taking little note of the food that was placed before them.

It was Reb Moshe's practice to eat his Succos meals in Rav Shisgal's *succah*, before he, too, moved to the high-rise apartments

on FDR Drive. One *Erev Succos*, it rained with such intensity that Rav Shisgal's *succah*, which had no protective covering, was clearly not usable for the *yom tov* meal that night. Although it had stopped raining, the table and benches were drenched and water dripped from the *s'chach*. Reb Moshe, his son-in-law and a third *talmid chacham* who usually joined them for the Succos meals made arrangements to eat in the *succah* of the Kapitshnitzer *Rebbe*, Rabbi Avraham Yehoshua Heschel, whose *succah* had been protected by a strong cover.

That night, as the three made their way to the *succah*, the Kapitshnitzer *Rebbe* was already seated in his *succah*, surrounded by his *chassidim*. When the guests entered his *succah*, the *rebbe* said, "*Chazal* tell us that rain on Succos is not a good omen. However, for me it is a *good* omen, for it has brought me such exalted guests!"

❊   ❊   ❊

In the winter of 1969, New York was hit with a blizzard that blanketed it with more than a foot of snow. A wedding, to which Reb Moshe and his family were invited, was scheduled for that night at a mid-town Manhattan hotel. That afternoon, Rav Shisgal and his *Rebbetzin* trudged through the snow to Reb Moshe's apartment building, from which a limousine was to take them to the wedding. The limousine never arrived. Someone present suggested to Reb Moshe, "The *Rosh Yeshivah* cannot go to the wedding in such weather — no one will go!" Reb Moshe responded, "No one will go? Then we *must* go!"

They succeeded in borrowing a car but soon after they started out the car broke down. Reb Moshe, Rav Shisgal, Reb Reuven and their wives plowed through the snow to a subway station, and went to the wedding by subway. They returned the same way.

The next morning, Rav Shisgal rose early and made his way through the deserted streets to Reb Moshe's building, where *minyanim* were sometimes formed in inclement weather. He met Reb Moshe in the building's lobby; it seemed that there was no *minyan* that morning, so the two set out together on the long walk to Tifereth Jerusalem. Not another soul was in sight on the streets, where huge drifts of snow made their journey a strenuous task. They had gone only a few blocks when a passing patrol car stopped them. What emergency, the officers wanted to know, had caused the rabbis to venture out in such treacherous conditions? When Rav Shisgal explained the situation, the officers offered to drive them to the yeshivah. Before Reb Moshe and his son-in-law left the car, the officers extracted a promise from them that they would call the precinct for a ride home later that day.

IN THE SPRING OF 1973, Rav Shisgal became seriously ill. When he realized how grave his condition was, he began a study session with **Illness** a Holocaust survivor, who had been with a number of *tzaddikim* prior to their death. He once chided himself for asking his doctor what the future held for him. The future, he reasoned, was entirely in the hands of *Hashem*, regardless of the doctor's prognosis.

When his illness became known, a Catholic neighbor approached the Shisgal family to say that he prayed for Rabbi Shisgal's recovery every day.

❀ ❀ ❀

Rav Shisgal's family wanted him to have a private room during his hospital stays. However, he resisted this suggestion, saying that having roommates afforded one the opportunity for performing *chesed.* He assisted his roommates not only physically, but also spiritually, teaching those who were not religious to recite blessings over foods. One of his roommates would shout violently at anyone who attempted to speak with him — except for Rav Shisgal, with whom he conversed quite normally.

He always kept cake and fruit in his room to serve his visitors and would escort them to the elevator on their way out, despite the constant pain. Interestingly, Reb Moshe, who would do the same for his company in his last, infirm years, tried to discourage his son-in-law from escorting him out. However, Rav Shisgal would not relent.

On a Friday in July of 1973, Rav Shisgal was discharged from the hospital for what would be his last time. Rabbi Peretz Steinberg, who took him home that day, recalls that after Rav Shisgal's belongings were packed, he went from room to room saying goodbye to all the patients. Having made his farewells, he began heading towards the elevator. A nurse who spotted him leaving called to the nurses' station, "Come, everyone! The rabbi's leaving!" The nurses, every last one of them, walked behind him. As he entered the elevator, a nurse exclaimed, "There goes a beautiful man!"

On the way home, he asked that Rabbi Steinberg take him to the home of Rabbi Yosef Eliyahu Henkin. Rav Shisgal requested that Rabbi Henkin, who was then well past ninety, bless him. Rabbi Henkin, with whom Rav Shisgal was very close, blessed him and then said, "Now, you bless me."

They passed away but ten days apart. *

During the two-month-long illness that took Rav Shisgal's life, Reb Moshe visited his son-in-law every day. Mr. David H. Schwartz, a brother-in-law of Rav Shisgal, recalls spending an entire night with Reb Moshe in a hospital waiting room when Rav

---

* When Rav Shisgal was to marry off a daughter, he extended a personal invitation to Rabbi Henkin, who said, "I know that many prominent *rabbanim* and *roshei yeshivah* will attend your daughter's wedding. I will be happy to attend, but I do not want to be accorded any honor at the *chupah.*"

Rav Shisgal discussed the matter with Reb Moshe, who said that Rabbi Henkin's request should be ignored. At the *chupah,* he was called to recite the first two of the *sheva berachos,* a most esteemed honor.

Shisgal was rushed there for emergency treatment. Toward morning, Mr. Schwartz dozed for a while and awoke with a start. Reb Moshe, who was reciting *Tehillim*, smiled at him and nodded reassuringly.

ON THE NIGHT OF 3 MENACHEM AV, 5733 (1973), Rabbi Nissan Alpert looked out the window of his apartment, which overlooked

The End that of Reb Moshe, and saw Reb Moshe returning home from a visit to the hospital where Rav Shisgal lay in a coma. A short while later the lights in Reb Moshe's apartment went out as he and his *Rebbetzin* retired for the night.

At around midnight of that night, Reb Nissan noticed that the lights in the Feinstein apartment were on and Reb Moshe was pacing back and forth. Reb Nissan understood that the worst had happened; Rav Shisgal had passed away.

> A member of Reb Moshe's family recalls, "We learned how to handle even tragedy from the *Rosh Yeshivah*. When we came to the door we had to ring the bell because of the chain. The *Rosh Yeshivah* opened the door and understood at once what had happened. 'We will not wake *der mama,'* he said. 'She will have time to grieve. Let her sleep so that she will have strength.'
>
> "He then took the telephone book and instructed each of us whom to call. The *Rosh Yeshivah* himself called about the gravesite. He asked that the site be 'a worthy one.' After all the details and arrangements had been completed, he allowed his grief to take over. As he wiped the tears streaming down his face he said, 'Now I will go tell *der mama.'* "

At 6:00 the next morning, Reb Nissan watched as Reb Moshe sat on his terrace, recording his *chiddushei Torah*. He would be occupied with the funeral for most of the day and, in spite of his deep sense of grief over the tragedy, he still utilized every available moment for Torah study.

In his eulogy, Reb Moshe wept as he began, but brought himself under control as he quoted the verse — הַצוּר תָּמִים פָּעֳלוֹ ..., *The Rock (Hashem)! — perfect is His work, for all his paths are just; a G-d of faith without iniquity, righteous and fair is He* (Deuteronomy 32:4).

"We do not understand," he said, "but we know that the

Ribbono shel Olam is just. He is righteous and fair and whatever He does is an expression of His mercy."

❀ ❀ ❀

Reb Moshe's profound grief did not interfere even for a moment with his concern for others. As the funeral entourage stood together at Kennedy Airport, from where Rav Shisgal would be flown to Jerusalem for burial, Reb Moshe had the presence of mind to ask an acquaintance if he had a ride back home. When he saw a second coffin being carried, he walked in back of it as well, fearing that the huge crowd that had come to pay respects to his son-in-law would indirectly cause hurt to the other family and shame to the deceased.

❀ ❀ ❀

Two weeks after the funeral, someone called Reb Moshe to extend his condolences. When the person started to speak of the enormity of the loss, Reb Moshe interrupted him in mid-sentence. "We must accept *Hashem's* decrees with love — *And Aharon remained silent!*" — a reference to Aharon's silent acceptance of the death of his two sons *(Leviticus* 10:3).

❀ ❀ ❀

The inaugural issue of the *Am HaTorah* journal was dedicated to Rav Shisgal's memory. In a letter of appreciation to the journal's editors, Reb Moshe described his late son-in-law.

"He was a *gadol b'Torah;* he toiled strenuously in it all his days, literally. His mouth did not cease uttering its words, nor did his mind ever stop delving into its depth. He was a *tzaddik* and *chassid* and his every word and deed was in accordance with Torah. His *middos* were exceptional and he was pleasing to all; his every action was for the sake of Heaven ...

... Let it be recognized and understood that even in this country a man as great as he developed, so that many other students of Torah will follow in his path to become great in Torah and in deed.

One who signs with great pain, but with the hope that many will follow in his path, which will be a merit for his soul and pleasing to it,

Moshe Feinstein"

CHAPTER ELEVEN

Humblest of Men

"And the man Moshe was exceedingly humble." It was because of this that Moshe merited that the Torah be given through him and that the Divine Presence rest upon him. Thus said the prophet Yeshayahu: רוּחַ ה' אֱלֹקִים עָלָי, יַעַן מָשַׁח ה' אֹתִי לְבַשֵּׂר עֲנָוִים, *The spirit of HASHEM/ELOKIM is upon me, because HASHEM has elevated me to bring good tidings to the humble (Isaiah 61:1) From this we can derive that humility is the most desirable trait of all (Midrash Aseres HaDibros, Numbers 12:3).*

R ABBI SHMUEL GERTZ, one of Reb Moshe's first *talmidim* in America, applied the above *Midrash* to his revered *rebbi.* Reb Moshe's humility was true and natural; it was apparent to anyone who was privileged to know him. He honored others at every opportunity, but he sought to escape honor. And when it came to helping his fellow Jew, no deed was beneath his dignity.

Respect for Everyone

In Tifereth Jerusalem, it was not uncommon to see Reb Moshe hurrying from his seat near the *Aron HaKodesh* to greet a bedraggled stranger in the back of the *beis midrash.* "Can I do something for you?" he would ask, his eyes radiating the inner warmth he felt for every Jew.

A poor man once entered the *beis midrash* while Reb Moshe's *shiur* was in progress and began to ask the students for money. The man was asked to wait until the *shiur* ended, but he refused. So great a commotion did he cause that Reb Moshe had no choice but to have a few *talmidim* escort him out. As soon as the lecture ended, Reb Moshe, instead of donning his hat in preparation for *Minchah*, hurried to the back of the *beis midrash*. He rushed over to the beggar and, holding the poor man's hand, humbly begged forgiveness for what had happened.

Once Reb Moshe had to send his son, Reb David, on an important mission. At the time, Reb David was helping a child with his studies. While Reb Moshe felt it necessary for his son to leave at once, he did not want the child to suffer because of it — so he sat down and tutored the boy himself.

On a hot summer day, someone came with a halachic query. Wishing to discuss the matter in private, Reb Moshe took the visitor to his private office — but it was occupied. A student seeking relief from the heat had gone to the office with his *gemara* and was sitting there with the air conditioner on full blast. Not even remarking on the unauthorized use of his office, Reb Moshe apologized to the student for disturbing him — and went back to the *beis midrash*.

Without the slightest hesitation, Reb Moshe would stand on a bench to shut the lights in the *beis midrash* after everyone else had left; climb on the desk in his office to lower the setting on a three-in-one light fixture, in order not to waste the yeshivah funds; or prepare breakfast for the student who had come to assist him with his morning needs. When, on one occasion, the student protested this, Reb Moshe responded, "What is wrong? Am I not permitted to do a kindness for someone?"

When the *shamash* of Tifereth Jerusalem was not well, Reb Moshe climbed up on a bench to turn on a *yahrzeit* bulb on the memorial plaque. He explained simply, "People pay for this service. It would be dishonest not to turn on the light."

❀   ❀   ❀

Rabbi Shimon Schwab, the distinguished *Rav* of K'hal Adas Yeshurun, recalls an occasion that, to him, epitomized Reb Moshe's humility. The *Rosh Yeshivah* had spent a Shabbos in Camp Agudah and when his car was leaving on Sunday morning, the driveway was lined with boys waving farewell and hoping to shake his hand through the open car window. Reb Moshe asked the driver to stop. He alighted from the car and walked to the end of the driveway to shake hands with each of the waiting boys.

❧   ❧   ❧

A Seattle court judge was having a difficult time deciding a case involving a Jewish litigant. He agreed to a suggestion that an authority on Jewish law be consulted to see how he would rule in such a matter.

Upon inquiry, the judge discovered that the aged dean of a Talmudic school on New York's Lower East Side was reputed to be the world's greatest authority on Jewish law. A meeting was arranged between an officer of the court and Rabbi Moshe Feinstein.

At the meeting's outset, the emissary respectfully asked, "Can you tell me how and when you were declared the greatest authority on Jewish law in our day?"

Reb Moshe replied, "I really don't know the answer to your question. All I do know is that people who come to me with halachic questions once, often return a second time with something else to ask. So I imagine that they are satisfied with the answers they receive."

To Rabbi Eliezer Shach he wrote a letter saying that he had difficulty sleeping at night because he felt that a title with which he had addressed the Ponevezher *Rosh Yeshivah* in some of their correspondences of earlier years was not befitting someone who had risen to become a leader of Torah Jewry — and he asked Rabbi Shach for his written forgiveness.

In a letter to an Israeli woman in quest of his blessing and prayers, Reb Moshe wrote, " ... there are many G-d-fearing men in *Eretz Yisrael* whose prayers are certainly desired by *Hashem*, so what is my role in such matters? However, because your anguish is great, I shall respond ... " (*Igros Moshe, Orach Chaim 4:47*).

ONCE, IN AN UNBELIEVABLE DISPLAY of thoughtlessness, someone called him before 5:00 a.m. to ask him a *sh'eilah* that was

Constant Self-Perfection not urgent. The next morning at the same time, the same person called with a question about a *Tosafos*. The next morning, it happened again. Finally, on the *fourth* morning, Reb Moshe softly told his pre-dawn caller, "The reason I arise so early to learn is so that I can be prepared to answer the questions people ask when they call me later." That was the last time the man called at that hour.

On another occasion, he complained to the *Rebbetzin*, "If I can't find time to learn, I will remain an *am ha'aretz.*" Coming from someone of such greatness, such fears sound as if said in jest, but Reb Moshe meant it, knowing the vastness of the Torah.

It is clear that Reb Moshe realized full well his position as a leader of *Klal Yisrael* and his role as a *posek.* His humility was rooted in the teaching of Rabbi Yochanan ben Zakkai: *If you have studied much Torah, do not take credit for yourself, for that is what you were created to do (Avos 2:9).* As *Mesillas Yesharim* explains, since intelligence is granted to a person for the purpose of acquiring knowledge, man may not become arrogant for having utilized this gift, any more than a bird may for using his wings to fly.

In this light, Reb Moshe's fear of remaining an *"am ha'aretz"* can be better understood. While we might be quite satisfied were we to amass a fraction of Reb Moshe's Torah knowledge, he was forever concerned lest he fall short of the potential inherent in the great mental gifts that *Hashem* had blessed him with.

In the same way that he was never satisfied with his achievements in Torah, so too did Reb Moshe never cease working to improve his *middos*, which seemed angelic to others even in his youth. The climb up the ladder of righteousness, as with the study of Torah, is endless. It is with this awareness that *tzaddikim* in all generations live with the everpresent thought that their piety is somehow lacking. This, too, was undoubtedly a prime source of Reb Moshe's humility.

> Reb Moshe was extremely mild mannered; in the most tense and provocative situations he would show not a trace of anger. In reference to this, he once remarked, "Do you think I was always like this? By nature, I have a fierce temper, but I have worked to overcome it."
>
> A similar comment was heard from him when a yeshivah student questioned him regarding humility. "It is years that I am working on perfecting this trait," he said.

One *Erev Yom Kippur*, Reb Moshe was seen studying *HaMeoros HaGedolim*, a collection of anecdotes about the great figures of the *Mussar* movement. As a preparation for the Day of

Atonement, he sought to discover avenues of improvement by examining the ways of these *tzaddikim*.

When arriving at a *chupah* ceremony, Reb Moshe would, for many years, take a seat in the back of the hall, though he would invariably be accorded an honor at the ceremony. Only in his later years — when, as the recognized *gadol hador*, he was the object of everyone's attention and such behavior would have seemed incongruous — did he take a seat toward the front.

Respect for Others IN MESIVTHA TIFERETH JERUSALEM, the *chazzan* would always pause at the conclusion of *Shema*, in line with the universal custom to wait for the congregation's leader at that point in the *tefillah*. Reb Moshe recited *Shema* with the proper cantillation *(trop)* and with intense concentration, and usually lagged far behind most of the congregation. Not wishing to keep the others waiting, he would signal to the *chazzan* to go on when he had completed only the first two portions of *Shema*.

Rabbi Reuven Feinstein once accompanied his father to a wedding at which *Ma'ariv* was recited. The *minyan* fell silent as the *chazzan* waited for Reb Moshe to complete the *Shema*. Departing from his normal custom, Reb Moshe recited the entire *Shema* without giving any signal. Well aware of his father's custom, Reb Reuven asked why he had not signaled the *chazzan* to go on. Reb Moshe explained. "In my own yeshivah, it is obvious that the *chazzan* is waiting only for me; therefore, there is nothing wrong in my signaling to him. However, at a wedding, where I am only a guest like everyone else, I have no right to assume that it is for *me* that the *chazzan* waits."

❈   ❈   ❈

Someone who assisted Reb Moshe for a number of years once asked him, "Why does the *Rosh Yeshivah* permit phone callers to disturb his learning at all hours of the day? Would it not be more practical to accept calls at specific hours only?"

Reb Moshe replied, "There is a trace of arrogance in telling someone that I cannot be disturbed and he must call me back at my convenience. That is not for me."

Reb Moshe was once walking along a street in his neighborhood, when he heard a voice calling, "Moshe,

Moshe!'' Looking up, he saw that the voice was that of an acquaintance, who was behind the wheel of his car. Without blinking an eye, Reb Moshe walked over to the car.

Upon realizing that Reb Moshe had assumed that he was being called, the man turned crimson with embarrassment. He said, ''I was calling my son, who happened to be on the street as I drove by. I would never have dreamed of addressing the *Rosh Yeshivah* in such a disrespectful manner. Besides, if I had had something to discuss with the *Rosh Yeshivah* I would have gotten out of my car and gone over to him — I would not have dared to ask the *Rosh Yeshivah* to come over to me ...''

Reb Moshe assured the man that there was nothing to be concerned about. ''It is already many years that these things mean nothing to me.''

A close aquaintance of Reb Moshe did not inform him of a grandson's upcoming *bris* out of embarrassment that someone other than Reb Moshe was being honored as *sandak*. How surprised this man was when Reb Moshe came uninvited and remained until the conclusion of the *seudas mitzvah!*

BUT REB MOSHE'S HUMILITY was not a product of weakness. He could be firm and unyielding if such was the proper course. As a **Strong** complete Torah personality, Reb Moshe would **When** respond forcefully when he felt the situation required such a reaction.

Necessary Once, when judging a *din Torah*, he caught someone offering testimony that was clearly false. Reb Moshe reprimanded the man and asked him to leave the room.

While judging a dispute, Reb Moshe stated a *halachah* that was not to the liking of one of the parties involved. The man had the audacity to accuse Reb Moshe of falsifying the law so that the case would be brought to a speedy conclusion. Reb Moshe rose to his full height and emphatically declared:

''My name is Moshe Feinstein. True, I do not know how to learn. But go in the streets and ask if I am a liar!''

When a manuscript commentary to *Chumash* attributed to Rabbi Yehudah *HaChassid* (twelfth-century *Tosafist)* was found to contain questionable statements, Reb Moshe issued a *teshuvah* condemning its publication and sale (see *Igros Moshe, Yoreh Deah*

III, § 114, 115). To Reb Moshe it was clear that even if Rabbi Yehudah *HaChassid* had written the bulk of the commentary, the statements in question were inserted by heretics. In order to deceive loyal Jews into accepting their views, these enemies of Torah would sometimes insert heresies into the manuscripts of acclaimed scholars who were no longer living.

When the manuscript was published despite his objections, Reb Moshe dispatched emissaries to Hebrew book stores, forbidding the sale of the *sefer*.

❀   ❀   ❀

A widow once accosted Reb Moshe as he was about to leave his yeshivah and, in a sharp and disrespectful manner, she complained about the way her son's *rebbi* was treating him. Reb Moshe listened in silence to the bereaved woman, allowing her to speak her piece. When she was finished, Reb Moshe assured her that he would look into the matter personally. He then asked the student who was waiting to drive him home to take the woman home instead. Reb Moshe went on foot.

Yet his reaction was altogether different when another widow expressed a determination to violate the *halachah*. She came to him insisting that her husband had been buried in the wrong grave, and she wanted to have his remains disinterred and reburied in the proper place. Reb Moshe dispatched a student to get the cemetery office on the phone so that he could verify the claim. The student could not reach the proper person. Reb Moshe explained to the widow that, in any case, it was forbidden to move the remains until some time had elapsed after burial. In the meantime, the facts could be established. She left, but came back a few minutes later insisting that it be done immediately. Again, he explained to her patiently that nothing could be done for the time being. She came back a third time. Then he told her sternly, "You will not change the *halachah* with tears!"

When the woman had left, Reb Moshe turned to his *talmid* to explain his behavior. "One should not raise his voice, especially to a person in pain — but sometimes it cannot be avoided, because that may be the only way to make them understand."

IN DEFINING THE WORD עָנָיו, *humble man*, as applied to Moshe *Rabbeinu*, *Rashi* writes (*Numbers* 12:3): a meek and tolerant

Ignoring Affronts person. In his commentary to *Avos* (2:9), *Rabbeinu Yonah* describes a tolerant person as: "One who distances himself from anger and responds in a soft tone. Even when he is wronged, he will tolerate it and no bitter word will escape his mouth ... "

Reb Moshe's tolerance of the personal wrongs committed against him was the most incredible aspect of his humility.

A student once asked to be forgiven for having once said something improper to him. Reb Moshe said, "You are right to ask forgiveness, but you should know that never in my life have I ever taken offense at something that was said to me."

He once judged a *din Torah* in which the money in question was held by a third party, who was to present it to the person in whose favor Reb Moshe would rule. The case was decided, but the man refused to hand the money over. When Reb Moshe asked why, the man replied, "I will not hand the money over, for your *p'sak* is invalid! You have overlooked an obvious *halachah*, namely that monetary disputes cannot be judged at night!"

Reb Moshe calmly explained to the man that he had not erred, and the money, therefore, should be handed over.

Five months later, this same man came before Reb Moshe, requesting that he be provided with a certificate attesting that he was a qualified *shochet*. Reb Moshe, who knew the man well, promptly picked up his pen and began to write.

Others present in the room were aware of this man's earlier insolent outburst and were convinced that he was unworthy of Reb Moshe's help. "The *Rosh Yeshivah* surely recalls the disrespect shown him by this man ... ," they began.

Reb Moshe replied adamantly, "Of what relevance is this? Yom Kippur has already passed, at which time I recited *Tefillah Zakah*, declaring my forgiveness of all who have sinned against me. This is not mere child's play! Besides, the man has certainly repented by now." And he continued writing the certificate requested of him.

❀　　❀　　❀

Many years ago, a respected *talmid chacham* published a *sefer* that bore a *haskamah* (approbation) from Reb Moshe. A number of points expressed in the *sefer* were sharply decried by some who found them contrary to their own strongly held traditions.

Some time later, a pamphlet appeared which viciously attacked the *sefer*, its author and even abused Reb Moshe for having given his *haskamah* to the work. There was widespread outrage at this attack on Reb Moshe, not only against the brazen author, but against the group to which he belonged. Most people were convinced that he would not have dared write that way about Reb Moshe unless he had been authorized to do so by his leaders.

A delegation of prominent members of this community visited Reb Moshe to disavow any involvement in the authorship or publication of the pamphlet. They made the point that their *Rebbe* and Reb Moshe had great mutual respect for one another and no one who heeded their *Rebbe's* word would have dared to write such slanderous comments.

Reb Moshe informed the delegation that he had not heard the rumors, nor seen the pamphlet; in fact, he was unaware of its contents. There was nothing, he assured them, to apologize for.

One of the delegates asked Reb Moshe if he would care to see a copy of the pamphlet. Reb Moshe replied, "No. If I read what has been written of me, I may become upset. For this alone (i.e., causing another Jew anguish) the author might incur Heavenly punishment, and I don't want that to happen."

Many years ago, Reb Moshe issued a *p'sak* that aroused opposition in many circles. Of those *rabbanim* who opposed the ruling, the vast majority did so with the great reverence due a *gaon* and *tzaddik* of Reb Moshe's stature. Most prominent among those who disagreed with the *p'sak* was the saintly *Rav* of Satmar, Rabbi Yoel Teitelbaum. A distinguished delegation of rabbis volunteered to visit Reb Moshe to convince him to retract his *p'sak*. Before going, they conferred with the Satmar *Rav* to seek his advice and blessing. The *Rav*, who was famous for his sparkling sense of humor, responded, "But what will you do if he speaks with you in learning?" The group went to Reb Moshe but failed to sway him. Reb Moshe, in turn, dispatched his own emissaries to the *Rav*, declaring his readiness to rescind the *p'sak* — if he could be convinced that his halachic logic in the matter was incorrect.

In the end, though Reb Moshe always made it clear that any qualified halachic authority had the right to disagree with him, he refuted all attempts at disproving his *p'sak* and stood by his ruling.

The Satmar Rav
Rabbi Yoel Teitelbaum

UNFORTUNATELY, not everyone involved in a controversy has the level-headedness of Torah giants like Reb Moshe or the Satmar *Rav*.

Above the Fray One fellow composed a *sefer*, containing chapter after chapter of refutations to various responsa found in *Igros Moshe*. Not content with the legitimate course of trying to show flaws in Reb Moshe's reasoning, the author filled his work with scornful and derogatory statements. Ridiculous as it may seem, the man somehow thought his efforts would help to undermine Reb Moshe's position as the foremost *posek* of the generation. For publication, he brought his manuscript to the very same typesetter-printer who produced Reb Moshe's *sefarim*. Seeing the *sefer's* contents, the printer immediately called Reb Moshe, gave him a quick outline of the situation, and asked him how to proceed.

"Well," Reb Moshe replied, "one who writes a *sefer* quite often needs it to supplement his income and achieve renown. One is obligated to do another Jew a favor. You, too, depend on printing to earn your livelihood. Go ahead with the *sefer's* publication."

When the above-mentioned controversy was at its height, one demented individual would call Reb Moshe at all hours of the day and night, shouting any insult that came to mind. Each time the fellow called, Reb Moshe would listen to the tirade in silence and say "Good-bye," when it finally came to an end.

Some understood this behavior as conforming to a teaching

cited in *Tiferes Yisrael:* The humble will listen carefully when berated by others, for amid a torrent of insults may lie some truths; by taking heed of such truths, one achieves some degree of self-improvement.

Reb Moshe once told a close *talmid*, "The best response to personal attacks is no response."

A certain rabbi attacked Reb Moshe's *p'sak* forcefully. The following summer, Reb Moshe spent some time vacationing not far from where this rabbi was staying. When Reb Moshe was asked to validate a *mikveh* in the area, he sent someone to ask the rabbi to accompany him on the inspection of the *mikveh.*

"What?" another person asked incredulously. "This is the man who wrote ... " As was so often the case, Reb Moshe's response was quiet, yet firm.

"I *must* have him with me on the inspection." Those close to Reb Moshe were understandably concerned with defending his honor — and why should he dignify someone who had been publicly disrespectful to him? Reb Moshe had a broader view. His stature would be measured by *Hashem*, not public opinion. If the status of the *mikveh* could be enhanced by that rabbi's participation, then he should participate in the inspection.

The *rav* accompanied Reb Moshe.

Rabbi Michel Barenbaum views this incident as an illustration of one of Rabbi Yisrael Salanter's teachings. Reb Yisrael taught that in perfecting the Torah's requirement not to bear a grudge for a wrong committed against oneself, it is necessary to eradicate totally any feeling of ill will toward the wrongdoer. The way to accomplish this is by actively seeking to benefit this very person. By repaying his misdeed with kindness, all bitterness will vanish.

In speaking of Reb Moshe, Reb Michel cites the following Talmudic teaching: "For three years, the academies of Shammai and Hillel argued. These said that the *Halachah* was as they saw it while the others took the opposite view. A Heavenly voice finally declared: 'Both these and those are the words of the living G-d! — but the *Halachah* follows the academy of Hillel.'

"If both are the words of the living G-d, then why did the academy of Hillel merit that the *Halachah* should follow their views? Because they were softspoken and bore disgrace (gracefully) ..." *(Eruvin* 13b).

If our era had a counterpart to the academy of Hillel who deserved recognition for the same reasons, surely it was Reb Moshe.

CHAPTER TWELVE
Transcending Nature

Moshe replied ..., 'The people come to me to seek Hashem'
(Exodus 18:15).
" ... the people come to me to seek Hashem," that I should
pray for their sick (Ramban).

I N THE EARLY YEARS, they would come at all hours of the day; more recently, when he was plagued by illness and his strength had to be conserved, an appointment had to be made in advance. Reb Moshe's "agenda" was unlimited. The **If People** halachic questions covered the full gamut of **Need Me** *Shulchan Aruch* from awesomely complex questions of life and death to matters of modern technology for which only someone of his caliber could find applicable precedents and principles in the classic sources, to questions that were so simple that one wondered why they had to be asked at all. There were other types of petitioners, too. They were of all ages, from all walks of life; men and women, young and old, *Ashkenazim* and *Sefardim*, *chassidim* and *misnagdim*. They sought blessings and prayers regarding anything that was important to a Jew: a *shidduch* for an older child, a baby for a childless couple, a cure for the sick, a livelihood for a breadwinner.

It was a matter of principle to Reb Moshe that he had to be available to anyone who needed him. He even had a telephone next to his seat in the *beis midrash*. As he grew older, one of his confidants put a note on Reb Moshe's apartment door giving hours when he could be reached. When Reb Moshe saw it, he removed it with annoyance, saying, "If someone comes to me now, he needs me *now*. I have no right to make him wait." Eventually he had to admit that he would have to limit his availability. This time, however, *he* composed the note giving the hours when he could see people. Its text and tone were apologetic, reflecting his sincere regret that troubled and tormented people would be forced to wait for *his* convenience.

He greeted each visitor with that warm smile that made people feel that he was their friend as much as their guiding light. He would listen patiently to each request, sometimes interjecting a question or two. He wanted to understand the situation well, because he cared.

When the entire picture had been presented, Reb Moshe would offer his advice or blessing. Often he would include the people in his prayers, especially the sick, either having them in mind during *Shemoneh Esrei* or by reciting *Tehillim* on their behalf.

Fortified by the blessing and prayers, the petitioner would take leave of Reb Moshe, his burden eased and his spirits raised.

A well-known *talmid chacham* once sat watching as a line of petitioners came before Reb Moshe, one by one, seeking his blessing. When the last person had gone, the scholar turned to Reb Moshe and related the following tale:

A woman once requested a blessing from Reb Yisrael, the *Maggid* of Koznitz, for a matter of major importance to her. The *Maggid* said, "I will grant your request, but only if you give me one hundred gold coins to distribute to the poor." The woman pleaded that it was impossible for her to meet such a demand. Yet the *Maggid* insisted that his condition be met.

Some time later the woman returned to the *Maggid* and placed a sack containing eighty gold coins before him. "I have gone through much sacrifice to raise this sum," she said. "Please consider it sufficient for my request to be granted."

"I will not," came the firm reply. "I made it clear that you were to return only if you had raised the specific sum. You should not have returned with less than the full amount. You have wasted your time in coming here."

That was enough for the distraught woman. She never dreamt that someone with a reputation for righteousness and benevolence could be so unbending toward someone in need. In her distress, the woman cried out, "I will manage without your blessing! I will rely on the *Ribbono shel Olam* alone and *He* will help me."

Upon hearing these words, the *Maggid's* demeanor suddenly changed. Gently he said, "*That* was what I have been waiting to hear. The first time you came before me, I sensed that you were placing your entire trust in my powers alone. But a Jew must never forget Who is the *real* source of all blessing. A Jew must show his faith in *Hashem* through prayer and good deeds. That will be a source of merit for him.

"I never wanted your money. I purposely demanded the impossible, to force you to change your way of thinking. Now that you realize toward Whom your prime trust should be directed, I offer you my blessings."

> Reb Moshe did not dispute the story's message, but he defended those who came before him with their requests. "They are fulfilling a teaching of our Sages that when misfortune strikes, one should ask a *chacham* to seek mercy on his behalf (*Bava Basra* 116a). I am not the *chacham* of whom our Sages speak, but if people think that I am and come before me for this reason, then I must honor their request."
>
> Others, however, could speak of Reb Moshe's powers in more open terms. The Steipler *Gaon*, whose blessings effected countless miracles, is reported to have remarked shortly before his own passing, "Reb Moshe has been given the keys to granting blessings in this generation."

ONCE AN EIGHT-YEAR-OLD BOY developed a malignant growth on his leg. The doctors said that the leg must be amputated — but

Concern for Petitioners
even then, there was no guarantee that the child's life could be saved. A friend of the family brought the distraught father with his son to the *beis midrash* of Tifereth Jerusalem, where the man told his story to Reb Moshe. The *Rosh Yeshivah* broke down in tears. The father, too, wept uncontrollably. After a few minutes, Reb Moshe took the man's hand in both of his and said, "I cried and you cried. The One Above will note our tears and your son will have a יְשׁוּעָה, *salvation*."

The amputation was performed, and there was no recurrence of the malignancy.

Reb Moshe's concern over a petitioner's troubles did not end when the person left him. Once, a *rosh yeshivah* called him requesting that he pray for a sick child. A few days went by without Reb Moshe having heard anything new about the child's condition. Then, he and the *rosh yeshivah* happened to meet. Reb Moshe anxiously asked, "How is the child? I have gone around for days without a head!"

❧ ❧ ❧

The phone in Reb Moshe's bedroom rang early one morning at three o'clock. The caller was a former *talmid* whose wife had given birth to a boy, who was experiencing life-threatening complications. Doctors had all but given up hope for the infant. The father asked Reb Moshe to pray for his son's recovery.

Two days later the young man held in his hands a special delivery letter from Reb Moshe, written only hours after the phone call of that fateful morning. In it, Reb Moshe assured the worried parents that their baby would get well. Sure enough, the baby recovered.

In relating this incident, Rabbi Chaskel Besser commented, "Reb Moshe always viewed a problem from every possible angle. All the parents sought was a salvation for their baby, but Reb Moshe also sought a salvation for the parents by giving them peace of mind."

Rebbetzin Feinstein recalled her husband's elation upon hearing that someone for whom his blessing had been sought had seen the wish fulfilled. She quickly added that never did Reb Moshe take credit for whatever had occurred. He was ecstatic only that another Jew's life had become happier.

One morning, Rabbi Elimelech Bluth heard Reb Moshe muttering; "Six months ... a miracle ... ?" Rabbi Bluth asked if the *Rosh Yeshivah* would explain the significance of these words, and he did:

Six months earlier, a childless couple had come to him for a blessing. As always, he had complied with their request, but in a somewhat strange fashion. "May you inform me in six months' time of happy tidings," he said. Now, six months later, the couple had called Reb Moshe with the news that they were going to have a baby, and expressed their appreciation for the "miracle he had brought about."

Reb Moshe summed up his feeling on the matter: "A miracle or not a miracle — what is the difference? As long as there are *simchos* among Jews!"

MANY STORIES ABOUT REB MOSHE indicate clearly that he had what can only be described as *ruach hakodesh*, the ability to see

Divine Insight beyond the visible. In the summer of 1970, Arab terrorists hijacked three TWA jets, forcing the pilots to land in the Jordanian desert, where the passengers were held hostage for some time. Among the hostages were Rabbi Yitzchak Hutner, *Rosh Yeshivah* of Mesivta Chaim Berlin and one of *Klal Yisrael's* leading Torah figures, and his family. While Jewry prayed for the safe release of *all* the prisoners, there was special concern for the fate of Rabbi Hutner, to whom so many turned for teaching and inspiration, and whose advanced age made prolonged captivity especially dangerous.

During the many days that the hostages were held, there was a heat wave in New York. Reb Moshe remarked to

With Rabbi Yitzchak Hutner (left) and Rabbi Yaakov Yitzchak Ruderman (right)

his *talmid*, Rabbi Yosef Brick, that *Hashem* brought the intense heat upon us so that we should feel the suffering of the hostages.

One afternoon, Reb Moshe entered the *beis midrash* of Mesivtha Tifereth Jerusalem in a jovial mood. "So, Rabbi Hutner has been released!" he smilingly told someone. The person, looking somewhat confused, informed Reb Moshe that the news reports had made no mention of the hostages' release.

That night it was learned that the crisis had indeed ended with the safe release of all hostages.

When Rabbi Shneur Kotler, revered *Rosh Yeshivah* of Beth Medrash Govoha, lay stricken with the illness that would eventually take his life, Reb Moshe prayed for him constantly, never forgetting to have his private *minyan* recite the *mi shebeirach* prayer on his behalf. Reb Moshe, who was then confined to his home because of his own poor physical state, would frequently ask his family to inquire as to Reb Shneur's current condition.

When Reb Shneur passed away on Thursday, the third of Tammuz, 5742 (1982), it was decided not to inform Reb Moshe, lest his own health be affected adversely. At the Torah reading on the

With Rabbi Shneur Kotler

following Shabbos, Reb Moshe made no request that a *mi shebeirach* be said. In fact, he never again asked about Reb Shneur's condition. When he happened to glance at a Yiddish newspaper which had been left lying in his apartment, Reb Moshe's face registered no shock or even faint surprise at the headlines telling of Reb Shneur's huge funeral.

❀   ❀   ❀

On one occasion, a childless couple asked for Reb Moshe's blessing. To their surprise, he asked if they had ever given a gift to their matchmaker. They had not. He told them that they were halachically required to do so and they should attend to it without delay. Within a year they had their first child and have had several more since then.

> It was common for yeshivah students to seek his blessing that they find their proper mate. One very diligent student was concerned that the mental and physical stress of *shidduchim* would hamper his learning; however, he made no mention of this when coming before Reb Moshe for a blessing. He was therefore quite amazed when Reb Moshe concluded his blessing with, " ... and may your quest cause only minimal loss to your Torah study."
>
> When this same young man was married and his wife was expecting their first child, he again requested Reb Moshe's blessing. After conferring his usual good wishes for mother and child, Reb Moshe added cryptically, "At times, complications arise at childbirth; one need not be alarmed by this." Sure enough, as the pangs of childbirth set in, doctors detected a problem that posed a danger to the child — but concern soon gave way to joy as a healthy baby was born.

Another student was debating whether or not he was ready for marriage. While he mulled the matter over in his mind, he was certain of one thing: it was not too early to receive Reb Moshe's blessing that all go well whenever he would seek a *shidduch*. Again, the petitioner made no mention to Reb Moshe of his personal considerations; all he asked for was a blessing. Reb Moshe said, "May *Hashem* help you find ... and you should begin the search now!"

Once he was called from Memphis, Tennessee with a halachic query about a married couple. He gave his ruling, and then said,

"One must seek grounds to rule leniently for them, because they have not had children yet after twelve years of marriage." The caller gasped. Reb Moshe was right — but no one had ever told him of that poignant fact.

IN HIS CLASSIC *Nefesh HaChaim*, Rabbi Chaim of Volozhin writes (4:18), "A person who accepts upon himself the yoke of Torah, for

Nature Will Be His

its own sake *(Torah lishmah)*, will be raised above everything in this world. *Hashem* will watch over him with a Providence that will transcend the laws of nature ... for he is attached to the Torah and to *Hashem*, as it were ... *The laws of nature will be placed in his power, according to what he will decree upon them ...* "

Mr. Heshy Jacob, leader of the East Side Hatzalah, was very devoted to Reb Moshe and often had *Shalosh Seudos* with him in his apartment. Once Mr. Jacob's six-year-old son was hit in the eye by a thrown rock, and suffered a cut cornea. The eye was badly bloodshot, and the ophthalmologist said the wound would take about thirty days to heal. The next Shabbos, Mr. Jacob took his son to Reb Moshe's apartment for *Minchah* and *Shalosh Seudos*. Reb Moshe noticed the eye and asked what had happened. Seeing Reb Moshe's anguish, Mr. Jacob regretted having brought the child, but it was too late. He told Reb Moshe the story. Reb Moshe held the boy's face between his hands and stared into his eyes without saying a word. By the following Shabbos the eye was completely healed! The ophthalmologist said that in his thirty years of practice he had never seen such a recovery.

❈ ❈ ❈

A mother of four in the Midwest went into labor, and her husband called Reb Moshe for a blessing. The woman's family was from the East Side, and had a close personal relationship with Reb Moshe. Whenever there was a family celebration or crisis, they would share the news with him. In response to the present call, Reb Moshe said, "Your wife will have a complete recovery and the four children will be well." The father retorted that he wanted a blessing for the fifth child — the newborn. Reb Moshe repeated himself, "Your wife will have a complete recovery and the four children will be well." But he added, "Whatever *Hashem* does is for the best and you and your wife should accept it."

When the father came to the hospital and saw his new baby, he noticed that the infant was breathing heavily. The doctor said it was normal, but the condition worsened. Reb Moshe was called again and once more he would not give a blessing for the new baby, but urged the father to strengthen his wife and encourage her to have faith that whatever *Hashem* wills is for the best. The baby died soon after.

Only a few months later, the same woman began to get severe headaches. She underwent tests to find the cause of the malady, and her family doctor told her there was nothing to worry about; the condition would correct itself within a week or two. A few days later, shortly after *Havdalah*, the phone rang. The husband answered. It was the doctor. "Is your wife listening?" he asked. After being assured that she was not on the line, the doctor said that she had a brain tumor, but that he had not wanted to tell them until he had made arrangements for a hospital bed and the best surgeon in the area. She was to enter the hospital on Monday and the operation was scheduled for Tuesday.

But she *had* been listening to the conversation and, not surprisingly, was frozen with fear. Again they called Reb Moshe. The *Rebbetzin* said that he was at a *Melaveh Malkah* for Tifereth Jerusalem, but would call back as soon as he got home. The call came after midnight, and Reb Moshe assured husband and wife that the operation would be a complete success and she would be perfectly healthy again.

Their spirits were as high as could be expected, until Monday. The surgeon told the husband, "The tumor is accessible and operable. I can remove it completely, but I have to cut through tissue and your wife will be paralyzed permanently on her left side."

Again to the telephone to consult Reb Moshe. He laughed and told the caller to ignore the doctor; his wife would have a complete recovery.

The operation was performed and, when the surgeon came to the waiting room to report to the husband, he said, "The operation was a success and there is no paralysis. It is a phenomenon."

With the husband was a local rabbi who also served as the hospital chaplain. He exclaimed, "Why do you call it a phenomenon? Why can't you admit it was a miracle?"

Sullenly, the doctor said, "That's what I meant. There is no medical explanation for it."

Rabbi Bluth was present when a woman came to Reb

Moshe with a request. She was childless after many years of marriage and had suffered through a long succession of traumatic occurrences related to her problem. Her husband had come to Reb Moshe each year for the blessing that he hoped would finally bring the longed-for child; so far, this hope had not been fulfilled. Now, she desired something more than a blessing.

"I want the *Rosh Yeshivah* to decree that Heaven grant me a child," she said amid sobs.

Reb Moshe was taken aback by the woman's request. "I should decree ... ? What power have I to do such things ...?"

"Yes, the *Rosh Yeshivah* can decree ... he can ..."

Her incessant weeping became so intense that at one point Rabbi Bluth took the initiative in trying to comfort her. Reb Moshe, however, stopped him. "No, no ... it is good, it is good," was all he said. His intention may have been, simply, that crying can unburden a person of anguish that is welled up inside, or, as Rabbi Bluth suggests, the bitter tears of a righteous Jewish woman can help bring about her own salvation by arousing Heavenly mercy on her behalf.

Finally, as the woman continued crying, Reb Moshe said, "I cannot decree, but I will say this. In merit of your faith in the power of Torah scholars — for this, you *deserve* a child."

Reb Moshe's words calmed his broken-hearted petitioner; her pure faith, which Reb Moshe had found so praiseworthy, told her that with the *Rosh Yeshivah's* utterance, her wish had been granted. However, she was not yet finished.

"*Rebbi* — when?" she persisted.

Reb Moshe was not disturbed by the question. He thought and began counting off the Hebrew months on his fingers. The ninth month was Kislev, the month of Chanukah. "It can't be before Chanukah," he said. "Right after Chanukah."

On the last day of the next Chanukah, her child was born.

A young woman, stricken with a debilitating disease, had received frightening news from her doctor. She was pregnant and according to her doctor, because of her illness neither she nor her child would survive a full-term pregnancy. The doctor insisted that drastic measures be taken to save her life.

The woman's husband consulted a prominent Chassidic *rav*, seeking his guidance. "This is not a question for me," the *rav* replied honestly. "This is a question for Reb Moshe."

The couple soon found themselves in the dining room of Reb Moshe's small apartment. The aged sage gently asked the woman to repeat exactly what the doctor had said. He questioned her on a number of points to make certain that he understood the facts clearly. Then he stated his opinion.

"Do not be frightened by what the doctor said. You are going to give birth to a healthy child, and in fact, your own condition will improve. There is nothing to fear."

A few months later, Reb Moshe's prediction came true.

The story, however, did not end there. One *Erev Shabbos* a year after the baby's birth, the phone rang in the kitchen of the woman's home.

"Hello, this is Moshe Feinstein calling. How are you feeling? ... Good, very good ... and how is your baby? ... *Baruch Hashem* ... Today is your baby's birthday — may *Hashem* bless your entire family with good health and success!"

IN TRUTH, MANY OF REB MOSHE'S MIRACLES were intertwined with strands of his compassion, loving-kindness and other

Source of Miracles

outstanding traits. This is not merely coincidental, as someone remarked after hearing the following two incidents:

A young man had taken a vocational course after spending several years in a *kollel*, but for many months had been unable to find a job. His concerned mother was granted an appointment with Reb Moshe so that she could request a blessing for her son. Reb Moshe assured the worried mother that her son would find a means of livelihood. A few days later, the young man was called for an interview by someone who had rejected his application some months earlier; this time, he was hired. The story, though, did not end there.

Some time later, the above story was repeated to a prominent senior *rosh yeshivah*, who exclaimed in amazement, "Now I understand!" He explained that the young man's employer was his former *talmid* and the mother of the young man had once implored him to call the employer on behalf of her son. He tried a few times but had been unable to get through for one reason or another, and eventually forgot about it. Then, one night, he dreamt that Reb Moshe was asking him to speak to this same person on behalf of the unemployed young man. He made the call the next day and the former *talmid* promised to cooperate.

The dates were checked. The dream had come on the night of Reb Moshe's blessing.

The second story is not a miraculous one — or perhaps it is, if we have a true appreciation of Reb Moshe's greatness.

> Years ago, Reb Moshe would have *Shalosh Seudos* and recite *Tehillim* in his yeshivah every Shabbos afternoon. One Shabbos, as he was reciting *Tehillim*, a mildly retarded child stood watching him. The boy went over and turned Reb Moshe's *Tehillim* on an angle to the right, and Reb Moshe continued reciting. Then the boy turned the *Tehillim* to the left and Reb Moshe continued reciting. The boy took the *Tehillim* and turned it completely around and Reb Moshe continued reciting. Not satisfied, the boy turned the page, but Reb Moshe was still not disturbed.
>
> A man sitting nearby had watched all this and, although people went out of their way to be patient with the boy, the man had seen what he felt was too much. He snapped, "Stop it already. Let the *Rosh Yeshivah daven!*"
>
> Reb Moshe turned to the man and said, "He is only playing with me. I *enjoy* it when he plays with me. I love him like my own child!" With that, Reb Moshe embraced the boy and kissed him.

Said one person after hearing the above two stories, "Stories like the first one could happen because stories like the second one happened."

Reb Moshe himself once said as much, though in an opposite sense, when someone came to him with a bizarre story. A stranger claiming Kabbalistic powers had frightened someone terribly by accosting him suddenly and announcing that it had been revealed to him that one of the man's close kin was deathly ill. The stranger told the man that his relative's illness would soon become apparent unless the family followed an order of prayer and repentance that he would prescribe.

The man had accepted all the stranger had said as fact. However, he asked someone close to Reb Moshe to relate the story to the *Rosh Yeshivah*, and ask if any additional repentance was necessary.

After hearing the story, Reb Moshe was visibly upset. He said, "The man has nothing to worry about. The stranger's telling of his 'revelation' in a manner that frightened the poor man so, shows a total lack of sensitivity on his part. He is lacking in *middos* and *Hashem* does not communicate with someone lacking in *middos*. He did not have a revelation."

If *middos* and Divine inspiration are so intertwined, then it is no wonder that Reb Moshe was among the very few in our generation to whom the hidden was revealed.

CHAPTER THIRTEEN

The Final Years

N THE FINAL YEARS of his long life, Reb Moshe suffered from a number of physical ailments. Until his very last day, he strained to carry on his holy mission in this world with every last ounce of his waning strength.

Fighting Infirmity
A heart ailment, which necessitated the insertion of a pacemaker into his chest, forced him to curtail the heavy schedule of public appearances that had been part of his life for decades. However, this condition did not prevent him from rising at dawn to study Torah as he always had, nor did it prevent him from continuing to rule on matters of *Halachah*, and publish *sefarim* on both Talmud and *Halachah*.

In 1981, in his preface to the sixth volume of *Igros Moshe*, Reb Moshe writes, " ... I have already reached, through the kindness of *Hashem* and His infinite mercy, into my eighties ... He continues to grant me the strength to clarify the *Halachah* properly, with knowledge and understanding, as in my earlier years ..."

Those who were privileged to take part in the *minyan* in his apartment during periods of illness could see clearly how he ignored pain and infirmity during his *tefillos*. During periods of excruciatingly painful sciatica attacks, when standing was an agony for him and he needed assistance to rise from his chair, he insisted on standing for *Baruch She'amar* and then, a few minutes later, getting up again for *Mizmor L'Sodah* and of course, for *Shemoneh Esrei*. He would stand again for *Modim D'Rabbanan*. Despite the

With (left to right)
Rabbi Naftoli Borchardt,
Rabbi Baruch Borchardt
and Rabbi
Mordechai Tendler

pain in his back, he maintained his constant practice of bowing very deeply during *Shemoneh Esrei.* During that time, someone once observed how Reb Moshe's knees buckled from pain as he was reciting *Shemoneh Esrei.* As he began to fall forward, his hands pressed against a wall, helping him regain his balance, and he continued *davening.*

As Purim approached that year, Reb Moshe was still in great pain. Those close to him assumed that a *minyan* would be convened in his home for the *Megillah* reading. However, Reb Moshe insisted on *davening* in Tifereth Jerusalem in order to proclaim the miracle in the presence of a large multitude [פְּרְסוּמֵי נִיסָא]. The *Rebbetzin* pleaded with him not to exert himself. He compromised by having a *minyan* in his apartment in the evening, but going to the yeshivah in the morning.

❀　　❀　　❀

When he spent Yom Kippur at the Yeshivah of Staten Island, he was implored, for the sake of his health, not to fall to the floor and bow, as is customary during the *Mussaf* prayer. Reb Moshe, however, could not be dissuaded. ''How can I remain standing when

everyone else *is* bowing?'' he demanded.

The last two years of his life, his failing health forced him to spend Yom Kippur at home, where a *minyan* was convened. His close ones appealed to him not to bow, and he agreed to step out of the room at that part of the service. When the time came to bow, however, someone peeked into the hallway — and there was Reb Moshe, bowing along with the *minyan*.

His failing vision caused him to fall behind in his study of *Daf Yomi*. Yet, he continued to press on as he strove to complete *Shas* for yet another time. He was observed engrossed in *Maseches Bechoros* (using a magnifying glass), studying not only the basic text, but all the amendations of *Bach* and *Shitah Mekubetzes* in a very small print on the side of the *gemara!* It was a source of

The last picture taken with the Rebbetzin

satisfaction to him that he eventually did complete the cycle of *Daf Yomi*, even though he did not complete it in time for the world-wide *siyum* celebration in the fall of 1983.

He sought to help others as much as his strength allowed. He would obtain the phone numbers of some of the many sick people for whom he was asked to pray, speak with them for a while and wish them well. On Friday nights, he would knock on the door of a widow living on his floor to wish her a *Gut Shabbos*. And, of course, he continued to advise both individuals and organizations on matters affecting them.

One hot, humid summer day a neighbor was asked to try to repair a broken air conditioner in Reb Moshe's apartment. When the neighbor arrived, he found Reb Moshe sweltering in the heat as he recited *Tehillim* for a sick woman.

During this very difficult period of his life, his grandson, Rabbi Mordechai Tendler, assumed even greater responsibility for assisting and protecting Reb Moshe. There was regular tension between Reb Moshe's sense of responsibility to be available and the opposing need to conserve his strength, protect his health, and differentiate between those who genuinely *needed* him and those who wanted simply to be near him. Most of the time, the buffer, protector and screener was Reb Mordechai.

AS TIME PROGRESSED, Reb Moshe weakened steadily. In the winter of 5745 (1985), he was hospitalized with a condition that, for a time, caused him to drift in and out of a semi-coma.

In the Hospital Jews the world over poured out their hearts in prayer for him. *Baruch Hashem*, their entreaties were accepted, and Reb Moshe, though still extremely weak, was eventually discharged from the hospital. Approximately a year later, in the winter of 5746, he was again hospitalized and subsequently released.

Proclamation issued by the Moetzes Gedolei HaTorah,
calling for prayer on Reb Moshe's behalf (winter, 1985)

קול צעקה

לעורר רחמים ותחנונים

עבור פאר דורנו גאון עוזנו

מרן

משה בן פייא גיטל

פינשטיין

הצריך רפואה שלימה וישועה בתוך שאר חולי ישראל.

נא להרבות בתפילות ובקשות

והשי״ת ישמע קול שועתנו ברחמים

חברי מועצת גדולי התורה בארה״ב

יעקב קמנצקי   יעקב יצחק הלוי רודרמן   ישראל שפירא (מבלוזב)   מרדכי גיפטר
אברהם פאם   אלי׳ שוועי   משה הלוי הורוויץ (מבוסטון)

It was obvious to the hospital staff that, in treating Rabbi Moshe Feinstein, they were in the presence of holiness. He strained to get dressed for *davening;* at the very least, he would don his hat. All were amazed how he would often stand for *Shemoneh Esrei* despite excruciating pain. When too weak to stand, but strong enough to sit, he would be careful not to lean back or even to make use of the arm-rests. Amazingly, he would force himself up from his wheelchair to bow at *Modim.*

However, it was more than his performance of deeds "between man and G-d" that impressed the doctors and nurses. They saw before their eyes an angel whose concern for other human beings was of a quality they had never seen.

When someone would come to administer an injection or some other treatment, he would force himself closer to the person to make his or her task easier. He never forgot a "thank you" for anything that was done for him. Before leaving the hospital he again thanked and blessed all who had come to his aid. He strained not to cry out when painful treatments were performed, so as not to cause anguish to the one administering them.

His solicitude for the feelings and welfare of others was undiminished by his own suffering. Several times a day he would inquire about the *Rebbetzin* and wanted to be sure that the concern for him did not cause her to be neglected.

Someone who administered a treatment known to cause excruciating pain asked Reb Moshe how he was able to bear the suffering without crying out. He replied, "You are doing what must be done for my benefit. It is worthwhile for me to have a little more pain, rather than to cause you aggravation."

During one hospital stay, the ladies of the family brought cakes to the hospital and distributed slices to doctors, nurses, orderlies, attendants — anyone who had rendered Reb Moshe a service in any way. Instead of eating their portions, they showed them off and treasured them, and most took them home to their families. To them, these were not ordinary pastries, but mementos of an extraordinary man. The hospital staff was so devoted to Reb Moshe that many of them wept when they heard about his death.

ABOUT A YEAR BEFORE Reb Moshe's passing, someone came to

Rabbi David Feinstein with the delicate question of whether or not a member of his family should undergo major surgery. Reb David presented the question to Reb Moshe, who was then so weak that he could barely speak. Reb Moshe advised that the surgery be performed. When Reb David relayed his father's decision, the sick person's family expressed reservations. Reb Moshe was extremely ill; perhaps he had not fully grasped the problem? Was it possible that in healthier times he would have advised differently?

Siyata DiShmaya

Reb David told the family members that they need not be concerned. "If the *Rosh Yeshivah* understood the question properly, then you certainly must listen to him. And even if he did not understand it, he still had the *siyata diShmaya* to say what is correct." The surgery was performed with successful results.

It had been Reb Moshe's practice for many years to spend Shavuos at the Yeshivah of Staten Island. For his last Shavuos, in 5745 (1985), he remained at home. Mr. and Mrs. Jaeger, the yeshivah's cooks, had always prepared a special cake and blintzes in Reb Moshe's honor. This time, they sent these foods, prepared in accordance with Reb Moshe's strict diet, to his East Side apartment. After *Yom Tov* was over, Reb Moshe wanted to call the Jaegers and thank them. Someone attempted to dissuade him, saying that he was too weak even to hold the telephone receiver. Reb Moshe said, "To give the Jaegers some pleasure by thanking them, the *Ribbono shel Olam* will give me the strength to hold the phone."

One day, a great-granddaughter came to insert drops into Reb Moshe's eyes. As she was preparing to administer them, the *Rebbetzin* entered. "But you were already given those drops a little while ago!" she exclaimed. "Yes," replied Reb Moshe, "but I know that our granddaughter takes pleasure in giving them to me. Better that I be given them again than for her to have come for nothing."

For a time, a gentile male nurse cared for Reb Moshe at his home. A yeshivah student would also sleep in the apartment, in case of emergency. Once, a substitute nurse was there, who was unfamiliar with the accommodations in the apartment. Realizing that the nurse might not know how to set up the makeshift bed, Reb Moshe sent the student to make sure the nurse was resting comfortably.

In the summer of 1985, someone saw Reb Moshe straining his eyes to study *Sidra Vayikra* more than two months after it had been read as the weekly Torah portion. The person was apprehensive lest Reb Moshe's memory was failing him and he was confused as to which was the *Sidra* of that week. Delicately, the person mentioned that *Vayikra* had been read some time ago. Reb Moshe said, "The *halachah* states that one who is G-d-fearing should review the weekly *Sidra* with both *Targum* and *Rashi*. I fell behind while I was in the hospital so now I am simply paying up my debts!"

The Light Glows ...

ON *CHANUKAH* of his final year, Reb Moshe stood ready to kindle his *menorah*, as his *Rebbetzin* and a yeshivah student who often attended him looked on. Reb Moshe recited the blessing and then directed the lit candle which he held toward the wick in the *menorah*. He lit the first wick, but with his weak eyesight he could not find the next one. He tried moving the candle about, but still could not locate the wick. The student came over and gently took Reb Moshe's hand and started to guide it, but Reb Moshe would not let him. He wanted to fulfill the *mitzvah* without assistance. He tried once more, but again was not successful. Reb Moshe seemed on the verge of tears. He loved every *mitzvah* so ... he wanted so badly to fulfill it ... Suddenly the flame found the wick and it caught. Immediately, Reb Moshe's mood changed. He lit the remaining wicks and, joyfully, began to chant *HaNeiros Hallalu*.

Reb Moshe's lack of strength during those last months made it difficult for him to concentrate. Still, he tried his utmost to persevere. When a young man told him a *chiddush* with which he disagreed, Reb Moshe immediately contended with him. Not wanting to cause Reb Moshe undue strain, the young man said, "We can discuss it another time." But Reb Moshe could not rest knowing that someone believed something to be true when, in fact, it was false. To remain silent would be a greater strain for Reb Moshe than to speak. He patiently showed the young man where he had erred.

❦ ❦ ❦

When it became too strenuous for him to pray the long Shabbos morning *davening* with a *minyan*, he would recite the

Shacharis prayers alone and later a *minyan* would come to his apartment for the Torah reading and *Mussaf*. On Shabbos *Parshas Zachor*, the last Shabbos of his life, an *aufruf* was held at Tifereth Jerusalem. Since those who regularly formed Reb Moshe's *minyan* would be attending the *aufruf* and would not be at his home until much later than usual, it was thought best for Reb Moshe that he *daven Mussaf* privately, and hear the Torah reading with a *minyan* later in the day.

Rabbi Reuven Feinstein hurried to his father's home that day well before the *minyan* was to gather. He suggested to Reb Moshe that he recite *Mussaf* and eat something before the *minyan* arrived for the Torah reading.

"Why won't there be a *minyan* for *Mussaf?*" Reb Moshe wanted to know. Reb Reuven explained that the *aufruf* had made this impractical. Reb Moshe, however, was adamant. He wanted to daven *Mussaf* with a *minyan*, as he had always done. It was already past noon and most people had already *davened*, but Reb Reuven, seeing how distressed his father was, made the effort to gather a *minyan*. His quest was successful and a *minyan* soon formed in Reb Moshe's dining room for *Krias haTorah* and *Mussaf*.

Later, as they sat eating the *Seudas Shabbos*, Reb Moshe turned to Reb Reuven and said, "*Gedenk, men darf arein chappen vifil men ken*" (Remember! One must squeeze in as many *mitzvos* as he can).

ON THE FOLLOWING SUNDAY NIGHT, the eve of Ta'anis Esther, 5746 (1986), a call was sounded to the Hatzalah emergency rescue squad: Rabbi Moshe Feinstein had to be rushed to the hospital immediately.

... and Flickers

As the ambulance was speeding to the hospital he felt his strength waning. He said, "*Ich hob mehr nisht kein ko'ach*" (I have no more strength). Those were his last words.

How much strength had he had for the last several years? Very little, but whatever strength was left in him was devoted to *Hashem*, to Torah and to *Klal Yisrael*. As long as he had strength — *any* strength — his service continued. He would not stop working at his full capacity, as he had for ninety-one years. And then he had no more strength.

In the *beis midrash* at the Yeshivah of Staten Island, boys and young men were fervently reciting *Tehillim*, imploring *Hashem* to spare him. At 9:50 p.m. the light fixture over his seat near the *Aron HaKodesh* flickered and went out. Then it glowed for a moment and went out again.

Reb Moshe was gone and the light went dark.

It has been pointed out that the 5746th verse in the Torah reads, *And it came to pass after Moshe had finished writing down the words of this Torah in a book to the very end (Deuteronomy 31:24).*

THE NEWS SPREAD QUICKLY that night, casting a pall on the merry preparations for Purim. Everywhere there was a sense of having been orphaned. It had been a world *with* Reb Moshe, and now it was a world *without* Reb Moshe. True he had been very ill and virtually inaccessible, but he had still

Farewell

Poster announcing the funeral in New York

been among us. He was like a sun obscured by clouds. We could not see it but we were warmed and comforted by the knowledge that it was there. But now, the sun had set and was gone — and we knew the sky was empty. People heard the news and gasped. Then wept.

The *chevra kadisha* members who prepared Reb Moshe for burial were some of the most respected and experienced practitioners of this ultimate kindness. They shook their heads in reverent amazement. The body radiated such holiness, such purity!

All night, devoted disciples met with the family and police to plan the funeral. A plot was designated in *Har HaMenuchos*, Jerusalem. It was near his *rebbi*, Reb Isser Zalman; his friend, Reb Aharon; his son-in-law, Rav Shisgal; and in the close proximity of the holy Belzer *Rebbe*. In New York, the Police Department prepared for the largest funeral American Orthodoxy had ever known. As the *niftar* lay in the *beis midrash* — his own *beis midrash* — of Mesivtha Tifereth Jerusalem surrounded by reverent Jews from four generations reciting *Tehillim*, the subways and highways

were somber arteries of grief, as mourners converged on the East Side.

The cross-section of people was breathtaking: Chassidic *rebbes*, rabbis, *roshei yeshivah*, yeshivah students, Bais Yaakov girls, teachers, merchants, professionals, civil servants, black hats and long coats, crocheted skullcaps and sport jackets, community leaders, elected officials. Businesses chartered buses so that groups of employees could take turns going to the funeral. Schools and offices closed for the day. Orthodoxy had lost its father, and 75,000 of his children crowded the Lower East Side to mourn their loss and share their grief. As the words of *Tehillim* boomed over the huge outdoor loudspeakers, it seemed as if all of creation was in mourning.

Rabbi Michel Barenbaum tearfully eulogized his mentor and friend, and poignantly said that if Reb Moshe could speak he would express his compassion for the tens of thousands of people who were standing in the street and would ask the speakers to be brief.

Rabbi Yaakov Yitzchak Ruderman — painfully thrust into the position of America's senior *rosh yeshivah* by the successive deaths of Rabbi Yaakov Kamenetzky and Reb Moshe — wept as he eulogized, "The teacher of us all ... a great *tzaddik* and *ba'al middos* ... his loss is so painful that one cannot find the words to express what he feels." Indeed, he couldn't. It was impossible for him to contain his sense of loss, and his unfettered emotions spilled out into the hearts of the multitude.

Other *roshei yeshivah* and *rabbanim* who eulogized him were, in order of their appearance, Rabbi David Lipschutz of Yeshivas Rabbi Yitzchak Elchonon; Rabbi Chaim Stein of the Telshe Yeshivah; Rabbi Shraga Moshe Kalmanowitz of the Mirrer Yeshivah; Rabbi Yaakov Joffen of Yeshivas Beis Yosef; Rabbi Levi Krupenia of the Kamenitzer Yeshivah; Rabbi Nissan Alpert; Rabbi Moshe David Tendler; the Satmar *Rav*; Rabbi Reuven Feinstein, and Rabbi Mordechai Tendler.

Speaker after speaker mourned the catastrophe. Only the facts that it was Taanis Esther and that the *niftar* had to be taken to the airport limited the eulogies.

By the time the eulogies were over, it was late afternoon. The crowd walked in mournful silence as the Hatzalah ambulance bearing Reb Moshe's coffin slowly made its way down East Broadway. From there the procession proceeded to Kennedy Airport.

The funeral
in Jerusalem

The funeral was over, the crowd dispersed ... it was difficult to imagine that Purim was just a few hours away.

On Shushan Purim in Jerusalem, 250,000 people paid their respects, in the largest funeral since the time of Rabban Yochanan ben Zakkai, some two thousand years ago.

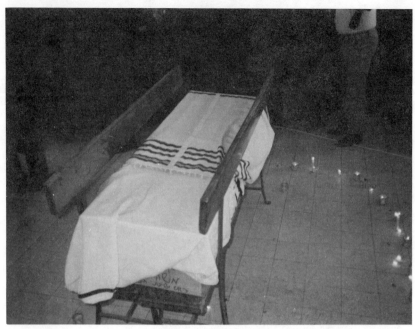

The coffin during the funeral at Yeshivas Etz Chaim in Jerusalem

Rabbi Eliezer Menachem Shach, his voice choked with tears, cried, "Torah, Torah, gird yourself in sackcloth! Prepare yourself to mourn for your only, unique son! ... Reb Moshe was the *gadol hador*, without embellishment, without exaggeration ... He was an only son to our generation."

He was followed by his colleague and Reb Moshe's boyhood friend, Rabbi David Povarsky; the Chief Rabbi of the *Eidah HaChareidus*, Rabbi Yaakov Yitzchak Weiss; Reb Moshe's nephew, Rabbi Michel Feinstein; the Sephardic *rosh yeshivah*, Rabbi Yehudah Tzadkah, and Rabbi Reuven Feinstein.

Reb Moshe had been in *Eretz Yisrael* only once in his lifetime, but he belonged to *Eretz Yisrael* as much as to America — and as much as to Uzda, Starobin, and Luban. He was the prince of Torah, and every citizen of the world of Torah was his subject and child.

At the conclusion of the eulogies, the mourners escorted Reb Moshe's coffin to *Har HaMenuchos*, where he was laid to rest.

A Postscript

SHORT WHILE AFTER Reb Moshe's passing, someone in *Eretz Yisrael* began experiencing excruciating headaches which no doctor was able to treat. Frightened, the man rushed to a leading *rav* in *Eretz Yisrael*, in search of his blessings and guidance.

Upon hearing that the man's troubles had begun around the time of the funeral, the *rav* asked if he had ever said anything disrespectful of Reb Moshe. The man replied that he had not. Then the *rav* offered counsel that was somewhat unusual. Rather than instruct him as to which doctor to use or the most preferred medical procedure to undergo, he told the man that the *goral HaGra* should be cast. Perhaps through this, the man would find the *real* source of his suffering.

The *goral* was cast. The verse it pointed to stared back at the man: " ... *and why did you not fear to speak against My servant, Moshe?*" *(Numbers* 12:8).

At first glance, these words meant nothing to the man. Then, suddenly, it hit him like a flash of lightning ...

Of course! He had been there, among the multitudes that had thronged the streets of Jerusalem on the day of Reb Moshe's funeral. Reb Moshe was a *gaon*, a *tzaddik* ... how could one not come and pay his respects?

He was upset, though, by the number of eulogies and the length of the funeral in general. It was Shushan Purim and Jerusalem was supposed to be engaged in the *mitzvos* of the festive holiday. It did not seem right, the man had felt, for a funeral — anyone's funeral — to ruin the Purim of hundreds of thousands of people.

The man had expressed his opinion to others.

"Why did you not fear to speak against My servant Moshe?"

The *rav* then told him that the *Shulchan Aruch* prescribes what he must do — indeed, the only solution to his suffering. He must gather ten people and, in their presence, ask forgiveness of Reb Moshe at his gravesite.

The man assembled a *minyan*, and, accompanied by them, made his way up *Har HaMenuchos* to the site of Reb Moshe's grave. There, he begged forgiveness for his words.

The man's headaches soon disappeared.

❀ ❀ ❀

All four sides of
Reb Moshe's monument on
Har HaMenuchos, Jerusalem

"Rabbi Chama bar Chanina said: *Tzaddikim are greater in death than in life*" (*Chulin* 7b). Reb Moshe himself once remarked that sometimes the *Ribbono shel Olam* takes a *tzaddik* away from this world, because it is only then that people take proper stock of his lofty ways and mighty deeds, in an effort to emulate him.

To follow in Reb Moshe's ways — how much there is to follow! As Rabbi Nissan Alpert expressed it, "Reb Moshe was so outstanding in every way, yet so simple in the way he went about things, that one tended to lose sight of his greatness."

Rabbi Elimelech Bluth said, "I don't think there was a mind in the world superior to that of the *Rosh Yeshivah* — and I'm really not sure which was greater, his mind or his heart."

Reb Moshe was loved and respected because he *offered* love and respect to all who knew him. He was admired by everyone for his greatness, but he devoted his life to teach that what he had accomplished could be attained by *anyone* who is willing to dedicate his life to serving *Hashem* with all his might. This is difficult, but not impossible. Reb Moshe was not a "miracle man," but, like the Moshe whose name he bore, was indeed a "man of G-d." Even more, he was an עֶבֶד ה', *servant of* HASHEM.

Rabbi Elchonon Wasserman explains that, by Torah law, an עֶבֶד has no personal rights or possessions; he exists only to serve his master. Moshe's utter devotion to *Hashem* was such that he dedicated every deed, thought and moment to His service. *Rambam* (*Hil. Teshuvah* 5:2) teaches, "Every person can be as great as Moshe our teacher." Can we really be as great as Moshe? Can we be as great as *Reb* Moshe? No. But we *can* aspire to equal their zeal to serve *Hashem*. That is what we should learn from Reb Moshe's life — every moment of it.

Reb Moshe lived for the day when there would be love and fear of *Hashem*, and when this would bring love and unity to all of *Klal Yisrael*. He longed to see peace among us, to know that each of us cared for our brethren — and he was convinced that such peace and love would bring *Mashiach*.

We thought that he would lead us to greet *Mashiach* — Hashem decreed otherwise. But if the lessons of Reb Moshe's life penetrate our minds and hearts, surely *Mashiach's* footsteps will not be far away.

Glossary

All entries are Hebrew unless otherwise noted: (Yid.) Yiddish, (Ar.) Aramaic.

Acharonim: Talmudic commentators and *poskim* from 16th century to the present

Aggadah: the philosophical, ethical, poetic and historical exposition of Scripture

agunah (pl. *agunos*): woman whose marital status is uncertain because she has neither a divorce nor evidence of her missing husband's death

Ahavas Yisrael: love for one's fellow Jew

al hamichyah: blessing recited after eating cake, cookies and the like

aliyah (pl. *aliyos*): call to the Torah for the public reading

anav: humble person

arba'ah minim: four species *(lulav, esrog,* myrtle, willow) used during Succos services

Aron HaKodesh: Ark for the Torah scrolls

Ashkenazi: Jew of European ancestry

aufruf (Yid.): special *aliyah* for a *chassan* on the Shabbos before his wedding

Avos: Pirkei Avos, Chapters of the Fathers

ba'al ga'avah: conceited person

ba'al middos: one with outstanding *middos*

ba'al mum: one with a physical defect

bachur (pl. *bachurim):* unmarried man

Bas Yisrael: Jewish girl

Baruch Hashem: "Thank G-d"

Baruch She'amar: opening blessing of *Pesukei D'Zimrah* in the morning service

Bavli: Babylonian Talmud

beis din: rabbinic court

Beis HaMikdash: Holy Temple in Jerusalem

beis midrash: study hall

bimah: podium for the Torah reading in *shul*

Bircas Kohanim: blessing recited by *Kohanim* on holidays

blatt (Yid.): one full leaf (two pages) of the Talmud

bris milah: circumcision

chas v'shalom: "G-d forbid"

Chasam Sofer: R' Moshe Sofer (1762 – 1839), *Rav* of Pressburg, halachic authority

Chashmonaim: Maccabees

chassan: bridegroom

chassid: pious person

Chassid: follower of Chassidic movement founded by R' Israel Baal Shem Tov

chavrusa: study partner

Chazal (acronym for *Chachameinu, zichronom livrachah):* our Sages, of blessed memory

cheder: Torah school, elementary level

chesed: kindness

Chevrah Mishnayos: society for studying chapters of *Mishnah*

chiddush (pl. *chiddushim), chiddushei Torah:* original analyses and interpretations of difficult points of Torah

chillul Hashem: desecration of *Hashem's* Name

chinuch: education

Chumash: the Five Books of Moses

chupah: marriage canopy or ceremony

daf: a *blatt*

Daf Yomi: systematic study of the entire Talmud in 7½ years, one *blatt* per day

daven, davening (Yid.): to pray, prayers

Dibros Moshe ("The Sayings of Moshe"): Reb Moshe's *chiddushim* on the Talmud

din Torah: case before a *beis din*

dinar: a coin common in Talmudic times

drashah (pl. *drashos):* sermon or discourse

drush: non-literal or Scriptural interpretation

d'var Torah: discourse on Torah subject

erev: the eve of (a Sabbath or Festival)

Eretz Yisrael: the Land of Israel

esrog: citron, one of *arba'ah minim*

gabbai: synagogue official

gadol hador: the prime Torah leader of the generation

gaon: brilliant Torah scholar

gedolei Yisrael, gedolim: The Torah leaders of the generation

gemara: [capitalized] the part of Talmud that elaborates on the *Mishnah;* [lower case] a volume of the Talmud

goral haGra: Vilna Gaon's method of casting lots to indicate a particular Scriptural verse as a solution to a problem

Gut Shabbos (Yid.): Sabbath greeting

Gut Yom Tov (Yid.): Festival greeting

hadran: prayer recited at a *siyum,* generally accompanied by a discourse

HaKadosh Baruch Hu: the Holy One, Blessed is He; i.e., G-d

Halachah: [capitalized] the body of Torah law; [lower case] a Torah law

Hallel: Psalms 113-118, recited on certain festive days

HaNeiros Hallalu: prayer following kindling of Chanukah *menorah*

Hashem ("the Name"): G-d

hasmadah: diligence

Hatzalah: volunteer first-aid corps operating in many Jewish communities

Havdalah: blessing recited over wine, candle and spices to mark the end of Shabbos

hosafos: additional *aliyos*

iluy: genius

Igros Moshe ("Correspondence of Moshe"): collection of Reb Moshe's *teshuvos*

kallah: bride

kashrus: the laws defining kosher food

kesubah: marriage contract

kibud av: mitzvah of honoring one's father

Klal Yisrael: the Jewish people

K'nessiah Gedolah: World Conference of Agudath Israel World Organization attended by many Torah leaders

Kohein (pl. *Kohanim*): male descendant of the priestly family of Aaron

Kohein Gadol: chief *Kohein* who served in the *Beis HaMikdash*

kollel: post-graduate yeshivah

Krias HaTorah: public Torah reading

Lag B'Omer: Thirty-third day of *Sefirah*

lamdan: Torah scholar

lulav: palm branch, one of the *arba'ah minim*

Ma'ariv: the evening prayer

maggid: preacher

Maharam: Rabbi Meir of Lublin (1558 — 1616), Talmudic commentator

Maharsha: R' Shmuel Eidelis (1555 — 1631); Talmudic commentator

masechta, maseches: Talmudic tractate

mashgiach: dean of students in a yeshivah who also acts as guide and advisor

Mashiach ("Anointed One"): the Messiah

matzah (pl. *matzos*): unleavened bread

Megillah, Megillas Esther: Scroll of Esther, read on Purim

melamed: teacher of young children

Melavah Malkah: meal eaten after *Havdalah* in honor of the departing Sabbath

menahel: school principal

menorah: eight-branched candelabrum kindled on Chanukah

mesader kiddushin: officiating rabbi at a wedding ceremony

Mesillas Yesharim: mussar classic written by R' Moshe Chaim Luzzato (1707 — 1747)

mi shebeirach: prayer recited on behalf of sick person, usually at public Torah reading

middos: character traits

Midrash: classical anthology of the Sages' teachings of the Torah

mikveh: ritualarium

Minchah: the afternoon prayer

minyan: quorum of ten men for conducting a prayer service

misnaged (lit. opponent): one opposed to Chassidism; loosely, any non-*Chassid*

Mishnah: Tannaitic dicta compiled by R' Yehudah HaNasi; together with *Gemara* comprises the Talmud

Mishneh L'Melech: classic commentary on *Rambam's Mishneh Torah*

mitzvah (pl. *mitzvos*): Torah commandment

Mizmor L'David: Psalm 23, customarily sung at *Shalosh Seudos*

Mizmor L'Sodah: Psalm 100, recited during *Pesukei D'Zimrah*

Modim: a blessing of *Shemoneh Esrei*

Modim d'Rabbanan: congregational response when *chazzan* reaches *Modim*

Moshe Rabbeinu: "Moses our Teacher"

Motza'ei Shabbos: Saturday night

Mussaf: the additional prayer of Shabbos, Festivals and *Rosh Chodesh*

mussar: ethical and moral teachings

Mussar movement: a movement founded by R' Yisrael of Salant which encouraged the study of *mussar* and self-improvement

na'anuim: the shaking of the *arba'ah minim* at certain points in the prayers

nachas: pleasure

Neilah: concluding service of Yom Kippur

nichum aveilim: comforting mourners

niftar: deceased

oleh: one called to Torah at public reading

oneg Shabbos: a gathering in honor of the Sabbath, usually with light refreshments

Parshas Zachor: portion of the Torah beginning "Zachor ... " (lit. Remember), read on the Sabbath before Purim

pasken (Yid.): decide a question of Torah law

pasuk: verse of Scripture

Pesach: Passover

Pesukei D'Zimrah: Psalms recited as part of *Shacharis*

P'nei Yehoshua: R' Yaakov Yehoshua Falk (1680 — 1756), Talmudic commentator

posek (pl. *poskim*): halachic authority

posek hador: the leading halachic authority of the generation

p'sak: decision of Torah law

Rambam: acronym for R' Moshe ben Maimon (Maimonides); codifier, halachist, commentator on *Mishnah*, and seminal figure of Jewish philosophy (1135 — 1204)

Ramban: acronym for R' Moshe ben Nachman (Nachmanides); Talmudist, Kabbalist and teacher, author of classic commentaries to Scripture and Talmud (1194 — 1270)

Rashi: R' Shlomo ben Yitzchak; most famous and widely studied commentator on Scripture and Talmud (1040 — 1105)

Rav (pl. *rabbanim*): rabbi

rebbe: leader of a Chassidic sect

Rebbetzin (Yid.): rabbi's wife

rebbi (pl. *rebbeim*): teacher or master

Ribbono shel Olam: Master of the Universe, G-d

Rishonim: early Talmudic commentators and poskim, 10th to 15th centuries

Rosh Chodesh: first day of a Jewish month

rosh yeshivah (pl. roshei yeshivah): dean of a Torah institution

ruach hakodesh: Divine inspiration

sandak: one who holds the baby during circumcision

Sanhedrin: Supreme Rabbinic Court in the times of the Holy Temple

s'chach: succah-covering, such as branches

Seder Zeraim: one of the six orders of the Mishnah

Sefardi (pl. Sefardim): Jew of Spanish or Oriental ancestry

sefer (pl. sefarim): book

sefer Torah (pl. sifrei Torah): Torah scroll

Sefirah: period between Passover and Shavuos during which certain mourning customs are observed

segulah: spiritual remedy

semichah: rabbinic ordination

seudas mitzvah: meal in honor of a mitzvah

Shabbos (pl. Shabbosos): Sabbath

Shabbos HaGadol: the Sabbath before Passover

Shabbos Shuvah: the Sabbath between Rosh Hashanah and Yom Kippur

Shach: commentary on Shulchan Aruch, by R' Shabsai HaKohein (1621 — 1662)

Shacharis: morning prayer service

shalach manos: gifts of food sent on Purim

Shalosh Seudos: third Sabbath meal, eaten in the afternoon

shamash: synagogue caretaker

Shas: the Talmud

Shechinah: Divine Presence

sh'eilah (pl. sh'elilos): question of Torah law

Shema: Jew's declaration of faith recited at morning and evening services

Shemoneh Esrei: the Amidah prayer

sheva berachos: seven blessings recited during wedding ceremony, and week following

shidduch (pl. shidduchim): marriage match

shiur (pl. shiurim): lecture

shivah (lit. seven): seven days of mourning following death of a close relative

shmad: religious persecution; apostasy

shochet: ritual slaughterer

shul (Yid.): synagogue

Shulchan Aruch: Code of Jewish Law, written by Rabbi Yosef Caro (1488 — 1575)

Shushan Purim: the day after Purim, celebrated in Jerusalem as Purim

Sidra: weekly Torah portion

siyata d'Shmaya: the help of Heaven

siyum: conclusion of the study of a book of Scriptures or Talmud

succah: booth in which the Jew is commanded to dwell during Succos

Ta'anis Esther: the Fast of Esther, observed the day before Purim

tahor: ritually pure

tallis kattan: small tallis worn beneath a man's outer garments during the day

talmid (pl. talmidim): student

talmid chacham: Torah scholar

Tanach: Scripture

Targum: Aramaic translation of Chumash by the proselyte Onkelos

techias hameisim: resurrection of the dead

tefillah (pl. tefillos): prayer

Tefillah Zakah: prayer recited before Kol Nidrei in which, among other things, supplicant declares his forgiveness of all who have wronged him

Tehillim: Psalms

teshuvah (pl. teshuvos): responsum

Tosafos: (12th cent.) commentary printed in all editions of the Talmud

Tur: classic halachic text by R' Yaakov ben R' Asher (c.1275 — c. 1340)

tzaddik (pl. tzaddikim): a saintly person

tzedakah: charity

tzelem Elokim: the image of G-d in which every person was created

tzidkus: righteousness

Tzom Gedaliah: fast day observed day after Rosh Hashanah

Vilna Gaon: R' Eliyahu of Vilna (1720 — 1797), one of the greatest spiritual leaders of Jewry in post-medieval times

Yam shel Shlomo: Talmudic commentary, by R' Shlomo Luria (1510 — 1573)

Yerushalmi: Jerusalem Talmud

yetzer hara: evil inclination

yetzer tov: good inclination

zemiros: songs of praise, especially those sung at the Sabbath and Festival meals